Formal Methods

Flemming Nielson • Hanne Riis Nielson

Formal Methods

An Appetizer

 Springer

Flemming Nielson
Department of Applied Mathematics
and Computer Science
Technical University of Denmark
Kgs. Lyngby, Denmark

Hanne Riis Nielson
Department of Applied Mathematics
and Computer Science
Technical University of Denmark
Kgs. Lyngby, Denmark

ISBN 978-3-030-05155-6   ISBN 978-3-030-05156-3   (eBook)
https://doi.org/10.1007/978-3-030-05156-3

This Springer imprint is published by the registered company Springer Nature Switzerland AG
The registered company address is: Gewerbestrasse 11, 6330 Cham, Switzerland

Preface

Motivation   This book is an introduction to the use of *formal methods* ranging from semantics of key programming constructs to techniques for the analysis and verification of programs. We use *program graphs* as the mechanism for representing the control structure of programs in order to find a balance between generality (should be able to accommodate many programming constructs and support many analysis techniques) and conceptual complexity (should not require students to be able to manipulate proof trees and the like).

We cover a wide selection of formal methods while at the same time intending to overcome some of the learning difficulties that many students have when studying formal methods. In particular, many of our students find the compositional approach taken in our book *Semantics with Applications: An Appetizer* (Springer Undergraduate Topics in Computer Science) challenging — especially when it comes to proofs. Hence the aim of this book is to rely more on the intuition that students have about graphs.

Teaching from the book   We are using the book in the bachelor course *02141: Computer Science Modelling* at The Technical University of Denmark. Our students have some background in functional programming so that recursive definitions are somewhat familiar to them. Still it may be useful to explicitly point out that the recursive definitions are sufficently detailed that they can easily be converted to functional programs (as briefly sketched in Appendices B and C). Since our students have different skills we have added bonus material in most chapters; this may challenge the more advanced students but is not required.

Our intention is that the chapters of the book are largely plug-and-play. Chapters 1 and 2 suffice for the treatment of the majority of the remaining material; the few cross references, examples or exercises that do not adhere to this can safely be ignored in teaching. These two chapters cover our model of program graphs and an example programming language.

Chapters 3, 4, 5 and 6 cover formal methods for analysing the behaviour of programs in various ways ranging from verification, via program analysis and language-based

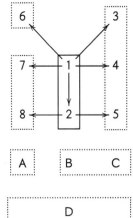

Figure 0: Dependencies.

v

security, to model checking.

Chapters 7 and 8 present language extensions with procedures and concurrency and cover their semantics.

Appendix A describes a fragment of the C programming language that may be useful for assignments.

Appendix B contains ideas for a number of programming projects related to the development in Chapters 1 to 5 with Appendix C providing further suggestions for how to tackle them in F#. This constitutes the basis for the learning environment described in Appendix D.

Appendix D describes part of the learning environment at `FormalMethods.dk`, which allows students to play with the development and hence create examples beyond those covered in the main text.

Further teaching material and a list of typographical errors will be made available at `FormalMethods.dk` in due course.

Studying the book   The text in this book is not only black text on a white background. We use a yellow background for definitions and other key notations; we use a grey background for examples; we use a magenta background for key results; and we use a cyan background for comments that paint a wider picture or impose restrictions on our treatment. The simplest exercises are labelled 'Try It Out' and should be attempted before reading any further, the more normal exercises are labelled 'Exercises' and can be solved right away or during an exercise session, and the 'Teasers' may be too challenging for most students. We strongly recommend reading all exercises and teasers even if they are not solved; those central to the subsequent development are labelled 'Essential Exercise'.

We have intended the book to be short and concise and leave it to the students to provide further examples using the learning environment available at `FormalMethods.dk` and introduced in Appendix D.

Acknowledgement   We have received many comments and suggestions from students and colleagues when writing this book; in particular, we should like to thank Andreas Viktor Hess, Alberto Lluch Lafuente, Kasper Laursen, Hugo A. López, Mike Castro Lundin and Panagiotis Vasilikos for their enthusiasm.

About the authors   The authors are full professors at *The Technical University of Denmark*, working in the section on *Formal Methods for Safe and Secure Systems* in the *Department of Applied Mathematics and Computer Science*.

In recent decades they have written several books on semantics and analysis and have lectured on semantics and analysis at *Aalborg University, Aarhus University, University of Kiel, Saarland University,* and *The Technical University of Denmark.*

October 2018
Flemming Nielson
Hanne Riis Nielson

Prologue

Formal Methods Society becomes ever more dependent on IT systems and is increasingly vulnerable to cyber attacks and programming errors. The slogan of *safe and secure by design* emphasises that ideally IT systems should be constructed in such a way that they are mostly immune to such vulnerabilities. The use of *formal methods* offers a wide variety of techniques and tools for mitigating these vulnerabilities. When working with existing IT systems the aim is instead to *retrofit safety and security* to the extent possible.

This book is an introduction to the use of formal methods for describing and analysing the software components that constitute IT systems. The IT systems may be small stand-alone apps or they may be part of larger cyber-physical systems or the Internet of Things. Constructs that look similar in different programming languages may have subtle differences, and constructs that look rather different may turn out to be fairly similar after all. It is the role of *semantics* to make these issues precise.

Often we need to ensure that software components behave in certain ways – methods such as *program verification*, *program analysis*, *language-based security* and *model checking* are useful for this. Together they provide a variety of means for ensuring a safe and secure IT infrastructure for our society. Let us briefly compare the methods. *Program verification* is very powerful as to the behaviour that can be expressed but unfortunately the verification process cannot be fully automated. This is in contrast to *program analysis*, which is fully automatic but less precise. The approach of *model checking* supports more general properties and it is also fully automatic but the performance is often not as good as for program analysis.

In the remainder of this prologue we provide an overview of the approach taken in this book. For a well-written account of what formal methods can do for safety and security of IT systems you might take a look at

Kevin Hartnett: *Hacker-Proof Code Confirmed*. Quanta Magazine, 2016.

(https://www.quantamagazine.org/formal-verification-creates-hacker-proof-code-20160920), which describes how one can prove certain programs to be error-free with the same certainty that mathematicians prove theorems, and how this is being used to secure everything from unmanned drones to the Internet.

Program Graphs   Sometimes we want to analyse existing software components and sometimes we want to analyse software components that are in the process of being designed – to ensure that we do not waste effort on implementing a software component that eventually falls short of meeting its aims.

To present a uniform approach to these goals we make use of *models* of software components or IT systems. A model is an *abstraction* of the system – it will focus on some parts of the system and ignore others. It may focus on the workflow of an organisation and ignore details about how the individual steps are carried out. It may describe the logic of a vending machine offering tea, coffee and chocolate at different prices and ignore construction details. It may dig into the details of how a cryptographic protocol or a sorting algorithm works. It may be extremely concrete and model the detailed bit-level operation of computers. What is common is that a model should describe not only the structure of the IT system but also its meaning – at an appropriate level of abstraction.

In this book we shall focus on a graphical representation of models called *program graphs*. Program graphs focus on how a system proceeds from one point to the next by performing one of the actions identified by the abstraction. The meaning of the actions is formalised by defining their *semantics* and this gives rise to a precise description of the meaning of the program graphs themselves. Depending on our focus the semantics may be at the level of bit strings, mathematical integers, or data structures such as arrays. We refer to Chapter 1 for this development.

Guarded Commands   When programming we use a programming language such as C, Java or F# to construct the software components needed. The *syntax* of a programming language is usually specified by a BNF grammar and sometimes there are additional well-formedness conditions that need to be adhered to. There are many approaches to how to define the *semantics* of the programming language – that is, to formally define the meaning of programs written in the programming language. Some approaches are very mathematical in nature and others are more operational, and in general the approaches have their own strengths and weaknesses. As an example, some of the approaches lend themselves easily to programming languages with concurrency whereas others do not.

To present a uniform approach to the semantics of a variety of programming languages we shall take the view that programs give rise to program graphs. This means that we will show how to transform programs in programming languages into program graphs. We shall focus on the language *Guarded Commands* introduced by Dijkstra in 1975. Our treatment covers the syntax and the construction of program graphs. We also cover a number of extensions, including more advanced control structures. We refer to Chapter 2 for this development. Guarded Commands is a tiny and probably unfamiliar language but the techniques used can be extended to more familiar languages as discussed in Appendix A.

Program Verification   Having a precise understanding of the meaning of models and programs is a precursor to being able to reason about their behaviour. We can investigate whether the model has the functionality we envisioned, whether it provides the required safety or security guarantees, and we can look into performance issues. We shall cover four methods for how to achieve this: program verification, program analysis, language-based security and model checking. They differ widely in the degree to which they can be automated and the precision that can be obtained.

The basic idea of *program verification* is to attach a predicate to each node in the program graph. This should be done in such a way that a predicate at a node is fulfilled whenever we reach the node during execution – when this is the case the predicate is said to be an *invariant*. As an example, we may want to express that whenever the execution of a program graph for a sorting routine reaches its final node then the array given as input to the routine has indeed been sorted. Program verification allows such properties to be verified in a very systematic manner.

We will cover how to express predicates and how it suffices to have predicates only for the nodes corresponding to loop entries. We will explain what needs to be verified about the predicates in order that they are proper invariants. And we will show how to integrate the development with the Guarded Commands language. We refer to Chapter 3 for this development.

Program Analysis   The main shortcoming of program verification is that it cannot be fully automated – due to the expressive power of the predicates used.

In *program analysis* the properties attached to the nodes in the program graph are made less expressive and we accept that the properties often describe more memories than can actually arise at a node – we say that program analysis is *over-approximating* in nature. We illustrate the approach by developing a program analysis for keeping track of the signs of integers and of arrays of integers: we introduce the properties and show how to define the analysis functions.

It is possible to develop a number of algorithms for automatically computing the properties to be attached to the nodes and these algorithms often have good performance. Consequently, program analysis techniques are used extensively in the advanced implementation of programming languages as well as in ensuring correctness properties of potentially large programs. We refer to Chapter 4 for this development.

Language-Based Security   Formal Methods constitute a key set of techniques for ensuring that we can rely on our IT systems to provide a safe and secure infrastructure.

Security is often said to consist of three components: *Confidentiality*, meaning that data is only told to those we trust; *Integrity*, meaning that data is only influenced by those we trust; *Availability*, meaning that data is not inaccessible when needed.

We show how to achieve confidentiality and integrity by limiting the *information flow* permitted by programs. This can only partially be done by checking the information flow dynamically so static checks will be needed and we develop a security analysis for the Guarded Commands language to do so. We refer to Chapter 5 for this development.

Model Checking   Another fully automatic method for the analysis of models is that of *model checking*.

The key novelty of the model checking approach is the use of a *computation tree logic* for expressing the properties. The use of logic for expressing properties retains some of the flavour of program verification but the expressive power is sufficiently reduced with respect to that of the predicates so that full automation can be achieved. The approach earned its inventors the Turing award.

Model checking is more precise than program analysis but also more costly as it analyses a transition system built from a program graph by having multiple copies of each node – one for each of the memories possible at that node. This gives rise to the so-called 'state explosion problem', which is the real hindrance to applying model checking on very large systems. We refer to Chapter 6 for this development.

Procedures   One of the key abstraction mechanisms in programming languages is that of procedures, or equivalently those of functions and methods. To study this we extend the Guarded Commands language of Chapter 2 with recursive *procedures* with input and output parameters as well as blocks with local declarations of variables.

The key novelty when giving the semantics to this language is that the memory model is changed to be a stack of frames. The program graphs are extended with appropriate actions for manipulating the stack: when a block is entered a new frame is pushed on the stack and it is popped when the block is left – and similarly a new frame is pushed on the stack when a procedure is called and it is popped when the call returns.

Our first treatment of procedures gives rise to *dynamic scope*; we then show how a slight modification of the development suffices for obtaining *static scope*. Our only focus is on defining the semantics and we refer to Chapter 7 for this development.

Concurrency   Another key abstraction mechanism in programming languages is that of *concurrency*. The idea here is that a system consists of a number of processes that execute in parallel and interact with one another by exchanging information.

We shall assume here that the individual processes are in an extended version of the Guarded Commands language of Chapter 2.

The key challenge in this setting is that the memory model must keep track of the configurations of all the processes. We shall first consider the simple setting where the processes interact through *shared variables*. We then extend it to channel-based communication, by which we mean that the Guarded Commands language is extended with constructs for input and output over channels. First we consider asynchronous communication by means of buffered channels and next we consider synchronous communication where two program graphs need to perform a step at the same time.

We finish with a treatment of some advanced communication constructs: 'broadcast', which sends a value to many recipients at the same time, and 'gathering', which obtains values from many senders at the same time. We refer to Chapter 8 for this development.

Programming Projects Our treatment of formal methods is sufficiently detailed that a number of programming projects can be formulated where the ideas are put into practice. This ranges from using the semantics to construct an interpreter to the implementation of a verification condition generator, a program analyser, and a security analysis. We refer to Appendices B and C for more on this. These projects can be adapted to the MicroC language of Appendix A as desired.

Contents

Chapter 1

Program Graphs

Sometimes we need to be very precise about the behaviour of our programs – there may be constructs in our programming language that are subtle or novel. Semantics is the part of Computer Science that deals with formalising the behaviour of programs. In this chapter we are going to develop an operational notion of semantics based on representing programs as so-called program graphs.

1.1   Program Graphs

A *program graph* is a graphical representation of the control structure of a program or system. A program graph is a directed graph so it has a set of *nodes* and a set of *edges*. However, there is a little more structure to a program graph. It has an *initial node* that intuitively represents the starting point of the executions modelled by the program graph and by symmetry it has a *final node* that represents a point where the execution will have terminated. Each of the edges is labelled with an *action* modelling the computation to take place when control follows the edge. The program graph does not specify the meaning of actions – so far they are just syntax and it is only when we come to the semantics in the next section that we give meaning to the actions.

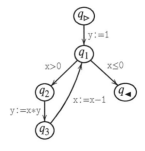

Figure 1.1: Program graph for the factorial function.

EXAMPLE 1.1: Figure 1.1 shows a program graph with five nodes: $q_{\triangleright}$ is the initial node, $q_{\blacktriangleleft}$ is the final node and then there are three additional nodes q_1, q_2 and q_3. The edges are labelled with the associated actions; as an example the action $y := x * y$ is associated with the edge with source q_2 and target q_3. The five actions $y := 1, x > 0, x \leq 0, y := x * y$ and $x := x - 1$ have been chosen so as to be suggestive of the meaning that we will be giving them when we come to the semantics – it should be no surprise that the program graph is

1

© Springer Nature Switzerland AG 2019
F. Nielson, H. Riis Nielson, *Formal Methods*, https://doi.org/10.1007/978-3-030-05156-3_1

intended to compute the factorial function: upon termination of the program the variable y should hold the value of the factorial of the initial value of x.

DEFINITION 1.2: A *program graph* **PG** consists of the following:

- **Q**: a finite set of *nodes*

- $q_{\rhd}, q_{\blacktriangleleft} \in$ **Q**: two nodes called the *initial node* and the *final node*, respectively

- **Act**: a set of *actions*

- **E** $\subseteq$ **Q** $\times$ **Act** $\times$ **Q**: a finite set of *edges*

An edge $(q_{\circ}, \alpha, q_{\bullet})$ has *source* node $q_{\circ}$ and *target* node $q_{\bullet}$, and it is labelled with the *action* α.

We shall *require* that the initial and final nodes are distinct and that there are no edges with source $q_{\blacktriangleleft}$.

We sometimes write **PG** $= ($**Q**$, q_{\rhd}q_{\blacktriangleleft},$ **Act**, **E**$)$ to summarise the components of the program graph.

EXAMPLE 1.3: Returning to the program graph of Figure 1.1, it can be represented by the three sets

$$\mathbf{Q} = \{q_{\rhd}, q_1, q_2, q_3, q_{\blacktriangleleft}\}$$
$$\mathbf{Act} = \{y := 1, x > 0, x \le 0, y := x * y, x := x - 1\}$$
$$\mathbf{E} = \{(q_{\rhd}, y := 1, q_1), (q_1, x > 0, q_2), (q_1, x \le 0, q_{\blacktriangleleft}),$$
$$(q_2, y := x * y, q_3), (q_3, x := x - 1, q_1)\}$$

where the first set lists the nodes, including the initial and final nodes, the second set lists the actions, and the third set lists the edges.

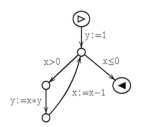

Figure 1.2: Program graph omitting names of nodes.

Often the names of the nodes of the program graph are of minor interest and we then omit them from the graphical representation, as illustrated in Figure 1.2; however, we shall always mark the initial node (with $\rhd$) and the final node (with $\blacktriangleleft$).

TRY IT OUT 1.4: Specify a program graph for the power function computing the power 2^n of a number $n \ge 0$: upon termination the variable y should hold the value of the x'th power of 2. As actions you should use simple tests and assignments similar to the ones used in Example 1.1. □

EXERCISE 1.5: Specify program graphs for the functions below using actions that are simple tests and assignments (similar to the ones used in Example 1.1):

(a) the modulo operation mod(n, m) returning the remainder after division of one number n by another m;

(b) the greatest common divisor $\gcd(n, m)$ of two numbers n and m;

(c) the n'th Fibonacci number.   □

The Formal Language View Program graphs are closely related to finite automata. Recall that a non-deterministic finite automaton is given by a set of states Q with one state q_0 being the initial state and a subset F of states being the final states; additionally, there is an alphabet Σ and a transition relation δ, which, given a state and a symbol from the alphabet, specifies a set of states. The alphabet corresponds to the set of actions of the program graph (so we have $\Sigma = \mathbf{Act}$) and the transition relation is nothing but an alternative representation of the edges of the program graph.

This leads us to the following definition of the formal language of a program graph as the sequences of actions obtained by following the edges of the graph. The *formal language* of a program graph **PG** from node $q_\circ$ to node $q_\bullet$ is given by

$$\mathbf{L}(q_\circ \rightsquigarrow q_\bullet)(\mathbf{E}) \;=\; \{\alpha_1 \cdots \alpha_n \mid \exists q_0, \cdots, q_n : \forall i \in \{0, \cdots, n-1\} : (q_i, \alpha_i, q_{i+1}) \in \mathbf{E},$$
$$q_0 = q_\circ, q_n = q_\bullet.\}$$

and we define the formal language of **PG** by

$$\mathbf{L}(\mathbf{PG}) = \mathbf{L}(q_\triangleright \rightsquigarrow q_\blacktriangleleft)(\mathbf{E})$$

using that $\mathbf{PG} = (\mathbf{Q}, q_\triangleright q_\blacktriangleleft, \mathbf{Act}, \mathbf{E})$ is as in Definition 1.2.

As an example, the language $\mathbf{L}(\mathbf{PG})$ for the program graph **PG** of Figures 1.1 and 1.2 is given by the regular expression

$$\mathtt{y := 1} \quad (\mathtt{x > 0} \quad \mathtt{y := x * y} \quad \mathtt{x := x - 1})^* \quad \mathtt{x \le 0}$$

where for example $\mathtt{y := 1}$ is an element of the alphabet $\Sigma = \mathbf{Act}$.

One can show that $\mathbf{L}(\mathbf{PG})$ is a regular language whenever **PG** is a program graph.

> You may have seen programs represented as *flow charts* and wonder about the relationship between program graphs and flow charts. Basically they swap the way edges and nodes are used. In a program graph the nodes correspond to *program points* whereas the edges represent the actions (say assignments). In a flow chart the nodes represent the actions (say sequences of assignments) whereas the edges roughly correspond to program points.

1.2 Semantics

The next task is to be precise about the meaning of the actions in the program graphs. An action represents a transformation on a semantic domain: an element of the semantic domain will describe the memory of the program or system at a given point and the *semantics* of the action tells us how this information is modified when the action is executed – if indeed it can be executed.

As an example, suppose that we have only two variables x and y and that we use pairs like $(3, 5)$ to indicate the memory where $x = 3$ and $y = 5$. Then the semantics of an assignment $y := 1$ is given by the total function $S[\![y := 1]\!]$ defined by $S[\![y := 1]\!](v_x, v_y) = (v_x, 1)$. We then have $S[\![y := 1]\!](3, 5) = (3, 1)$ showing that if the memory is $(3, 5)$ before the execution of the action $y := 1$ then the memory is $(3, 1)$ afterwards. Furthermore, the semantics of the test $x > 0$ is given by the partial function $S[\![x > 0]\!]$ defined by $S[\![x > 0]\!](v_x, v_y) = (v_x, v_y)$ when $v_x > 0$ and undefined otherwise. We then have $S[\![x > 0]\!](3, 5) = (3, 5)$ because $3 > 0$ is true, whereas $S[\![x > 0]\!](0, 5)$ is undefined because $0 > 0$ is false.

DEFINITION 1.6: A *semantics* of a program graph consists of

- a non-empty set **Mem** called the *memory* (or semantic domain)

- a semantic function $S[\![\cdot]\!]$: **Act** → (**Mem** ↪ **Mem**) specifying the meaning of the actions

Whenever $S[\![\alpha]\!]\sigma = \sigma'$ the idea is that if σ is the memory before executing α then σ' is the memory afterwards.

Recall that a *partial function* f : **Mem** ↪ **Mem** is defined on a subset $\mathrm{dom}(f)$ of **Mem** and for each element in $\mathrm{dom}(f)$ it gives an element of **Mem**; if $\mathrm{dom}(f) =$ **Mem** then it is a *total function*.

Also recall that a *higher-order function* g : **Act** → (**Mem** ↪ **Mem**) takes a first parameter α and gives rise to a (partial) function $g(\alpha)$: **Mem** ↪ **Mem**; so if $\sigma \in$ **Mem** we have that either $g(\alpha)(\sigma) \in$ **Mem** or $g(\alpha)(\sigma)$ is undefined.

EXAMPLE 1.7: Continuing Example 1.1 we shall take **Mem** to be sets of pairs of integers; the first component of a pair (v_x, v_y) will be the value of the variable x while the second component will be the value of the variable y. The program graph has five different actions and we shall define the semantic function $S[\![\cdot]\!]$ in each of the five cases:

$$S[\![y := 1]\!](v_x, v_y) = (v_x, 1)$$

$$S[\![x > 0]\!](v_x, v_y) = \begin{cases} (v_x, v_y) & \text{if } v_x > 0 \\ \text{undefined} & \text{otherwise} \end{cases}$$

$$S[\![x \le 0]\!](v_x, v_y) = \begin{cases} (v_x, v_y) & \text{if } v_x \le 0 \\ \text{undefined} & \text{otherwise} \end{cases}$$

$$S[\![y := x * y]\!](v_x, v_y) = (v_x, v_x * v_y)$$

$$S[\![x := x - 1]\!](v_x, v_y) \;=\; (v_x - 1, v_y)$$

Notice that we specify partial functions for the two actions testing on the value of x: rather than formally modelling that the test evaluates to true, we model it as an application of the identity function, and rather than formally modelling that the test evaluates to false, we model it as an application of the undefined function.

TRY IT OUT 1.8: Returning to Try It Out 1.4, define the semantics for the actions used in the program graph (in the manner of Example 1.7). □

EXERCISE 1.9: Returning to Exercise 1.5, define the semantics for the actions used in each of the program graphs (in the manner of Example 1.7). □

Configurations and Transitions   When defining the semantics of program graphs we will be looking at configurations consisting of nodes from the program graphs and memories.

DEFINITION 1.10: A *configuration* is a pair $\langle q; \sigma \rangle$ where $q \in \mathbf{Q}$ and $\sigma \in \mathbf{Mem}$; an *initial configuration* has $q = q_{\triangleright}$ and a *final configuration* has $q = q_{\blacktriangleleft}$.

Next we will use the semantics to explain how to move between configurations.

DEFINITION 1.11: Whenever $(q_\circ, \alpha, q_\bullet) \in \mathbf{E}$ we have an *execution step*

$$\langle q_\circ; \sigma \rangle \xMapsto{\alpha} \langle q_\bullet; \sigma' \rangle \text{ if } S[\![\alpha]\!]\sigma = \sigma'$$

Note that $S[\![\alpha]\!]\sigma = \sigma'$ means that σ is in the domain of $S[\![\alpha]\!]$ as well as that the result of the function is σ'; if σ is not in the domain of $S[\![\alpha]\!]$ there is no execution step.

A configuration $\langle q; \sigma \rangle$ is called *stuck* if it is not a final configuration and if there is no execution step of the form $\langle q; \sigma \rangle \xMapsto{\alpha} \langle q'; \sigma' \rangle$; in this case we write $\langle q; \sigma \rangle \not\Longrightarrow$.

EXAMPLE 1.12: Continuing Examples 1.1 and 1.7, we have the execution step

$$\langle q_{\triangleright}; (3, 5) \rangle \xMapsto{y := 1} \langle q_1; (3, 1) \rangle$$

and next we have the following execution step

$$\langle q_1; (3, 1) \rangle \xMapsto{x > 0} \langle q_2; (3, 1) \rangle$$

$\langle q_{\triangleright}; (3,7)\rangle \overset{\text{y}:=1}{\Longrightarrow}$

$\langle q_1; (3,1)\rangle \overset{\text{x}>0}{\Longrightarrow}$

$\langle q_2; (3,1)\rangle \overset{\text{y}:=\text{x}*\text{y}}{\Longrightarrow}$

$\langle q_3; (3,3)\rangle \overset{\text{x}:=\text{x}-1}{\Longrightarrow}$

$\langle q_1; (2,3)\rangle \overset{\text{x}>0}{\Longrightarrow}$

$\langle q_2; (2,3)\rangle \overset{\text{y}:=\text{x}*\text{y}}{\Longrightarrow}$

$\langle q_3; (2,6)\rangle \overset{\text{x}:=\text{x}-1}{\Longrightarrow}$

$\langle q_1; (1,6)\rangle \overset{\text{x}>0}{\Longrightarrow}$

$\langle q_2; (1,6)\rangle \overset{\text{y}:=\text{x}*\text{y}}{\Longrightarrow}$

$\langle q_3; (1,6)\rangle \overset{\text{x}:=\text{x}-1}{\Longrightarrow}$

$\langle q_1; (0,6)\rangle \overset{\text{x}\leq 0}{\Longrightarrow}$

$\langle q_{\blacktriangleleft}; (0,6)\rangle$

Figure 1.3: Execution sequence for the factorial function.

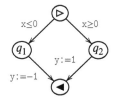

Figure 1.4: There may be more than one complete execution sequence.

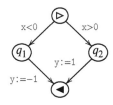

Figure 1.5: There may be no complete execution sequence.

We may put this together as follows

$$\langle q_{\triangleright}; (3,5)\rangle \overset{\text{y}:=1}{\Longrightarrow} \langle q_1; (3,1)\rangle \overset{\text{x}>0}{\Longrightarrow} \langle q_2; (3,1)\rangle$$

Figure 1.3 gives a complete execution sequence for the program graph in the case where the initial values of x and y are 3 and 7: the initial memory is $(3,7)$ and the final memory is $(0,6)$, showing that the factorial of 3 is 6.

DEFINITION 1.13: We write $\langle q; \sigma\rangle \overset{\omega}{\underset{*}{\Longrightarrow}} \langle q'; \sigma'\rangle$ for the *reflexive and transitive closure* of the execution relation.

An *execution sequence* is a sequence of the form $\langle q; \sigma\rangle \overset{\omega}{\underset{*}{\Longrightarrow}} \langle q'; \sigma'\rangle$; a *complete execution sequence* is a sequence of the form $\langle q_{\triangleright}; \sigma\rangle \overset{\omega}{\underset{*}{\Longrightarrow}} \langle q_{\blacktriangleleft}; \sigma'\rangle$, that is, it begins in an initial configuration and ends in a final configuration.

We may dispense with the superscript action sequence if it is of little interest.

TRY IT OUT 1.14: Continuing Examples 1.1 and 1.7, determine the complete execution sequence

$$\langle q_{\triangleright}; (4,4)\rangle \overset{\omega}{\underset{*}{\Longrightarrow}} \langle q_{\blacktriangleleft}; (v_{\text{x}}, v_{\text{y}})\rangle$$

What are the length of the action sequence ω and the values v_{x} and v_{y}? ☐

EXAMPLE 1.15: Sometimes an initial memory may give rise to more than one complete execution sequence. For the semantics of Example 1.7 this arises for the program graph of Figure 1.4. Here we have the complete execution sequence

$$\langle q_{\triangleright}; (0,0)\rangle \overset{*}{\Longrightarrow} \langle q_{\blacktriangleleft}; (0,-1)\rangle$$

as well as

$$\langle q_{\triangleright}; (0,0)\rangle \overset{*}{\Longrightarrow} \langle q_{\blacktriangleleft}; (0,1)\rangle$$

This means that the program graph of Figure 1.4 is a non-deterministic system.

Sometimes an initial memory might not have a complete execution sequence. For the semantics of Example 1.7 this arises for the program graph of Figure 1.5. Here the configuration $\langle q_{\triangleright}; (0,0)\rangle$ is stuck because both of the edges leaving $q_{\triangleright}$ have a semantics that is undefined on $(0,0)$. This means that the program graph of Figure 1.5 does not always successfully terminate.

You may not have seen the special brackets ⟦···⟧ before. We shall exclusively use them around arguments that relate to syntactic constructs. Historically, they come from an approach to semantics called Denotational Semantics and are a stylised form of what could be written (⌈···⌉). The outermost (···) is the usual kind of parentheses that we might use around arguments to functions. The innermost ⌜···⌝ is Quine quasi-quotation; you can read more about this on Wikipedia.

1.3 The Structure of the Memory

So far we have modelled memories as tuples: when we have n variables $x_1, \cdots, x_n$ we have modelled the memory as an n-tuple $\sigma = (v_1, \cdots, v_n)$ (or $\sigma = (v_{x_1}, \cdots, v_{x_n})$) where $v_i \in$ **Int** gives the value of x_i.

Writing **Var** for the set $\{x_1, \cdots, x_n\}$ we shall now model memories as mappings

$$\sigma : \textbf{Var} \rightarrow \textbf{Int}$$

and then we write $\sigma(x_i)$ for the value of x_i. The set **Var** is called the domain of σ and is denoted $\mathsf{dom}(\sigma)$. This is illustrated in Figure 1.6 for a memory $\sigma : \{x, y\} \rightarrow$ **Int** with just two variables x and y.

x	12
y	5

Figure 1.6: Example memory: σ with $\sigma(x) = 12$ and $\sigma(y) = 5$.

We shall introduce the notation $\sigma[x \mapsto v]$ for the memory that is the same as σ except that the value of the variable $x \in \mathsf{dom}(\sigma)$ now has the value v. So if $\sigma(x) = 12$, $\sigma(y) = 5$ and $\sigma' = \sigma[x \mapsto 13]$, then $\sigma'(x) = 13$ and $\sigma'(y) = 5$ as is illustrated in Figure 1.7. With this notation we may for example write $\mathcal{S}[\![x := x + 1]\!]\sigma = \sigma[x \mapsto \sigma(x) + 1]$ for the semantics of the action incrementing the value of x. (It may be prudent to ensure that an entry for x is already present in σ and we shall do so when introducing the Guarded Commands language in Chapter 2.)

x	13
y	5

Figure 1.7: Updated example memory: $\sigma[x \mapsto 13]$.

Arrays Our programs may manipulate more complex structures, for example arrays. An *array* A has a fixed length, say k, and we refer to its elements as $A[0], A[1], \cdots, A[k-1]$. We shall therefore extend memories to hold information about the values of these elements, as illustrated in Figure 1.8. Here we have three variables n, i and j and an array A of length 4, and the memory specifies the values in each of the cases. If we index outside the bounds of the array and ask for the value of, say A[4], then the result is undefined – the memory has no information.

n	4
i	1
j	2
A[0]	4
A[1]	2
A[2]	17
A[3]	9

Figure 1.8: Example memory with an array of length 4.

For the general formulation assume that we have a finite set of variables **Var** and a finite set of arrays **Arr**; each array $A \in$ **Arr** has a length given by $\mathsf{length}(A)$. We shall then take

$$\sigma : \big(\ \textbf{Var} \cup \{A[i] \mid A \in \textbf{Arr}, 0 \leq i < \mathsf{length}(A)\}\ \big) \rightarrow \textbf{Int}$$

Thus $\sigma(A[i])$ will be the value of the i'th entry of the array A – provided that i is a proper index into the array, that is, $0 \leq i < \mathsf{length}(A)$. The notation $\sigma[A[i] \mapsto v]$ stands for the memory that is the same as σ except that the i'th entry of the array A now has the value v; again this is provided that $0 \leq i < \mathsf{length}(A)$.

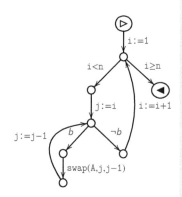

Figure 1.9: Program graph for insertion sort.

EXAMPLE 1.16: Figure 1.9 shows a program graph for an algorithm intended to sort the elements of an array A of length n. The algorithm is known as *insertion sort* and the sorting is performed using two integer-valued variables i and j and the action $\text{swap}(A, j, j-1)$. For typographical reasons we write b for $j > 0$ && $A[j-1] > A[j]$, and $\neg b$ for its negation, where && is a *short-circuit* version of conjunction $\wedge$ which does not attempt to evaluate the right argument if the left argument is false. This means that if $j = 0$ we do not get an error from $A[j-1]$.

The memory of the semantics will specify the values of the elements of the array A as well as the values of the variables n, i and j; Figure 1.8 gives an example of a memory. The semantics will specify the meaning of the actions; most of these are fairly straightforward and we shall therefore concentrate on the action $\text{swap}(A, j, j-1)$. As the name suggests it is intended to swap two entries in the array and leave the rest of the memory unchanged. We may formalise this as follows:

$$S[\![\text{swap}(A, j, j-1)]\!]\sigma = \begin{cases} \sigma[A[j] \mapsto v_{j-1}][A[j-1] \mapsto v_j] \\ \quad \text{if } \sigma(j) = j \text{ and } A[j], A[j-1] \in \text{dom}(\sigma) \\ \quad \text{and } v_j = \sigma(A[j]) \text{ and } v_{j-1} = \sigma(A[j-1]) \\ \text{undefined} \quad \text{otherwise} \end{cases}$$

The test in the first branch ensures that $A[j]$ as well as $A[j-1]$ refer to existing entries in the array A; if this is not the case then the semantics is undefined, as recorded in the second branch of the formula.

TRY IT OUT 1.17: Modify the program graph for the insertion sort algorithm to use a temporary variable to do the swapping of array entries and define the corresponding semantics. How is indexing outside the array bounds captured in your semantics?☐

EXERCISE 1.18: Construct a program graph for the bubble sort algorithm and define the semantics of the actions being used; be careful to capture when you are indexing outside the bounds of the arrays.   ☐

EXERCISE 1.19: Let A and B be arrays corresponding to two vectors of length n and m, respectively. Construct program graphs for the following operations:

(a) the *inner product* being the number defined by $\Sigma_{i=0}^{n-1}\Sigma_{j=0}^{m-1} A[i] \cdot B[j]$;

(b) the *outer product* being an $n \times m$ matrix C with the (i,j)'th entry given by $C[i,j] = A[i] \cdot B[j]$.

Define the semantics of the actions being used; in the case of the outer product this also involves defining the structure of the memories, as they now have to represent matrices.   ☐

TEASER 1.20: Argue as convincingly as you can that every complete execution sequence of the insertion sort algorithm of Figure 1.9 ensures that the array is eventually sorted. (We shall return to this in Chapter 3.)   ☐

1.4   Properties of Program Graphs

Often programs are expected to compute some output values based on some input values. For a complete execution sequence $\langle q_\triangleright; \sigma \rangle \overset{\omega}{\underset{*}{\Longrightarrow}} \langle q_\blacktriangleleft; \sigma' \rangle$ we would say that σ' contains the output values corresponding to the input values in σ.

Deterministic System   We would often expect the value computed to be the same each time we perform the computation and that the same computations are performed. This leads to the notion of a deterministic system.

> DEFINITION 1.21: A program graph **PG** and its semantics S constitute a *deterministic system* whenever
>
> $$\langle q_\triangleright; \sigma \rangle \overset{\omega'}{\underset{*}{\Longrightarrow}} \langle q_\blacktriangleleft; \sigma' \rangle \text{ and } \langle q_\triangleright; \sigma \rangle \overset{\omega''}{\underset{*}{\Longrightarrow}} \langle q_\blacktriangleleft; \sigma'' \rangle$$
>
> imply that $\sigma' = \sigma''$ and that $\omega' = \omega''$

To ensure that a program graph and its semantics give rise to a deterministic system we may use the following sufficient condition (illustrated in Figure 1.10), which is relatively straightforward to check.

> PROPOSITION 1.22: A program graph **PG** and its semantics S constitute a *deterministic system* whenever distinct edges with the same source node have semantic functions that are defined on non-overlapping domains:
>
> $$\forall (q, \alpha_1, q_1), (q, \alpha_2, q_2) \in \mathbf{E} : \left(\begin{array}{l} (\alpha_1, q_1) \neq (\alpha_2, q_2) \Rightarrow \\ (\mathrm{dom}(S[\![\alpha_1]\!]) \cap \mathrm{dom}(S[\![\alpha_2]\!]) = \{\ \}) \end{array} \right)$$

Figure 1.10: $S[\![\alpha_1]\!]\sigma$ or $S[\![\alpha_2]\!]\sigma$ undefined.

PROOF: First we prove that

$$\text{if} \quad \langle q_\triangleright; \sigma \rangle \overset{\omega'}{\underset{*}{\Longrightarrow}} \langle q'; \sigma' \rangle, \quad \langle q_\triangleright; \sigma \rangle \overset{\omega''}{\underset{*}{\Longrightarrow}} \langle q''; \sigma'' \rangle \quad \text{and} \quad |\omega'| = |\omega''|$$
$$\text{then} \quad q' = q'', \quad \sigma' = \sigma'' \quad \text{and} \quad \omega' = \omega''$$

We conduct the proof by mathematical induction on the length $|\omega'|$ of ω'. If $|\omega'| = 0$ we have $q' = q'' = q_\triangleright$, $\omega' = \omega'' = \varepsilon$ (the empty string) and $\sigma' = \sigma'' = \sigma$ so the result is immediate.

If $|\omega'| = n+1$ for some $n \geq 0$ we can write $\omega' = u'\alpha'$ and expand $\langle q_\triangleright; \sigma \rangle \overset{\omega'}{\underset{*}{\Longrightarrow}} \langle q'; \sigma' \rangle$ to $\langle q_\triangleright; \sigma \rangle \overset{u'}{\underset{*}{\Longrightarrow}} \langle q_0'; \sigma_0' \rangle \overset{\alpha'}{\Longrightarrow} \langle q'; \sigma' \rangle$; similarly we can write $\omega'' = u''\alpha''$ and expand $\langle q_\triangleright; \sigma \rangle \overset{\omega''}{\underset{*}{\Longrightarrow}} \langle q''; \sigma'' \rangle$ to $\langle q_\triangleright; \sigma \rangle \overset{u''}{\underset{*}{\Longrightarrow}} \langle q_0''; \sigma_0'' \rangle \overset{\alpha''}{\Longrightarrow} \langle q''; \sigma'' \rangle$. It follows from the induction hypothesis that $q_0' = q_0''$, $\sigma_0' = \sigma_0''$ and $u' = u''$.

We clearly have edges (q_0', α', q') and (q_0'', α'', q'') such that $S[\![\alpha']\!]\sigma_0' = \sigma'$, and $S[\![\alpha'']\!]\sigma_0'' = \sigma''$. It follows from the assumptions of the proposition that $(q_0', \alpha', q') = (q_0'', \alpha'', q'')$ and hence that $\alpha' = \alpha''$ and $\sigma' = \sigma''$. This concludes the proof in the inductive case.

The above result suffices to establish the property of Definition 1.21. So assume $\langle q_\triangleright; \sigma \rangle \stackrel{\omega'}{\Longrightarrow}^* \langle q_\triangleleft; \sigma' \rangle$ and $\langle q_\triangleright; \sigma \rangle \stackrel{\omega''}{\Longrightarrow}^* \langle q_\triangleleft; \sigma'' \rangle$. If $|\omega'| = |\omega''|$ the property follows directly from the above. If $|\omega'| \neq |\omega''|$ then we can, without loss of generality, assume that ω' is shorter than ω'' so $\omega'' = \omega_1''\omega_2''$ where $|\omega'| = |\omega_1''|$. Now consider the prefix

$$\langle q_\triangleright; \sigma \rangle \stackrel{\omega_1''}{\Longrightarrow}^* \langle q'''; \sigma''' \rangle$$

of the second execution sequence. The result proved above gives that $q_\triangleleft = q'''$ and since there are no edges leaving $q_\triangleleft$ it cannot be the case that $|\omega'| \neq |\omega''|$. This completes the proof. □

TRY IT OUT 1.23: Continuing Examples 1.1 and 1.7, determine whether or not the factorial program constitutes a deterministic system. □

The conditions mentioned in the proposition are sufficient for obtaining a deterministic system but they are not necessary – meaning that it is possible to have a deterministic system even when the conditions of the proposition do not hold. An example is shown in Figure 1.11 where the key point is that $x \leq 0$ and $x \geq 0$ overlap exactly when $x = 0$.

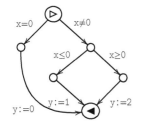

Figure 1.11: A deterministic system.

Evolving System   We would generally like that a value is always computed. This is clearly not always the case because programs may loop, and proving the absence of looping behaviour requires careful analysis of the program.

A weaker demand is that a program does not stop in a stuck configuration. This leads to the notion of an evolving system.

DEFINITION 1.24: A program graph **PG** and its semantics S constitute an *evolving system* whenever

$$\langle q_\triangleright; \sigma \rangle \stackrel{\omega'}{\Longrightarrow}^* \langle q'; \sigma' \rangle \text{ with } q' \neq q_\triangleleft \text{ can always be extended to}$$

$$\langle q_\triangleright; \sigma \rangle \stackrel{\omega''}{\Longrightarrow}^* \langle q''; \sigma'' \rangle \text{ for some } \omega'' \text{ of the form } \omega'' = \omega'\alpha'$$

To ensure that a program graph and its semantics give rise to an evolving system we may use the following sufficient condition (illustrated in Figure 1.12), which is relatively straightforward to check.

PROPOSITION 1.25: A program graph **PG** and its semantics S constitute an *evolving system* if for every non-final node and every memory there is an edge leaving it such that the memory is in the domain of the semantic function for that edge:

$$\forall q \in \mathbf{Q} \setminus \{q_{\blacktriangleleft}\} : \forall \sigma \in \mathbf{Mem} : \exists (q, \alpha, q') \in \mathbf{E} : \sigma \in \mathrm{dom}(S[\![\alpha]\!])$$

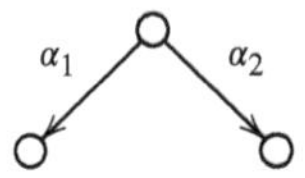

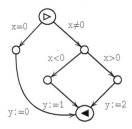

Figure 1.12: $S[\![\alpha_1]\!]\sigma$ or $S[\![\alpha_2]\!]\sigma$ defined.

PROOF: Straightforward: simply use the assumption on the last configuration of the execution sequence considered in Definition 1.24. □

TRY IT OUT 1.26: Continuing Examples 1.1 and 1.7, determine whether or not the factorial program constitutes an evolving system. □

The conditions mentioned in the proposition are sufficient for obtaining an evolving system but they are not necessary – meaning that it is possible to have an evolving system even when the conditions of the proposition do not hold. An example is shown in Figure 1.13 where the key point is that $x > 0$ and $x < 0$ have a gap exactly when $x = 0$.

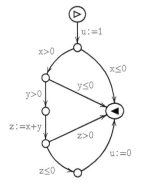

Figure 1.13: An evolving system.

1.5   Bit-Level Semantics (Bonus Material)

When looking at the numbers occurring in the actions of program graphs we may take them to be the integers, as we know them from mathematics. But to be more faithful to the fact that program graphs are to be executed by actual computers we could take them to be bit strings interpreted in certain ways. In this section we are going to consider three scenarios for how to model the semantics of numbers.

We will consider the program graph in Figure 1.14 throughout this section. The semantics will operate on a memory that gives values to the four variables x, y, z and u; we shall write $\sigma = (\sigma_x, \sigma_y, \sigma_z, \sigma_u)$. We use the notation $x := e$ to indicate that the result of evaluating e gives rise to the new value of the variable x. We will be interested in answering the following two questions:

- Is it always possible to reach a final configuration?
  To be precise: $\forall \sigma : \exists \sigma' : \langle q_{\triangleright}; \sigma \rangle \Longrightarrow^* \langle q_{\blacktriangleleft}; \sigma' \rangle$?

- Will the final value of u always be 1?
  To be precise: $\forall \sigma, \sigma' : (\langle q_{\triangleright}; \sigma \rangle \Longrightarrow^* \langle q_{\blacktriangleleft}; \sigma' \rangle) \Rightarrow \sigma'_u = 1$?

Scenario 1: Mathematical Integers   In this approach to the semantics of numbers we consider them to be the *integers* as we know them from mathematics, and the

Figure 1.14: Example program.

operations $+$, $>$ and $\leq$ are the familiar ones. (This is the approach that we have implicitly taken so far and will be taking throughout the book.) It is straightforward that the answer to both questions is affirmative because clearly the sum of positive integers is a positive integer.

Scenario 2: Unsigned Byte   In this approach to the semantics of numbers we consider them to be bit strings of length 8 that are interpreted as *unsigned numbers*. (This is called `unsigned char` in C.) To be precise the mathematical integer denoted by the bit string $b_7 \cdots b_0$ is

$$[\![b_7 \cdots b_0]\!]_U = \Sigma_{i<8} \ b_i 2^i$$

and as an example $[\![10000000]\!]_U = 128$.

The operation $+$ will be the familiar addition on bit strings where we start from the right and produce a carry (either 0 or 1) that is repetitively brought to the next position. To avoid confusion we write $+$ for this operation on bits. In general we write

$$b_7' \cdots b_0' \ + \ b_7'' \cdots b_0'' = c : b_7 \cdots b_0$$

Figure 1.15: Adding bit strings.

where c is the value of the final carry bit. As an example $10010101 + 10011001 = 1 : 00101110$; this is illustrated in Figure 1.15. We need to consider when this operation might be incorrect with respect to the mathematical integers, that is when

$$[\![b_7' \cdots b_0']\!]_U + [\![b_7'' \cdots b_0'']\!]_U \neq [\![b_7 \cdots b_0]\!]_U$$

and the answer is that this is the case precisely when $c = 1$. There is nothing we can do about this because in this case the correct result cannot be represented in 8 bits. We have two choices for how to deal with the overflow situation where $c = 1$. One is to *halt* the program and the other is to *ignore* the problem; the latter would seem more familiar from actual computers.

Returning to the program graph of Figure 1.14 let us merely assume that the operations $>$ and $\leq$ work as expected. Next, let us take both x and y to be 10000000 (representing the integer 128) and note that $10000000 + 10000000 = 1 : 00000000$ and that $[\![10000000]\!]_U > 0$ but $[\![00000000]\!]_U \leq 0$. It is then clear that the answer to the first question above is affirmative only if we *ignore* the overflow. Also, that the answer to the second question is affirmative only if we *halt* the program. Clearly the magnitude of x and y becomes critical to the correctness of the program graph.

TEASER 1.27: Suppose that the initial value of x is chosen with equal probability among the 256 possibilities (representing numbers from 0 to 255) and similarly for y. Furthermore, assume that we ignore the overflows. Show that the probability that u has a final value of 1 is 99.6%. (Hint: Determine the number of cases where the final value of u is 0, then divide by 256^2, and finally subtract from 1.)   □

Scenario 3: Signed Byte In this approach to the semantics of numbers we consider them to be bit strings of length 8 that are interpreted as *signed numbers*. (This is called `signed char` in C.) To be precise, the mathematical integer denoted by the bit string $sb_6 \cdots b_0$ is

$$\llbracket sb_6 \cdots b_0 \rrbracket_S = (-s)2^7 + \Sigma_{i<7} \, b_i 2^i = (-s)2^7 + \llbracket b_6 \cdots b_0 \rrbracket_U$$

and as an example $\llbracket 10000001 \rrbracket_S = -127$.

As before, the operation + will be the familiar addition on bit strings where we start from the right and produce a carry (either 0 or 1) that is repetitively brought to the next position and to avoid confusion we write + for this operation on bits. In general we write

$$s'b'_6 \cdots b'_0 + s''b''_6 \cdots b''_0 = c : sb_6 \cdots b_0$$

where c is the value of the final carry bit. As an example $00001001 + 10000000 = 0 : 10001001$ and as yet another example $10001001 + 10000000 = 1 : 00001001$. We need to consider when this operation might be incorrect with respect to the mathematical integers, that is when

$$\llbracket s'b'_6 \cdots b'_0 \rrbracket_S + \llbracket s''b''_6 \cdots b''_0 \rrbracket_S \neq \llbracket sb_6 \cdots b_0 \rrbracket_S$$

and it is helpful to consider the sub-computation $b'_6 \cdots b'_0 + b''_6 \cdots b''_0 = o : b_6 \cdots b_0$ and to note that $0s' + 0s'' + 0o = cs$ and that this makes it possible to determine o from s', s'', s and c. As we shall see in the exercise below, the erroneous situation arises when $s' = s'' \neq o$. There is nothing we can do about this because the correct result cannot be represented in 8 bits when interpreted as signed numbers. We have two choices for how to deal with the erroneous situation where $s' = s'' \neq o$. One is to *halt* the program and the other is to *ignore* the problem; the latter would seem more familiar from actual computers.

Returning to the program graph, let us merely assume that the operations > and $\leq$ work as expected. Next let us take both x and y to be 01000000 (representing the integer 64) and note that $01000000 + 01000000 = 0 : 10000000$ and that $\llbracket 01000000 \rrbracket_S > 0$ but $\llbracket 10000000 \rrbracket_S \leq 0$. It is then clear that the answer to the first question is affirmative only if we *ignore* the overflow. Also, that the answer to the second question is affirmative only if we *halt* the program. Clearly the magnitude of x and y becomes critical to the correctness of the program graph.

EXERCISE 1.28: Consider each of the eight cases in Figure 1.16 and argue that they correctly explain whether or not $\llbracket s'b'_6 \cdots b'_0 \rrbracket_S + \llbracket s''b''_6 \cdots b''_0 \rrbracket_S = \llbracket sb_6 \cdots b_0 \rrbracket_S$. Finally note that the two offending cases are characterised by $s' = s'' \neq o$.

As an example, let us consider the last entry. From $s' = 1$, $s'' = 1$ and $o = 1$ we know that $c = 1$ and $s = 1$ and hence that $1b'_6 \cdots b'_0 + 1b''_6 \cdots b''_0 = 1 : 1b_6 \cdots b_0$. From $o = 1$ we know that $\llbracket b'_6 \cdots b'_0 \rrbracket_U + \llbracket b''_6 \cdots b''_0 \rrbracket_U = 2^7 + \llbracket b_6 \cdots b_0 \rrbracket_U$ and hence

s'	s''	o	
0	0	0	ok
0	0	1	wrong
0	1	0	ok
0	1	1	ok
1	0	0	ok
1	0	1	ok
1	1	0	wrong
1	1	1	ok

Figure 1.16: Case analysis.

that

$$\llbracket 1b'_6 \cdots b'_0 \rrbracket_S + \llbracket 1b''_6 \cdots b''_0 \rrbracket_S =$$
$$\llbracket b'_6 \cdots b'_0 \rrbracket_U - 2^7 + \llbracket b''_6 \cdots b''_0 \rrbracket_U - 2^7 =$$
$$\llbracket b_6 \cdots b_0 \rrbracket_U - 2^7 =$$
$$\llbracket 1b_6 \cdots b_0 \rrbracket_S$$

as was to be shown.   □

TEASER 1.29: Suppose that the initial value of x is chosen with equal probability among the 256 possibilities (representing numbers from -128 to 127) and similarly for y. Furthermore, assume that we ignore the overflows. Show that the probability that u has a final value of 1 is 87.6%. (Hint: Find the number of cases where the final value of u is 0, then divide by 256^2, and finally subtract from 1.)   □

EXERCISE 1.30: One method for carrying out subtraction of numbers in signed byte representation is based on the mathematical equality $x - y = -(y + (-x))$. For the calculation of $-x$ one often uses the formula

$$-\ sb_6 \cdots b_0 = \text{flip}(sb_6 \cdots b_0)\ +\ 00000001$$

where $\text{flip}(sb_6 \cdots b_0) = (1 - s)(1 - b_6) \cdots (1 - b_0)$; as an example $\text{flip}(01010101) = 10101010$. Determine when $-\llbracket sb_6 \cdots b_0 \rrbracket_S \neq \llbracket \text{flip}(sb_6 \cdots b_0)\ +\ 00000001 \rrbracket_S$.   □

Chapter 2

Guarded Commands

Programs are written in programming languages and in this chapter we are going to show how we can construct program graphs for all programs in a programming language. The programming language will be the (probably unfamiliar) language of Guarded Commands introduced by Dijkstra in 1975.

2.1 Syntax

In Dijkstra's language of *Guarded Commands* a basic command has one of two forms: either it is an assignment $x := a$ or it is a skip command; the latter has no effect but is useful when no memory change is wanted. Commands can be combined in three different ways. Sequencing is written $C_1 ; \cdots ; C_k$ and indicates that the commands should be executed in the order they are written. The conditional takes the form if $b_1 \to C_1 [] \cdots [] b_k \to C_k$ fi; as an example, to express that C_1 should be executed when b holds and that otherwise C_2 should be executed, we shall write if $b \to C_1 [] \neg b \to C_2$ fi. The iteration construct takes the form do $b_1 \to C_1 [] \cdots [] b_k \to C_k$ od; as an example, to express that C should be executed as long as b holds, we shall write do $b \to C$ od.

EXAMPLE 2.1: Figure 2.1 is a program intended to compute the factorial function. In addition to assignments, it makes use of sequencing (as indicated by the semicolons) and the iteration construct do $\cdots$ od. The body of the construct is a single guarded command consisting of a guard and a command; here the guard is the test $x > 0$ and the command is the sequence of assignments $y := x * y; x := x - 1$. The idea is that as long as the guard is satisfied the associated command will be executed. When the guard fails, the construct terminates.

```
y := 1;
do x > 0 →  y := x * y;
            x := x - 1
od
```

Figure 2.1: Example program for the factorial function.

15

© Springer Nature Switzerland AG 2019
F. Nielson, H. Riis Nielson, *Formal Methods*, https://doi.org/10.1007/978-3-030-05156-3_2

```
if x ≥ y → z := x
[] y > x → z := y
fi
```

Figure 2.2: Example program for the maximum function.

EXAMPLE 2.2: Figure 2.2 is a program computing the maximum of two values. It makes use of the conditional `if ··· fi` and contains two guarded commands separated by the choice symbol `[]`. The idea is to select a guard that is satisfied and to execute the corresponding command – in our program exactly one of the guards will be satisfied.

If none of the guards are satisfied the execution stops; for example, this will be the case if we change the first guard to x > y and start in a memory where x and y are equal.

It might also be the case that more than one guard is satisfied and then one of the alternatives will be selected non-deterministically for execution; for example, this will be the case if we change the second guard to y ≥ x and start in a memory where x and y are equal.

DEFINITION 2.3: The syntax of the commands C and guarded commands GC of the *Guarded Commands* language are mutually recursively defined using the following *BNF notation*:

$$C \quad ::= \quad x := a \mid \texttt{skip} \mid C_1 ; C_2 \mid \texttt{if } GC \texttt{ fi} \mid \texttt{do } GC \texttt{ od}$$
$$GC \quad ::= \quad b \to C \mid GC_1 \, [] \, GC_2$$

We make use of arithmetic expressions a and boolean expressions b given by

$$a \quad ::= \quad n \mid x \mid a_1 + a_2 \mid a_1 - a_2 \mid a_1 * a_2 \mid a_1 \,\hat{}\, a_2$$
$$b \quad ::= \quad \texttt{true} \mid a_1 = a_2 \mid a_1 > a_2 \mid a_1 \geq a_2 \mid b_1 \wedge b_2 \mid b_1 \, \&\& \, b_2 \mid \neg b_0$$

The syntax of variables x and numbers n is left unspecified.

Figure 2.3: Abstract syntax trees for x ∗ (y + z) and (x ∗ y) + z.

The definition specifies an *abstract syntax tree* for commands, guarded commands and arithmetic and boolean expressions. As an example, $a ::= x$ tells us that an arithmetic expression can be a tree consisting of a single node representing the variable x, whereas $a ::= a_1 * a_2$ tells us that it can be a binary tree with root $*$ and a subtree corresponding to a_1 and another subtree corresponding to a_2.

The definition specifies the *syntactic tree structure* (rather than a linear sequence of characters) and therefore we do not need to introduce explicit *brackets* in the syntax, although we shall feel free to use *parentheses* in textual presentations of programs in order to disambiguate the syntax. This is illustrated in Figure 2.3; when the precedence of operators is clear we write x ∗ y + z for (x ∗ y) + z.

Figure 2.4: Abstract syntax trees for $C_1 ; (C_2 ; C_3)$ and $(C_1 ; C_2) ; C_3$.

Similar comments hold for commands, guarded commands and boolean expressions; see Figure 2.4 for an example. In the case of sequencing we consider the sequencing operator to associate to the right so that $C_1 ; C_2 ; C_3$ is shorthand for $C_1 ; (C_2 ; C_3)$. In the case of choice we consider the choice operator to associate to the right so that $GC_1 \, [] \, GC_2 \, [] \, GC_3$ is shorthand for $GC_1 \, [] \, (GC_2 \, [] \, GC_3)$. Figure 2.5 gives the

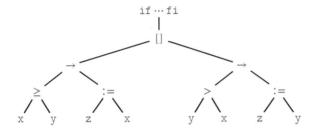

Figure 2.5: Abstract syntax tree for the program in Figure 2.2.

abstract syntax tree for the program of Figure 2.2.

TRY IT OUT 2.4: Draw the abstract syntax tree for the program of Figure 2.1. □

TRY IT OUT 2.5: Construct a Guarded Commands program for the power function computing the power 2^n of a number n without using exponentiation (^). □

EXERCISE 2.6: Construct programs in the Guarded Commands language computing

(a) the modulo operation $\text{mod}(n, m)$ returning the remainder after division of one number n by another m;

(b) the greatest common divisor $\gcd(n, m)$ of two numbers n and m;

(c) the n'th Fibonacci number. □

Usually we write programs as linear sequences of characters so how do we get them in the form of the abstract syntax trees required here? The answer is that this task is carried out by *parsing* the programs. How to do this is specified using a context-free grammar that differs from our BNF notation in having to deal with issues like precedence of operators. Hence parsing produces parse trees that need to be 'simplified' to the abstract syntax trees used here.

2.2 Program Graphs

In Chapter 1 we constructed program graphs manually and given a program in the Guarded Commands language we should be able to do the same. However, we would like the construction of program graphs from programs to be fully specified in such a way that it could be carried out by an algorithm (which might be part of an interpreter for the Guarded Commands language).

To this end we will define a function **edges**, which works on commands and guarded commands and produces the set of edges of a program graph – given the factorial program of Figure 2.1 we expect the function to construct the edges of a program graph like the one in Example 1.3. We are particularly interested in the initial and final nodes and want to restrict the function **edges** to use the intended initial and final nodes; they are therefore supplied as parameters. So for a command C the result of $\textbf{edges}(q_\circ \rightsquigarrow q_\bullet)[\![C]\!]$ should be the set of edges of a program graph with initial node $q_\circ$ and final node $q_\bullet$. During the construction of program graphs we will be able to create *fresh nodes*; however, we shall refrain from covering the machinery needed to really ensure that fresh nodes are indeed only chosen once.

DEFINITION 2.7: For commands the edges are constructed as follows:

$$\textbf{edges}(q_\circ \rightsquigarrow q_\bullet)[\![x := a]\!] \;=\; \{(q_\circ, x := a, q_\bullet)\}$$

$$\textbf{edges}(q_\circ \rightsquigarrow q_\bullet)[\![\texttt{skip}]\!] \;=\; \{(q_\circ, \texttt{skip}, q_\bullet)\}$$

$$\textbf{edges}(q_\circ \rightsquigarrow q_\bullet)[\![C_1 \,;\, C_2]\!] \;=\; \begin{aligned} &\text{let } q \text{ be fresh} \\ &\quad E_1 = \textbf{edges}(q_\circ \rightsquigarrow q)[\![C_1]\!] \\ &\quad E_2 = \textbf{edges}(q \rightsquigarrow q_\bullet)[\![C_2]\!] \\ &\text{in } E_1 \cup E_2 \end{aligned}$$

$$\textbf{edges}(q_\circ \rightsquigarrow q_\bullet)[\![\texttt{if } GC \texttt{ fi}]\!] \;=\; \textbf{edges}(q_\circ \rightsquigarrow q_\bullet)[\![GC]\!]$$

$$\textbf{edges}(q_\circ \rightsquigarrow q_\bullet)[\![\texttt{do } GC \texttt{ od}]\!] \;=\; \begin{aligned} &\text{let } b = \text{done}[\![GC]\!] \\ &\quad E = \textbf{edges}(q_\circ \rightsquigarrow q_\circ)[\![GC]\!] \\ &\text{in } E \cup \{(q_\circ, b, q_\bullet)\} \end{aligned}$$

For an assignment $x := a$ we simply create an edge from $q_\circ$ to $q_\bullet$ that is labelled $x := a$. This is illustrated in Figure 2.6(a). The construct $\texttt{skip}$ is handled in a similar way.

For a sequence of commands $C_1 \,;\, C_2$ we create a new node that will glue the edges for the C_i's together; the idea is that the final node of C_1 becomes the initial node of C_2. This is illustrated in Figure 2.6(b).

DEFINITION 2.8: For guarded commands the edges are constructed as follows:

$$\textbf{edges}(q_\circ \rightsquigarrow q_\bullet)[\![b \rightarrow C]\!] \;=\; \begin{aligned} &\text{let } q \text{ be fresh} \\ &\quad E = \textbf{edges}(q \rightsquigarrow q_\bullet)[\![C]\!] \\ &\text{in } \{(q_\circ, b, q)\} \cup E \end{aligned}$$

$$\textbf{edges}(q_\circ \rightsquigarrow q_\bullet)[\![GC_1 \,[]\, GC_2]\!] \;=\; \begin{aligned} &\text{let } E_1 = \textbf{edges}(q_\circ \rightsquigarrow q_\bullet)[\![GC_1]\!] \\ &\quad E_2 = \textbf{edges}(q_\circ \rightsquigarrow q_\bullet)[\![GC_2]\!] \\ &\text{in } E_1 \cup E_2 \end{aligned}$$

For a single guarded command $b \rightarrow C$ we create an edge labelled b to a new node q that is then used as the initial node for the following command. This is illustrated

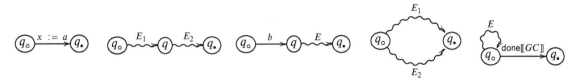

(a) assignment   (b) sequencing   (c) single guarded   (d) choice guarded   (e) iteration
    command   of commands   command   command   command

Figure 2.6: Figures explaining the construction of program graphs.

in Figure 2.6(c). If we have a choice between two guarded commands we use the same source and target nodes for both of them as illustrated in Figure 2.6(d).

Returning to the conditional if GC fi, we simply construct the edges of the program graph for the embedded guarded command using the given source and target nodes; it will automatically take care of the various tests within the guarded commands. As an example, for a conditional of the form if $b_1 \rightarrow C_1 \,[]\, b_2 \rightarrow C_2$ fi we obtain a graph of the form shown in Figure 2.7 (where each E_i arises from C_i).

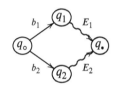

Figure 2.7: A conditional with two guarded commands.

The iteration construct do GC od is slightly more complex as the program graph has to record the looping structure as shown in Figure 2.6(e). We construct the edges of the embedded guarded command using $q_\circ$ as source as well as target node, thereby reflecting the iterative nature of the construct. When none of the tests of the guarded command are satisfied the iteration should terminate and therefore we add an edge from $q_\circ$ to $q_\bullet$ labelled with the boolean expression done$[\![GC]\!]$ expressing this condition. It is defined by

$$\text{done}[\![b \rightarrow C]\!] = \neg b$$
$$\text{done}[\![GC_1 \,[]\, GC_2]\!] = \text{done}[\![GC_1]\!] \wedge \text{done}[\![GC_2]\!]$$

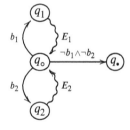

Figure 2.8: An iteration construct with two guarded commands.

As an example, for an iteration construct of the form do $b_1 \rightarrow C_1 \,[]\, b_2 \rightarrow C_2$ od we obtain a graph of the form shown in Figure 2.8; note that done$[\![b_1 \rightarrow C_1 \,[]\, b_2 \rightarrow C_2]\!]$ amounts to $\neg b_1 \wedge \neg b_2$.

EXAMPLE 2.9: Let us apply the function **edges**$(q_\rhd \leadsto q_\lhd)[\![\cdot]\!]$ to the program in Figure 2.1. We calculate

$$\textbf{edges}(q_\rhd \leadsto q_\lhd)[\![\text{y} := 1; \text{do } \text{x} > 0 \rightarrow \text{y} := \text{x} * \text{y}; \text{x} := \text{x} - 1 \text{ od}]\!]$$
$$= \quad \textbf{edges}(q_\rhd \leadsto q_1)[\![\text{y} := 1]\!]$$
$$\quad \cup \quad \textbf{edges}(q_1 \leadsto q_\lhd)[\![\text{do } \text{x} > 0 \rightarrow \text{y} := \text{x} * \text{y}; \text{x} := \text{x} - 1 \text{ od}]\!]$$

$$= \{(q_\triangleright, \text{y} := 1, q_1)\}$$
$$\cup \ \mathbf{edges}(q_1 \rightsquigarrow q_1)[\![\text{x} > 0 \rightarrow \text{y} := \text{x} * \text{y}; \text{x} := \text{x} - 1]\!]$$
$$\cup \ \{(q_1, \neg(\text{x} > 0), q_\blacktriangleleft)\}$$

$$= \{(q_\triangleright, \text{y} := 1, q_1), (q_1, \text{x} > 0, q_2)\}$$
$$\cup \ \mathbf{edges}(q_2 \rightsquigarrow q_1)[\![\text{y} := \text{x} * \text{y}; \text{x} := \text{x} - 1]\!]$$
$$\cup \ \{(q_1, \neg(\text{x} > 0), q_\blacktriangleleft)\}$$

$$= \{(q_\triangleright, \text{y} := 1, q_1), (q_1, \text{x} > 0, q_2)\}$$
$$\cup \ \mathbf{edges}(q_2 \rightsquigarrow q_3)[\![\text{y} := \text{x} * \text{y}]\!] \ \cup \ \mathbf{edges}(q_3 \rightsquigarrow q_1)[\![\text{x} := \text{x} - 1]\!]$$
$$\cup \ \{(q_1, \neg(\text{x} > 0), q_\blacktriangleleft)\}$$

$$= \{(q_\triangleright, \text{y} := 1, q_1), \ (q_1, \text{x} > 0, q_2), \ (q_2, \text{y} := \text{x} * \text{y}, q_3),$$
$$(q_3, \text{x} := \text{x} - 1, q_1), \ (q_1, \neg(\text{x} > 0), q_\blacktriangleleft)\}$$

The resulting graph is shown in Figure 2.9.

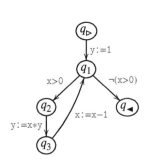

Figure 2.9: $\mathbf{edges}(q_\triangleright \rightsquigarrow q_\blacktriangleleft)[\![\cdot]\!]$ applied to the factorial function.

TRY IT OUT 2.10: Use the algorithm of Definitions 2.7 and 2.8 to construct a program graph for the program of Try It Out 2.5. Discuss the extent to which you get the same program graph as you constructed in Try It Out 1.4. □

EXERCISE 2.11: Use the algorithm of Definitions 2.7 and 2.8 to construct program graphs for the programs of Exercise 2.6. Discuss the extent to which you get the same program graphs as you constructed in Exercise 1.5. □

Recall that the edges of a program graph are triples $\mathbf{E} \subseteq \mathbf{Q} \times \mathbf{Act} \times \mathbf{Q}$ and given the initial node $q_\triangleright$ and the final node $q_\blacktriangleleft$ we define $\mathbf{E} = \mathbf{edges}(q_\triangleright \rightsquigarrow q_\blacktriangleleft)[\![C]\!]$ for the command C of interest. The set $\mathbf{Act}$ consists of three kinds of actions: one is an assignment, $x := a$, another is skip, and the third is a boolean condition, b. The set $\mathbf{Q}$ of nodes consists of $\{q_\triangleright, q_\blacktriangleleft\}$ together with all the nodes occurring as first or third components of tuples in $\mathbf{E}$.

PROPOSITION 2.12: Given a command C the result of $\mathbf{edges}(q_\triangleright \rightsquigarrow q_\blacktriangleleft)[\![C]\!]$ is a set $\mathbf{E}$ of edges of a program graph $\mathbf{PG}$ where $\mathbf{Act}$ and $\mathbf{Q}$ are as explained previously (and where we ensure that $q_\triangleright \neq q_\blacktriangleleft$).

SKETCH OF PROOF: It is immediate that $\mathbf{edges}(q_\triangleright \rightsquigarrow q_\blacktriangleleft)[\![C]\!]$ produces a set of edges and we need to show that $q_\blacktriangleleft$ is not the first component of any edge in $\mathbf{edges}(q_\triangleright \rightsquigarrow q_\blacktriangleleft)[\![C]\!]$ (using that $q_\triangleright \neq q_\blacktriangleleft$).

Formally this can be done by induction on the size of the argument C or GC to the call of $\mathbf{edges}(q_\circ \rightsquigarrow q_\bullet)[\![\cdot]\!]$; here we take the size to be the number of nodes in the abstract syntax tree. The actual proof boils down to considering each of the defining clauses for $\mathbf{edges}(q_\circ \rightsquigarrow q_\bullet)[\![\cdot]\!]$ in Definitions 2.7 and 2.8 one by one and showing that if $q_\circ \neq q_\bullet$ then $q_\bullet$ cannot be the first component of any edge in $E = \mathbf{edges}(q_\circ \rightsquigarrow q_\bullet)[\![\cdot]\!]$.

Suppose that $E' = \mathbf{edges}(q_\circ' \rightsquigarrow q_\bullet')[\![\cdot]\!]$ and $E'' = \mathbf{edges}(q_\circ'' \rightsquigarrow q_\bullet'')[\![\cdot]\!]$ arise from two distinct calls on the right-hand side of the same clause. Let N' be the set of nodes in

E' and N'' be the set of nodes in E''. The freshness of the generated nodes ensures that $(N' \setminus \{q_\circ', q_\bullet'\}) \cap (N'' \cup \{q_\circ'', q_\bullet''\}) = \{\}$ and $(N' \cup \{q_\circ', q_\bullet'\}) \cap (N'' \setminus \{q_\circ'', q_\bullet''\}) = \{\}$.

It now follows from the induction hypothesis that if $q_\circ \neq q_\bullet$ then $q_\bullet$ cannot be the first component of any edge in $E = \mathbf{edges}(q_\circ \leadsto q_\bullet)[\![\cdot]\!]$. $\qquad\square$

TEASER 2.13: Argue that the construction of $\mathbf{edges}(q_\circ \leadsto q_\bullet)[\![C_1; C_2]\!] = E_1 \cup E_2$ for $E_1 = \mathbf{edges}(q_\circ \leadsto q)[\![C_1]\!]$ and $E_2 = \mathbf{edges}(q \leadsto q_\bullet)[\![C_2]\!]$ (for some fresh node q) might be incorrect if we did not ensure that the final node cannot be a first component of any of the edges. $\qquad\square$

2.3 Semantics

We shall now define the semantics for Guarded Commands in accordance with Definition 1.6. This calls for defining a semantic domain and we shall use $\mathbf{Mem} = \mathbf{Var} \to \mathbf{Int}$ reflecting that the values of the variables will always be integers. It also calls for defining a semantic function $\mathcal{S}[\![\cdot]\!] : \mathbf{Act} \to (\mathbf{Mem} \hookrightarrow \mathbf{Mem})$ giving the meaning of the actions. Recall that the skip action does nothing so it is immediate to take $\mathcal{S}[\![\text{skip}]\!]\sigma = \sigma$; however we need a bit of preparation before we can define $\mathcal{S}[\![x := a]\!]$ and $\mathcal{S}[\![b]\!]$.

An arithmetic expression was defined to be one of n, x, $a_1 + a_2$, $a_1 - a_2$, $a_1 * a_2$ or $a_1 \,\hat{}\, a_2$, where a_1 and a_2 are also arithmetic expressions. This is a recursive definition of how to form an *abstract syntax tree* for an arithmetic expression.

When evaluating the arithmetic expressions we shall therefore define semantic functions

$$\mathcal{A}[\![a]\!] : \mathbf{Mem} \hookrightarrow \mathbf{Int}$$

recursively on the way the arithmetic expressions were formed; the idea being that $\mathcal{A}[\![a]\!]\sigma$ is the value of a in the memory σ:

$$\mathcal{A}[\![x]\!]\sigma = \begin{cases} \sigma(x) & \text{if } x \in \mathrm{dom}(\sigma) \\ \text{undefined} & \text{otherwise} \end{cases}$$

$$\mathcal{A}[\![n]\!]\sigma = n$$

$$\mathcal{A}[\![a_1 + a_2]\!]\sigma = \begin{cases} z_1 + z_2 & \text{if } z_1 = \mathcal{A}[\![a_1]\!]\sigma \text{ and } z_2 = \mathcal{A}[\![a_2]\!]\sigma \\ \text{undefined} & \text{otherwise} \end{cases}$$

$$\mathcal{A}[\![a_1 - a_2]\!]\sigma = \begin{cases} z_1 - z_2 & \text{if } z_1 = \mathcal{A}[\![a_1]\!]\sigma \text{ and } z_2 = \mathcal{A}[\![a_2]\!]\sigma \\ \text{undefined} & \text{otherwise} \end{cases}$$

$$\mathcal{A}[\![a_1 * a_2]\!]\sigma = \begin{cases} z_1 \cdot z_2 & \text{if } z_1 = \mathcal{A}[\![a_1]\!]\sigma \text{ and } z_2 = \mathcal{A}[\![a_2]\!]\sigma \\ \text{undefined} & \text{otherwise} \end{cases}$$

$$\mathcal{A}[\![a_1 \,\hat{}\, a_2]\!]\sigma = \begin{cases} z_1^{z_2} & \text{if } z_1 = \mathcal{A}[\![a_1]\!]\sigma,\ z_2 = \mathcal{A}[\![a_2]\!]\sigma \text{ and } z_2 \geq 0 \\ \text{undefined} & \text{otherwise} \end{cases}$$

Here we write merely n for the integer denoted by the number (or numeral) n, but we distinguish between the syntactic operations (e.g. $*$) and their mathematical counterparts (e.g. $\cdot$). If we had decided to use signed bytes (or signed words) as discussed in Section 1.5 we would have needed to take even more care in distinguishing syntax from semantics. When we write $z = \mathcal{A}[\![a]\!]\sigma$ this means that $\mathcal{A}[\![a]\!]\sigma$ is defined and that it gives the integer z. Note that $\mathcal{A}[\![x]\!]\sigma$ is undefined when $x \notin \mathsf{dom}(\sigma)$.

$$
\begin{aligned}
&\mathcal{A}[\![\mathtt{x}*3-5]\!]\sigma \\
=\ &\mathcal{A}[\![(\mathtt{x}*3)-5]\!]\sigma \\
=\ &\mathcal{A}[\![\mathtt{x}*3]\!]\sigma - \mathcal{A}[\![5]\!]\sigma \\
=\ &(\mathcal{A}[\![\mathtt{x}]\!]\sigma \cdot \mathcal{A}[\![3]\!]\sigma) - \mathcal{A}[\![5]\!]\sigma \\
=\ &(\sigma(\mathtt{x}) \cdot 3) - 5 \\
=\ &(7 \cdot 3) - 5 \\
=\ &16
\end{aligned}
$$

Figure 2.10: Calculating the value of $\mathtt{x}*3-5$.

EXAMPLE 2.14: Figure 2.10 shows in detail how to use the semantics to compute the value of $\mathtt{x}*3-5$ using the usual precedence of operators and a memory σ where $\mathtt{x}$ is 7.

The boolean expressions were defined to have one of the forms $\mathtt{true}$, $a_1 = a_2$, $a_1 > a_2$, $a_1 \geq a_2$, $b_1 \wedge b_2$, $b_1\ \&\&\ b_2$ or $\neg b_0$, where b_0, b_1 and b_2 are themselves boolean expressions. Once again this is a recursive definition of how the abstract syntax trees for boolean expressions are formed.

When evaluating boolean expressions we shall therefore define semantic functions

$$\mathcal{B}[\![b]\!] : \mathbf{Mem} \hookrightarrow \mathbf{Bool}$$

recursively on the way the boolean expressions were formed; here **Bool** denotes the set of truth values $\{\mathsf{true}, \mathsf{false}\}$:

$$\mathcal{B}[\![\mathtt{true}]\!]\sigma = \mathsf{true}$$

$$
\mathcal{B}[\![a_1 = a_2]\!]\sigma =
\begin{cases}
\mathsf{true} & \text{if } z_1 = \mathcal{A}[\![a_1]\!]\sigma, z_2 = \mathcal{A}[\![a_2]\!]\sigma, \text{ and } z_1 = z_2 \\
\mathsf{false} & \text{if } z_1 = \mathcal{A}[\![a_1]\!]\sigma, z_2 = \mathcal{A}[\![a_2]\!]\sigma, \text{ and } z_1 \neq z_2 \\
\mathsf{undefined} & \text{otherwise}
\end{cases}
$$

$$
\mathcal{B}[\![a_1 > a_2]\!]\sigma =
\begin{cases}
\mathsf{true} & \text{if } z_1 = \mathcal{A}[\![a_1]\!]\sigma, z_2 = \mathcal{A}[\![a_2]\!]\sigma, \text{ and } z_1 > z_2 \\
\mathsf{false} & \text{if } z_1 = \mathcal{A}[\![a_1]\!]\sigma, z_2 = \mathcal{A}[\![a_2]\!]\sigma, \text{ and } z_1 \leq z_2 \\
\mathsf{undefined} & \text{otherwise}
\end{cases}
$$

$$
\mathcal{B}[\![a_1 \geq a_2]\!]\sigma =
\begin{cases}
\mathsf{true} & \text{if } z_1 = \mathcal{A}[\![a_1]\!]\sigma, z_2 = \mathcal{A}[\![a_2]\!]\sigma, \text{ and } z_1 \geq z_2 \\
\mathsf{false} & \text{if } z_1 = \mathcal{A}[\![a_1]\!]\sigma, z_2 = \mathcal{A}[\![a_2]\!]\sigma, \text{ and } z_1 < z_2 \\
\mathsf{undefined} & \text{otherwise}
\end{cases}
$$

$$
\mathcal{B}[\![b_1 \wedge b_2]\!]\sigma =
\begin{cases}
\mathsf{true} & \text{if } \mathcal{B}[\![b_1]\!]\sigma = \mathsf{true} \text{ and } \mathcal{B}[\![b_2]\!]\sigma = \mathsf{true} \\
\mathsf{undefined} & \text{if } \mathcal{B}[\![b_1]\!]\sigma = \mathsf{undefined} \\
& \quad \text{or } \mathcal{B}[\![b_2]\!]\sigma = \mathsf{undefined} \\
\mathsf{false} & \text{otherwise}
\end{cases}
$$

$$\mathcal{B}[\![b_1 \,\&\&\, b_2]\!]\sigma \;=\; \begin{cases} \mathcal{B}[\![b_2]\!]\sigma & \text{if } \mathcal{B}[\![b_1]\!]\sigma = \text{true} \\ \text{false} & \text{if } \mathcal{B}[\![b_1]\!]\sigma = \text{false} \\ \text{undefined} & \text{if } \mathcal{B}[\![b_1]\!]\sigma = \text{undefined} \end{cases}$$

$$\mathcal{B}[\![\neg b]\!]\sigma \;=\; \begin{cases} \text{true} & \text{if } \mathcal{B}[\![b]\!]\sigma = \text{false} \\ \text{false} & \text{if } \mathcal{B}[\![b]\!]\sigma = \text{true} \\ \text{undefined} & \text{if } \mathcal{B}[\![b]\!]\sigma = \text{undefined} \end{cases}$$

TRY IT OUT 2.15: Give an example where the usual conjunction $b_1 \wedge b_2$ has a different semantics than the *short-circuit* conjunction $b_1 \,\&\&\, b_2$. ☐

EXERCISE 2.16: It is quite standard to use boolean expressions beyond those of true, $a_1 = a_2$, $a_1 > a_2$, $a_1 \geq a_2$, $b_1 \wedge b_2$, $b_1 \,\&\&\, b_2$ and $\neg b_0$. Extend the syntax and semantics to also incorporate false, $a_1 \neq a_2$, $a_1 < a_2$, $a_1 \leq a_2$, $b_1 \vee b_2$ and $b_1 \,||\, b_2$ (where the latter is a form of disjunction that does not attempt to evaluate b_2 if b_1 evaluates to true). Does this extend the expressive power of the boolean expressions or could we have managed without these extensions? ☐

DEFINITION 2.17: We are now ready to define the semantics for Guarded Commands. The semantic domain is

$$\mathbf{Mem} = \mathbf{Var} \to \mathbf{Int}$$

and the semantic function $\mathcal{S}[\![\cdot]\!] : \mathbf{Act} \to (\mathbf{Mem} \hookrightarrow \mathbf{Mem})$ is given by

$$\mathcal{S}[\![\text{skip}]\!]\sigma \;=\; \sigma$$

$$\mathcal{S}[\![x := a]\!]\sigma \;=\; \begin{cases} \sigma[x \mapsto \mathcal{A}[\![a]\!]\sigma] & \text{if } \mathcal{A}[\![a]\!]\sigma \text{ is defined and } x \in \text{dom}(\sigma) \\ \text{undefined} & \text{otherwise} \end{cases}$$

$$\mathcal{S}[\![b]\!]\sigma \;=\; \begin{cases} \sigma & \text{if } \mathcal{B}[\![b]\!]\sigma = \text{true} \\ \text{undefined} & \text{otherwise} \end{cases}$$

Whenever $\mathcal{S}[\![\alpha]\!]\sigma = \sigma'$ the idea is that if σ is the memory before executing α then σ' is the memory afterwards.

TEASER 2.18: Modify the development of the present section to use the semantic domain

$$\mathbf{Mem} = \mathbf{Var} \to \mathbf{Byte}$$

where **Byte** denotes signed bytes as considered in Section 1.5. Be careful in determining what to do in case of *overflow*: to *halt* the program or to *ignore* the problem. ☐

Arrays We shall now incorporate arrays as studied in Section 1.3 into the Guarded Commands language. For this we shall modify the syntax of Definition 2.3 as follows:

```
i := 0;
x := 0;
do i < 10 → x := x + A[i];
            B[i] := x;
            i := i + 1
od
```

Figure 2.11: Traversing an array.

$$C \quad ::= \quad A[a_1] := a_2 \mid \cdots \text{ as in Definition 2.3} \cdots$$
$$a \quad ::= \quad A[a] \mid \cdots \text{ as in Definition 2.3} \cdots$$

The new constructs give us a command for assigning to array entries and an arithmetic expression for indexing into an array. These constructs can be combined freely with the previous constructs. Figure 2.11 gives an example of a program constructing an array B such that $B[i] = A[0] + \cdots + A[i]$ for all values of $i < 10$, where the arrays A and B both have length 10.

The program graphs for commands (and guarded commands) of the extended language will have the same form as in Section 2.2 with the main exception being that we have a fourth kind of action, namely $A[a_1] := a_2$.

DEFINITION 2.19: We extend Definition 2.7 as follows:

$$\mathbf{edges}(q_\circ \rightsquigarrow q_\bullet)[\![A[a_1] := a_2]\!] \quad = \quad \{(q_\circ, A[a_1] := a_2, q_\bullet)\}$$

The memories of the semantics will be defined as in Section 1.3. Thus we shall assume that that each array $A \in \mathbf{Arr}$ has a length given by $\text{length}(A)$ and that the memories are given by

$$\mathbf{Mem} = \Big(\ \mathbf{Var} \cup \{A[i] \mid A \in \mathbf{Arr}, 0 \le i < \text{size}(A)\} \ \Big) \to \mathbf{Int}$$

ESSENTIAL EXERCISE 2.20: Extend Definition 2.17 to apply to the extended language. More precisely, use the above definition of **Mem** and complete the following partial definition of the semantic function $\mathcal{S}[\![\cdot]\!]$:

$$\mathcal{S}[\![A[a_1] := a_2]\!]\sigma \quad = \quad \begin{cases} \sigma[A[z_1] \mapsto z_2] & \text{if } z_1 = \mathcal{A}[\![a_1]\!]\sigma \\ & \text{and } z_2 = \mathcal{A}[\![a_2]\!]\sigma \\ & \text{and } A[z_1] \in \text{dom}(\sigma) \\ \text{undefined} & \text{otherwise} \end{cases}$$

To do so you should perform the necessary extensions of the functions $\mathcal{A}[\![\cdot]\!]$ and $\mathcal{B}[\![\cdot]\!]$.

2.4   Alternative Approaches

In Section 2.2 we presented one particular way of constructing the program graphs for the Guarded Commands language. In this section we shall discuss some alternatives that lead to different semantics of the syntactically same language. In order to avoid confusion we shall supply the function **edges** with an index reminding us of the alternative considered, and if the functions for commands and guarded commands have different functionality we shall use a prime to indicate the one for guarded commands.

A deterministic version Consider the following alternative way to define program graphs, where the function **edges** on guarded commands is modified: it is given an extra argument indicating which tests have been attempted previously and it returns an updated version of this information as well as the set of edges being constructed:

$$\mathbf{edges}_{\mathrm{d2}}(q_\circ \rightsquigarrow q_\bullet)[\![b \to C]\!](d) \;=\; \begin{aligned} &\text{let } q \text{ be fresh}\\ &\qquad E = \mathbf{edges}_{\mathrm{d}}(q \rightsquigarrow q_\bullet)[\![C]\!]\\ &\text{in } (\{(q_\circ, b \wedge \neg d, q)\} \cup E, b \vee d) \end{aligned}$$

$$\mathbf{edges}_{\mathrm{d2}}(q_\circ \rightsquigarrow q_\bullet)[\![GC_1 \,[]\, GC_2]\!](d) \;=\; \begin{aligned} &\text{let } (E_1, d_1) = \mathbf{edges}_{\mathrm{d2}}(q_\circ \rightsquigarrow q_\bullet)[\![GC_1]\!](d)\\ &\qquad (E_2, d_2) = \mathbf{edges}_{\mathrm{d2}}(q_\circ \rightsquigarrow q_\bullet)[\![GC_2]\!](d_1)\\ &\text{in } (E_1 \cup E_2, d_2) \end{aligned}$$

Note that we make use of the additional parameter in the construction of the edge in the case of a single guarded command and we pass the updated information from the first to the second guarded command in the case of the choice construct.

The new function is then used in the definition of the edges for the commands. Only the cases of conditional and iteration are affected so we modify Definition 2.7 to have

$$\mathbf{edges}_{\mathrm{d}}(q_\circ \rightsquigarrow q_\bullet)[\![\texttt{if } GC \texttt{ fi}]\!] \;=\; \begin{aligned} &\text{let } (E, d) = \mathbf{edges}_{\mathrm{d2}}(q_\circ \rightsquigarrow q_\bullet)[\![GC]\!](\texttt{false})\\ &\text{in } E \end{aligned}$$

$$\mathbf{edges}_{\mathrm{d}}(q_\circ \rightsquigarrow q_\bullet)[\![\texttt{do } GC \texttt{ od}]\!] \;=\; \begin{aligned} &\text{let } (E, d) = \mathbf{edges}_{\mathrm{d2}}(q_\circ \rightsquigarrow q_\circ)[\![GC]\!](\texttt{false})\\ &\text{in } E \cup \{(q_\circ, \neg d, q_\bullet)\} \end{aligned}$$

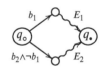

Figure 2.12: A conditional with two guarded commands.

As an example, for a conditional of the form if $b_1 \to C_1 \,[]\, b_2 \to C_2$ fi we now get a program graph of the form shown in Figure 2.12 (rather than as in Figure 2.7); here we have taken the liberty of simplifying $b_1 \wedge \neg\texttt{false}$ to b_1.

TRY IT OUT 2.21: Give an example of a command where **edges** and **edges$_{\mathrm{d}}$** give rise to different program graphs. □

EXERCISE 2.22: Argue that if $(E, d) = \mathbf{edges}_{\mathrm{d2}}(q_\circ \rightsquigarrow q_\bullet)[\![GC]\!](\texttt{false})$ then $\neg d$ is logically equivalent to done$[\![GC]\!]$. Argue that this means that all the resulting program graphs will give rise to *deterministic* systems in the sense of Section 1.4.□

An evolving version The semantics is such that a conditional if GC fi will be stuck at the source node if all of the tests in GC evaluate to false. As an example, consider a conditional of the form if $b_1 \to C_1 \,[]\, b_2 \to C_2$ fi; it will be stuck if both

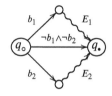

Figure 2.13: A non-blocking conditional with two guarded commands.

b_1 and b_2 evaluate to false. If we do not want this to be the case we can simply modify the construction of the edges of the program graph as follows:

$$\textbf{edges}_{\text{e}}(q_\circ \rightsquigarrow q_\bullet)[\![\texttt{if } GC \texttt{ fi}]\!] = \begin{aligned} &\text{let } b = \text{done}[\![GC]\!]\\ &\qquad E = \textbf{edges}_{\text{e}}(q_\circ \rightsquigarrow q_\bullet)[\![GC]\!]\\ &\text{in } E \cup \{(q_\circ, b, q_\bullet)\} \end{aligned}$$

The other definitions are as in Section 2.2. For a conditional $\texttt{if } b_1 \rightarrow C_1 \,[]\, b_2 \rightarrow C_2 \texttt{ fi}$ we now obtain a program graph of the form shown in Figure 2.13.

TRY IT OUT 2.23: Give an example of a command where **edges** and $\textbf{edges}_{\text{e}}$ give rise to different program graphs. □

EXERCISE 2.24: Assume that the semantics of arithmetic and boolean expressions are given by total functions. Argue that then the resulting program graphs will give rise to *evolving* systems in the sense of Section 1.4. □

An internal choice Returning to Definition 2.8 let us consider the following alternative for the case $GC_1 \,[]\, GC_2$:

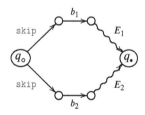

Figure 2.14: An internal choice for a conditional with two guarded commands.

$$\textbf{edges}_{\text{i}}(q_\circ \rightsquigarrow q_\bullet)[\![GC_1 \,[]\, GC_2]\!] = \begin{aligned} &\text{let } q_1 \text{ and } q_2 \text{ be fresh}\\ &\qquad E_1 = \textbf{edges}_{\text{i}}(q_1 \rightsquigarrow q_\bullet)[\![GC_1]\!]\\ &\qquad E_2 = \textbf{edges}_{\text{i}}(q_2 \rightsquigarrow q_\bullet)[\![GC_2]\!]\\ &\text{in } \{(q_\circ, \texttt{skip}, q_1), (q_\circ, \texttt{skip}, q_2)\} \cup E_1 \cup E_2 \end{aligned}$$

All the other cases are as in Definitions 2.7 and 2.8. Figure 2.14 illustrates the program graph obtained for a conditional $\texttt{if } b_1 \rightarrow C_1 \,[]\, b_2 \rightarrow C_2 \texttt{ fi}$ (where each E_i arises from C_i).

2.5   More Control Structures (Bonus Material)

Loop control commands Let us add two new constructs to the Guarded Commands language:

$$C ::= \texttt{break} \mid \texttt{continue} \mid \cdots \text{ as in Definition 2.3} \cdots$$

The idea is that a $\texttt{break}$ command encountered inside a $\texttt{do}$ command will terminate the execution of the loop and transfer control to the *end* of the command. On the other hand, the $\texttt{continue}$ construct will transfer control to the *beginning* of the loop.

EXAMPLE 2.25: The program in Figure 2.15 uses the variable x to compute the sum of some of the entries of the array A (of length 10) and y will count how many entries have been added up. The program terminates when the *first* negative entry is encountered.

If we replace the break command with a continue command then the program will sum *all* the non-negative entries in the array and count their number.

Note that if we replace the break command with skip then the intended relationship between x and y no longer holds.

```
i := 0;
x := 0;
y := 0;
do i < 10 →
    if  A[i] ≥ 0 → x := x + A[i];
                        i := i + 1
    []  A[i] < 0 → i := i + 1;
                        break
    fi;
    y := y + 1
od
```

Figure 2.15: Adding and counting some of the entries of an array.

To construct program graphs for the extended language we need to keep track of not only the source and target nodes $q_\circ$ and $q_\bullet$ of the program graph to be constructed but also the source and target nodes q_c and q_b of the immediately enclosing do command. The idea is that when we encounter a break command inside a do construct we have to transfer control to the target of the do construct, that is q_b (rather than $q_\bullet$). On the other hand, when we encounter a continue command we shall transfer control to the entry node of the do construct, that is q_c.

As in Section 2.2 the function **edges** is defined for commands and guarded commands. In addition to the parameters $q_\circ$, $q_\bullet$ and C or GC it will also take two nodes q_b and q_c as parameters.

DEFINITION 2.26: For commands the edges are constructed as follows:

$$\mathbf{edges}_{bc}(q_\circ \rightsquigarrow q_\bullet)[\![x := a]\!](q_b, q_c) \;=\; \{(q_\circ, x := a, q_\bullet)\}$$

$$\mathbf{edges}_{bc}(q_\circ \rightsquigarrow q_\bullet)[\![\texttt{skip}]\!](q_b, q_c) \;=\; \{(q_\circ, \texttt{skip}, q_\bullet)\}$$

$$\mathbf{edges}_{bc}(q_\circ \rightsquigarrow q_\bullet)[\![C_1; C_2]\!](q_b, q_c) \;=$$
$$\begin{aligned}
\text{let} \quad & q \text{ be fresh} \\
& E_1 = \mathbf{edges}_{bc}(q_\circ \rightsquigarrow q)[\![C_1]\!](q_b, q_c) \\
& E_2 = \mathbf{edges}_{bc}(q \rightsquigarrow q_\bullet)[\![C_2]\!](q_b, q_c) \\
\text{in} \quad & E_1 \cup E_2
\end{aligned}$$

$$\mathbf{edges}_{bc}(q_\circ \rightsquigarrow q_\bullet)[\![\texttt{if } GC \texttt{ fi}]\!](q_b, q_c) \;=\; \mathbf{edges}_{bc}(q_\circ \rightsquigarrow q_\bullet)[\![GC]\!](q_b, q_c)$$

$$\mathbf{edges}_{bc}(q_\circ \rightsquigarrow q_\bullet)[\![\texttt{do } GC \texttt{ od}]\!](q_b, q_c) \;=$$
$$\begin{aligned}
\text{let} \quad & b = \mathsf{done}[\![GC]\!] \\
& E = \mathbf{edges}_{bc}(q_\circ \rightsquigarrow q_\circ)[\![GC]\!](q_\bullet, q_\circ) \\
\text{in} \quad & E \cup \{(q_\circ, b, q_\bullet)\}
\end{aligned}$$

$$\mathbf{edges}_{bc}(q_\circ \rightsquigarrow q_\bullet)[\![\texttt{break}]\!](q_b, q_c) \;=\; \{(q_\circ, \texttt{skip}, q_b)\}$$

$$\mathbf{edges}_{bc}(q_\circ \rightsquigarrow q_\bullet)[\![\texttt{continue}]\!](q_b, q_c) \;=\; \{(q_\circ, \texttt{skip}, q_c)\}$$

Note that the parameters q_b and q_c are only modified when we enter a do command. The reason is that we only record the current looping context as the break and continue constructs are relative to the innermost enclosing do command. So in particular there is no need to record the information for all the enclosing loops.

DEFINITION 2.27: For guarded commands the edges are constructed as follows:

$$\mathbf{edges}_{bc}(q_\circ \rightsquigarrow q_\bullet)[\![b \to C]\!](q_b, q_c) =$$
$$\text{let } q \text{ be fresh}$$
$$E = \mathbf{edges}_{bc}(q \rightsquigarrow q_\bullet)[\![C]\!](q_b, q_c)$$
$$\text{in } \{(q_\circ, b, q)\} \cup E$$

$$\mathbf{edges}_{bc}(q_\circ \rightsquigarrow q_\bullet)[\![GC_1 \; [] \; GC_2]\!](q_b, q_c) =$$
$$\text{let } E_1 = \mathbf{edges}_{bc}(q_\circ \rightsquigarrow q_\bullet)[\![GC_1]\!](q_b, q_c)$$
$$E_2 = \mathbf{edges}_{bc}(q_\circ \rightsquigarrow q_\bullet)[\![GC_2]\!](q_b, q_c)$$
$$\text{in } E_1 \cup E_2$$

EXAMPLE 2.28: Let us use Definitions 2.26 and 2.27 to construct the program graph for the program in Figure 2.15. The result is shown in Figure 2.16. First a number of nodes are created for the sequence of initialising assignments. The program graph for the do command is then constructed using q_3 and $q_\blacktriangleleft$ as the source and target nodes and therefore its body will use $q_\blacktriangleleft$ and q_3 as its break and continue nodes. The two branches of the conditional are processed independently of one another; they both have $q_\blacktriangleleft$ and q_3 as their break and continue nodes but this information is only used in the second branch, which gives rise to an edge with target $q_\blacktriangleleft$ when it encounters the break command.

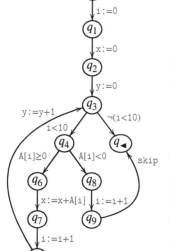

Figure 2.16: Program graph for the sum/counting function.

TRY IT OUT 2.29: Replace the break command with continue in the program in Figure 2.15 and construct the corresponding program graph. Repeat the exercise with skip in place of break. □

EXERCISE 2.30: Explain which parameters to give to $\mathbf{edges}_{bc}$ in order to generate the program graph for a command C of interest. Do you get the intended effect of a break or continue command that does not occur inside a do construct? □

EXERCISE 2.31: Add a command loop GC pool for which we generate edges as follows:

$$\mathbf{edges}_{bc}(q_\circ \rightsquigarrow q_\bullet)[\![\texttt{loop } GC \texttt{ pool}]\!](q_b, q_c) = \mathbf{edges}_{bc}(q_\circ \rightsquigarrow q_\circ)[\![GC]\!](q_\bullet, q_\circ)$$

Explain how its semantics differs from that of do GC od. Is there a way to use loop ⋯ pool and break to get the same behaviour as do ⋯ od? Is there a way to use do ⋯ od to get almost the same behaviour as loop ⋯ pool? □

Exceptions We shall now extend the Guarded Commands language of Section 2.1 with an exception mechanism. For this we introduce two new commands: one is the command throw e that will raise an exception named e and the other is a command try C catch e_1: C_1 [] $\cdots$ [] e_k: C_k yrt that specifies handlers for the exceptions $e_1, \ldots, e_k$. If the command throw e_i is encountered inside C then control will be transferred to C_i. In general when a command throw e is encountered, the control will be transferred to the appropriate innermost handler in an enclosing try command.

To summarise we shall modify the syntax of Definition 2.3 to have:

$$C \quad ::= \quad \text{try } C \text{ catch } HC \text{ yrt} \mid \text{throw } e \mid \cdots \text{as in Definition 2.3} \cdots$$
$$HC \quad ::= \quad e\colon C \mid HC_1 \,[]\, HC_2$$

The exceptions e are left unspecified but in examples we shall use strings, for example yes and no. The syntax of handler commands HC is patterned after that of guarded commands – the main difference is that the guards are now exception names rather than boolean expressions.

> EXAMPLE 2.32: The program of Figure 2.17 searches for a value in an array A (of length 10) and throws the exception yes if the value is present and no otherwise.

In order to construct the program graphs we need to keep track of a mapping γ from exceptions to the nodes in the program graph to which the control has to be transferred when the exception is thrown. The mapping is called a *handler environment* and we write $\gamma(e)$ for the node associated with the exception e.

The function **edges** needs to be supplied with a handler environment in order to construct the relevant edges. For the construct try C catch e_1: C_1 [] $\cdots$ [] e_k: C_k yrt we shall first extend the handler environment with information about the new exceptions $[e_1 \mapsto q_1, \cdots, e_k \mapsto q_k]$ and then use this when constructing the edges for C; here $q_1, \cdots, q_k$ are fresh nodes created when processing the handler commands, so the version of the **edges** function used for handler commands does not need to be supplied with a source node.

```
i := 0;
try
    do A[i] = x →
            throw yes
    [] ¬(A[i] = x) →
            if i < 9 →
                    i := i + 1
            [] i ≥ 9 →
                    throw no
            fi
    od
catch yes: ···
    []  no: ···
yrt
```

Figure 2.17: Searching for a value in an array.

For handler commands the edges and the updated handler environment are constructed as follows:

$$\mathbf{edges}_{\times 2}(\rightsquigarrow q_\bullet)[\![e\colon C]\!]\gamma \quad = \quad \begin{aligned}&\text{let} \quad q \text{ be fresh}\\ &\qquad E = \mathbf{edges}_{\times}(q \rightsquigarrow q_\bullet)[\![C]\!]\gamma\\ &\text{in} \quad (E, \gamma[e \mapsto q])\end{aligned}$$

$$\textbf{edges}_{x2}(\leadsto q_\bullet)[\![HC_1\, [\,]\, HC_2]\!]\gamma \quad = \quad \begin{array}{ll} \text{let} & (E_1,\gamma_1) = \textbf{edges}_{x2}(\leadsto q_\bullet)[\![HC_1]\!]\gamma \\ & (E_2,\gamma_2) = \textbf{edges}_{x2}(\leadsto q_\bullet)[\![HC_2]\!]\gamma_1 \\ \text{in} & (E_1 \cup E_2, \gamma_2) \end{array}$$

For the handler command $e\colon C$ we simply update the supplied handler environment γ with the relevant information for e. For the composite handler command $HC_1\,[\,]\,HC_2$ the definition expresses that first the handler environment γ is extended with the exceptions of HC_1 and the resulting environment γ_1 is then extended with the exceptions of HC_2 to produce the result for the composite construct.

For commands the edges are constructed as follows for the new constructs:

$$\begin{array}{l} \textbf{edges}_x(q_\circ \leadsto q_\bullet)[\![\texttt{try } C \texttt{ catch } HC \texttt{ yrt}]\!]\gamma = \\ \qquad\qquad \begin{array}{ll} \text{let} & (E',\gamma') = \textbf{edges}_{x2}(\leadsto q_\bullet)[\![HC]\!]\gamma \\ & E = \textbf{edges}_x(q_\circ \leadsto q_\bullet)[\![C]\!]\gamma' \\ \text{in} & E \cup E' \end{array} \end{array}$$

$$\textbf{edges}_x(q_\circ \leadsto q_\bullet)[\![\texttt{throw } e]\!]\gamma = \left\{ \begin{array}{ll} \{(q_\circ, \texttt{skip}, q)\} & \text{where } q = \gamma(e) \\ \{\,\} & \text{if } e \notin \text{dom}(\gamma) \end{array} \right.$$

Notice that the handler environment γ' constructed from HC in the construct $\texttt{try } C \texttt{ catch } HC \texttt{ yrt}$ is used when constructing the program graph for C. The construct $\texttt{throw } e$ then makes use of the handler environment when constructing the program graph.

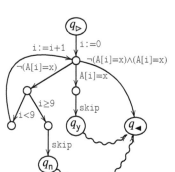

Figure 2.18: Program graph for the search function.

EXAMPLE 2.33: For the program in Figure 2.17 we obtain the program graph in Figure 2.18; we start with an empty handler environment and extend it to $[\texttt{yes} \mapsto q_y, \texttt{no} \mapsto q_n]$. The wavy edges represent the program graph for the unspecified parts of the program of Figure 2.17.

EXERCISE 2.34: Complete the specification of the function $\textbf{edges}_x$ for the commands and guarded commands of the extended language. □

EXERCISE 2.35: Consider each of the following scenarios. Determine what happens and discuss whether this is what we want:

(a) an exception is thrown and it has more than one handler in the same $\texttt{try}$ construct,

(b) an exception is thrown and it has a handler in more than one $\texttt{try}$ construct,

(c) an exception is thrown and it has no handler at all. □

Chapter 3

Program Verification

It is essential that programs are *correct* – meaning that their behaviour is as we intend. For example, a sorting routine should indeed sort the array given as input. To verify the correctness of programs one often writes invariants at various points in the program and checks their correctness. In this chapter we will illustrate this approach – working directly on program graphs.

3.1 Predicates

To be able to express the correctness of programs we need adequate notation; to set the scene we first consider a couple of examples.

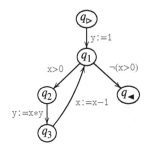

EXAMPLE 3.1: Let us consider the factorial function from Figure 3.1. Assuming that $x = \underline{n} \geq 0$ holds initially the aim is to establish that $y = fac(\underline{n})$ holds when the program terminates; here *fac* is the mathematical function defined by

$$fac(z) = \begin{cases} 1 & \text{if } z \leq 0 \\ z \cdot fac(z\text{-}1) & \text{if } z > 0 \end{cases}$$

So how do we define the correctness of the factorial function? One way is to say at $q_\triangleright$ that $x = \underline{n} \geq 0$, to say at $q_\blacktriangleleft$ that $y = fac(\underline{n})$, and to ensure that $\underline{n}$ never changes.

Figure 3.1: Program graph for the factorial function.

EXAMPLE 3.2: Consider the program graph for insertion sort explained in Example 1.16 and shown in Figure 3.2; recall that b abbreviates $j > 0 \,\&\&\, A[j-1] > A[j]$ and that $\neg b$ is its negation. It was intended to accept an array A of length n

31

© Springer Nature Switzerland AG 2019
F. Nielson, H. Riis Nielson, *Formal Methods*, https://doi.org/10.1007/978-3-030-05156-3_3

as input (at the node $q_{\triangleright}$) and to produce the sorted array A as output (at the node $q_{\blacktriangleleft}$).

How can we express that the array A is sorted? One possibility is to merely assume a predicate *sorted* and to write $sorted(\text{A}, 0, \text{n})$ to express this. Another possibility is to define $sorted(\text{A}, \text{m}, \text{n})$ by

$$\forall \underline{i}, \underline{j} : \text{m} \leq \underline{i} < \underline{j} < \text{n} \Rightarrow \text{A}[\underline{i}] \leq \text{A}[\underline{j}]$$

We may read this as saying that for all choices of indices i and j, whenever $i < j$ then $\text{A}[i] \leq \text{A}[j]$, assuming that i and j both stay within the bounds $\{\text{m}, \cdots, \text{n} - 1\}$.

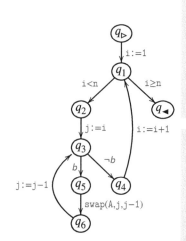

Figure 3.2: Program graph for insertion sort; b abbreviates $\texttt{j > 0 \&\&}$ $\texttt{A[j - 1] > A[j]}$.

EXAMPLE 3.3: Continuing Example 3.2, how can we express that the array A of length n is the result of sorting an array $\underline{\text{A}}$ also of length n? On top of $sorted(\text{A}, 0, \text{n})$ we need to say that A and $\underline{\text{A}}$ have the same elements. One possibility is to assume a predicate *permuted* and to write $permuted(\text{A}, \text{n}, \underline{\text{A}})$ to mean this. Another possibility is to define $permuted(\text{A}, \text{n}, \underline{\text{A}})$ by

$$\exists \underline{\pi} : \left(\begin{array}{l} (\forall \underline{i}, \underline{j} : 0 \leq \underline{i} < \underline{j} < \text{n} \Rightarrow 0 \leq \underline{\pi}(\underline{i}) \neq \underline{\pi}(\underline{j}) < \text{n}) \wedge \\ \forall \underline{i} : \text{A}[\underline{i}] = \underline{\text{A}}[\underline{\pi}(\underline{i})] \end{array} \right)$$

where the first line says that $\underline{\pi}$ is a permutation function and the second line says that A is a permuted version of $\underline{\text{A}}$.

How can we express that the output array A of length n is the sorted version of the input array $\underline{\text{A}}$ of length n? One way is to say at $q_{\triangleright}$ that $\text{A} = \underline{\text{A}}$, to say at $q_{\blacktriangleleft}$ that $sorted(\text{A}, 0, \text{n}) \wedge permuted(\text{A}, \text{n}, \underline{\text{A}})$, and to ensure that $\underline{\text{A}}$ never changes.

TRY IT OUT 3.4: Explain why it is problematic to define $permuted(\text{A}, \text{n}, \underline{\text{A}})$ by $\forall \underline{i} : 0 \leq \underline{i} < \text{n} \Rightarrow (\exists \underline{j} : 0 \leq \underline{j} < \text{n} : \text{A}[\underline{i}] = \underline{\text{A}}[\underline{j}])$.   □

The examples suggest that we would like to write predicates and expressions that go beyond what we can write in the boolean and arithmetic expressions of our program graphs. In particular, we would like to use universal quantifiers ($\forall$) and existential quantifiers ($\exists$); we would like to be able to quantify over functions and to use well-known mathematical functions; and we would like to have a supply of variables that cannot be changed by executing the actions of the program graph. The latter kind of variables will be called *logical variables* and we will use underlining to distinguish them from traditional *program variables*: only program variables can occur in the actions of the program graphs.

It will be inappropriate for us to fully specify the syntax of our predicates and expressions so we shall merely provide a partial specification of *predicates* (or formulae) ϕ and *expressions* e:

$$\phi \quad ::= \quad true \mid \phi_1 \wedge \phi_2 \mid \phi_1 \vee \phi_2 \mid \neg\phi_0 \mid \phi_1 \Rightarrow \phi_2 \mid$$
$$\exists \underline{x} : \phi_0 \mid \forall \underline{x} : \phi_0 \mid e_1 = e_2 \mid \cdots \mid p(e_1, \cdots, e_n)$$
$$e \quad ::= \quad x \mid \underline{x} \mid e_1 + e_2 \mid \cdots \mid f(e_1, \cdots, e_n)$$

Here p is a previously defined predicate (like *sorted*) and f is a well-known mathematical function (like *fac*).

When defining the meaning of predicates we shall write

$$(\sigma, \underline{\sigma}) \vDash \phi$$

to indicate that the predicate ϕ holds in a setting where the program variables are given by the (concrete) memory σ and the logical variables are given by the virtual memory $\underline{\sigma}$. We may provide the following partial definition:

$(\sigma, \underline{\sigma})$	$\vDash$	$true$	iff	true
$(\sigma, \underline{\sigma})$	$\vDash$	$\phi_1 \wedge \phi_2$	iff	$((\sigma, \underline{\sigma}) \vDash \phi_1) \wedge ((\sigma, \underline{\sigma}) \vDash \phi_2)$
$(\sigma, \underline{\sigma})$	$\vDash$	$\phi_1 \vee \phi_2$	iff	$((\sigma, \underline{\sigma}) \vDash \phi_1) \vee ((\sigma, \underline{\sigma}) \vDash \phi_2)$
$(\sigma, \underline{\sigma})$	$\vDash$	$\neg\phi_0$	iff	$(\sigma, \underline{\sigma}) \nvDash \phi_0$
$(\sigma, \underline{\sigma})$	$\vDash$	$\phi_1 \Rightarrow \phi_2$	iff	$((\sigma, \underline{\sigma}) \vDash \phi_1) \Rightarrow ((\sigma, \underline{\sigma}) \vDash \phi_2)$
$(\sigma, \underline{\sigma})$	$\vDash$	$\exists \underline{x} : \phi$	iff	$\exists v : (\sigma, \underline{\sigma}[\underline{x} \mapsto v]) \vDash \phi$
$(\sigma, \underline{\sigma})$	$\vDash$	$\forall \underline{x} : \phi$	iff	$\forall v : (\sigma, \underline{\sigma}[\underline{x} \mapsto v]) \vDash \phi$
$(\sigma, \underline{\sigma})$	$\vDash$	$e_1 = e_2$	iff	$[\![e_1]\!](\sigma, \underline{\sigma}) = [\![e_2]\!](\sigma, \underline{\sigma})$

It is essential that we ensure that $(\sigma, \underline{\sigma}) \vDash \phi$ always gives true or false (and hence cannot be undefined). The latter clause uses a function $[\![\cdot]\!]$ defined in part by

$$[\![x]\!](\sigma, \underline{\sigma}) \quad = \quad \sigma(x)$$
$$[\![\underline{x}]\!](\sigma, \underline{\sigma}) \quad = \quad \underline{\sigma}(\underline{x})$$
$$[\![e_1 + e_2]\!](\sigma, \underline{\sigma}) \quad = \quad [\![e_1]\!](\sigma, \underline{\sigma}) + [\![e_2]\!](\sigma, \underline{\sigma})$$

It is essential that we ensure that $[\![e]\!](\sigma, \underline{\sigma})$ always gives a value (and hence cannot be undefined).

Note how the definitions of $(\sigma, \underline{\sigma}) \vDash \phi$ and $[\![e]\!](\sigma, \underline{\sigma})$ make it clear that program variables are handled by the (concrete) memory and logical variables by the virtual memory.

Recall that a predicate ϕ is called a *tautology* when it is always true (meaning that $\forall (\sigma, \underline{\sigma}) : (\sigma, \underline{\sigma}) \vDash \phi$) and that a predicate ϕ is said to be *satisfiable* when it is not always false (meaning that $\exists(\sigma, \underline{\sigma}) : (\sigma, \underline{\sigma}) \vDash \phi$).

In both cases we only quantify over *suitable* pairs of memories that provide values to all the program variables and logical variables actually used. Note that ϕ is a tautology exactly when $\neg\phi$ is not satisfiable.

Often predicates are expressed in a first-order logic with interpreted base predicates. For some choices of predicates there are advanced tools known as SMT solvers (Satisfaction Modulo Theories) that can determine whether or not a predicate ϕ is satisfiable. The logic we used in Examples 3.2 and 3.3 is actually a form of second-order logic because of our quantification over functions.

3.2   Predicate Assignments

A key step in the verification of program graphs is to associate *invariants* with each node in the program graph. So let us consider a program graph **PG** given by **Q**, $q_{\triangleright}$, $q_{\blacktriangleleft}$, **Act** and **E** as in Definition 1.2.

DEFINITION 3.5: A *predicate assignment* is a mapping

$$\mathbf{P : Q \to Pred}$$

where **Pred** is a non-empty set of predicates as discussed in Section 3.1.

EXAMPLE 3.6: Returning to Example 3.1, define **P** as follows:

$$
\begin{aligned}
\mathbf{P}(q_{\triangleright}) &= \ \mathrm{x} = \underline{\mathrm{n}} \wedge \underline{\mathrm{n}} \geq 0 \\
\mathbf{P}(q_1) &= \ \underline{\mathrm{n}} \geq \mathrm{x} \wedge \mathrm{x} \geq 0 \wedge \mathrm{y} \cdot fac(\mathrm{x}) = fac(\underline{\mathrm{n}}) \\
\mathbf{P}(q_2) &= \ \underline{\mathrm{n}} \geq \mathrm{x} \wedge \mathrm{x} > 0 \wedge \mathrm{y} \cdot \mathrm{x} \cdot fac(\mathrm{x} - 1) = fac(\underline{\mathrm{n}}) \\
\mathbf{P}(q_3) &= \ \underline{\mathrm{n}} \geq \mathrm{x} \wedge \mathrm{x} > 0 \wedge \mathrm{y} \cdot fac(\mathrm{x} - 1) = fac(\underline{\mathrm{n}}) \\
\mathbf{P}(q_{\blacktriangleleft}) &= \ \mathrm{y} = fac(\underline{\mathrm{n}})
\end{aligned}
$$

This defines a predicate assignment for the program graph in Figure 3.1.

EXAMPLE 3.7: Returning to Examples 3.2 and 3.3, define the auxiliary predicate *almost*$(\mathrm{A}, \mathrm{m}, \mathrm{p}, \mathrm{n})$ by

$$\forall \underline{i}, \underline{j} : (\mathrm{m} \leq \underline{i} < \underline{j} < \mathrm{n}) \Rightarrow (\mathrm{A}[\underline{i}] \leq \mathrm{A}[\underline{j}] \vee \underline{j} = \mathrm{p})$$

Next define **P** as follows:

$$
\begin{aligned}
\mathbf{P}(q_\rhd) &= \mathtt{A} = \underline{\mathtt{A}} \\
\mathbf{P}(q_1) &= \mathit{sorted}(\mathtt{A}, 0, \mathtt{i}) \wedge \mathit{permuted}(\mathtt{A}, \mathtt{n}, \underline{\mathtt{A}}) \\
\mathbf{P}(q_2) &= \mathit{sorted}(\mathtt{A}, 0, \mathtt{i}) \wedge \mathit{permuted}(\mathtt{A}, \mathtt{n}, \underline{\mathtt{A}}) \wedge \mathtt{i} < \mathtt{n} \\
\mathbf{P}(q_3) &= \mathit{almost}(\mathtt{A}, 0, \mathtt{j}, \mathtt{i}+1) \wedge \mathit{permuted}(\mathtt{A}, \mathtt{n}, \underline{\mathtt{A}}) \\
\mathbf{P}(q_4) &= \mathit{sorted}(\mathtt{A}, 0, \mathtt{i}+1) \wedge \mathit{permuted}(\mathtt{A}, \mathtt{n}, \underline{\mathtt{A}}) \\
\mathbf{P}(q_5) &= \mathit{almost}(\mathtt{A}, 0, \mathtt{j}, \mathtt{i}+1) \wedge \mathtt{A}[\mathtt{j}-1] > \mathtt{A}[\mathtt{j}] \wedge \mathit{permuted}(\mathtt{A}, \mathtt{n}, \underline{\mathtt{A}}) \\
\mathbf{P}(q_6) &= \mathit{almost}(\mathtt{A}, 0, \mathtt{j}-1, \mathtt{i}+1) \wedge \mathit{permuted}(\mathtt{A}, \mathtt{n}, \underline{\mathtt{A}}) \\
\mathbf{P}(q_\blacktriangleleft) &= \mathit{sorted}(\mathtt{A}, 0, \mathtt{n}) \wedge \mathit{permuted}(\mathtt{A}, \mathtt{n}, \underline{\mathtt{A}})
\end{aligned}
$$

This defines a predicate assignment for the program graph in Figure 3.2.

To be useful, invariants must be preserved as we perform the actions in the program graph; for this we will need the semantic function S introduced in Definitions 1.6 and 2.17.

DEFINITION 3.8: A predicate assignment **P** is *correct* with respect to a semantics $S[\![\cdot]\!]$ when it satisfies the following constraints: whenever we have an edge

$$(q_\circ, \alpha, q_\bullet) \in \mathbf{E}$$

and whenever we have pairs of suitable memories $(\sigma, \underline{\sigma})$ we have that

$$\left(\; (\sigma, \underline{\sigma}) \vDash \mathbf{P}(q_\circ) \wedge \sigma' = S[\![\alpha]\!](\sigma) \; \right) \Rightarrow (\sigma', \underline{\sigma}) \vDash \mathbf{P}(q_\bullet)$$

where $\sigma' = S[\![\alpha]\!](\sigma)$ means that $S[\![\alpha]\!]$ is defined on σ and gives σ'.

TRY IT OUT 3.9: Show that the predicate assignment in Example 3.6 is correct for the program graph of Figure 3.1. ☐

EXERCISE 3.10: Show that the predicate assignment in Example 3.7 is correct with respect to the program graph of Figure 3.2 (using the semantics of Example 1.16).☐

PROPOSITION 3.11: Let **P** denote a correct predicate assignment. Whenever $(\sigma, \underline{\sigma}) \vDash \mathbf{P}(q_\circ)$ and $\langle q_\circ; \sigma \rangle \overset{\omega}{\Longrightarrow}{}^* \langle q_\bullet; \sigma' \rangle$ we have that $(\sigma', \underline{\sigma}) \vDash \mathbf{P}(q_\bullet)$.

PROOF: We prove the result by mathematical induction on the length $|\omega|$ of ω.

If $|\omega| = 0$ then $q_\circ = q_\bullet$ and $\sigma = \sigma'$ and the result is trivial.

If $|\omega| = n+1$ for some $n \geq 0$ we can write $\langle q_\circ; \sigma \rangle \overset{\omega}{\Longrightarrow}{}^* \langle q_\bullet; \sigma' \rangle$ as $\langle q_\circ; \sigma \rangle \overset{\omega'}{\Longrightarrow}{}^*$ $\langle q''; \sigma'' \rangle \overset{\alpha}{\Longrightarrow} \langle q_\bullet; \sigma' \rangle$ such that $\omega = \omega' \alpha$ and hence $|\omega'| = n$. From $(\sigma, \underline{\sigma}) \vDash \mathbf{P}(q_\circ)$ it follows using the induction hypothesis that $(\sigma'', \underline{\sigma}) \vDash \mathbf{P}(q'')$ and from the correctness of **P** (see Definition 3.8) we get that $(\sigma', \underline{\sigma}) \vDash \mathbf{P}(q_\bullet)$ as desired. ☐

The *partial correctness* of a program graph with respect to $\phi_{\rhd}$ and $\phi_{\blacktriangleleft}$ is a statement of the form

$$\left((\sigma', \underline{\sigma}) \vDash \phi_{\rhd} \wedge \langle q_{\rhd}; \sigma \rangle \overset{\omega}{\Longrightarrow}^{*} \langle q_{\blacktriangleleft}; \sigma' \rangle \right) \Rightarrow (\sigma', \underline{\sigma}) \vDash \phi_{\blacktriangleleft}$$

Proposition 3.11 shows that a correct predicate assignment **P** establishes the partial correctness of the program graph with respect to $\mathbf{P}(q_{\rhd})$ and $\mathbf{P}(q_{\blacktriangleleft})$.

TEASER 3.12: Let us assume that the arithmetic expressions a of Definition 2.3 are part of the expressions e considered in Section 3.1 – except for exponentiation – so that their semantics $\mathcal{A}[\![a]\!]$ gives rise to a total function; note that the arithmetic expressions a only mention program variables x but not logical variables $\underline{x}$. Furthermore, let us assume that the boolean expressions b of Definition 2.3 are part of the predicates ϕ considered in Section 3.1.

Define a predicate transformer $\mathcal{T}[\![\alpha]\!]$ mapping predicates into predicates such that $(\sigma, \underline{\sigma}) \vDash \mathcal{T}[\![\alpha]\!](\phi)$ if and only if $(\mathcal{S}[\![\alpha]\!]\sigma, \underline{\sigma}) \vDash \phi$, where α may be any one of skip, $x := a$ and b. (Adding array assignments $A[a_1] := a_2$ is more challenging.)   □

3.3   Partial Predicate Assignments

Predicate assignments often need to be provided by programmers and it is a bit demanding to require that a predicate should be given to each and every node in the program graph. To overcome this we shall introduce the notion of a partial predicate assignment together with conditions for when it encompasses sufficiently many nodes.

DEFINITION 3.13: A *partial predicate assignment* is a mapping $\mathbf{P} : \mathbf{Q} \hookrightarrow \mathbf{Pred}$.

EXAMPLE 3.14: Once more consider the program graph of Figure 3.1 and define **P** as follows:

$$
\begin{aligned}
\mathbf{P}(q_{\rhd}) &= x = \underline{n} \wedge \underline{n} \geq 0 \\
\mathbf{P}(q_1) &= \underline{n} \geq x \wedge x \geq 0 \wedge y \cdot fac(x) = fac(\underline{n}) \\
\mathbf{P}(q_{\blacktriangleleft}) &= y = fac(\underline{n})
\end{aligned}
$$

This defines a partial predicate assignment for the program graph in Figure 3.1.

EXAMPLE 3.15: Once more consider the program graph of Figure 3.2 and define **P** as follows:

$$
\begin{aligned}
\mathbf{P}(q_{\rhd}) &= \mathtt{A} = \underline{\mathtt{A}} \\
\mathbf{P}(q_1) &= \mathit{sorted}(\mathtt{A}, 0, \mathtt{i}) \wedge \mathit{permuted}(\mathtt{A}, \mathtt{n}, \underline{\mathtt{A}}) \\
\mathbf{P}(q_3) &= \mathit{almost}(\mathtt{A}, 0, \mathtt{j}, \mathtt{i}+1) \wedge \mathit{permuted}(\mathtt{A}, \mathtt{n}, \underline{\mathtt{A}}) \\
\mathbf{P}(q_{\blacktriangleleft}) &= \mathit{sorted}(\mathtt{A}, 0, \mathtt{n}) \wedge \mathit{permuted}(\mathtt{A}, \mathtt{n}, \underline{\mathtt{A}})
\end{aligned}
$$

This defines a partial predicate assignment for the program graph in Figure 3.2.

DEFINITION 3.16: A partial predicate assignment $\mathbf{P} : \mathbf{Q} \hookrightarrow \mathbf{Pred}$ *covers* the program graph $\mathbf{PG}$ with initial node $q_{\rhd}$ and final node $q_{\blacktriangleleft}$ whenenver

$$ q_{\rhd}, q_{\blacktriangleleft} \in \mathrm{dom}(\mathbf{P}) $$

each loop in $\mathbf{PG}$ contains a node in $\mathrm{dom}(\mathbf{P})$

and we also say that $\mathrm{dom}(\mathbf{P})$ *covers* the program graph when this holds.

Note that the partial predicate assignment of Example 3.14 covers the program graph of Figure 3.1.

EXERCISE 3.17: Argue that the partial predicate assignment of Example 3.15 covers the program graph of Figure 3.2. Can you find a smaller partial predicate assignment that also covers the program graph? □

DEFINITION 3.18: Define the set of *short path fragments* with respect to a partial predicate assignment $\mathbf{P}$ and program graph with edges $\mathbf{E}$ to be those paths that start and end at nodes in $\mathrm{dom}(\mathbf{P})$ but that do not pass through other nodes in $\mathrm{dom}(\mathbf{P})$:

$$
\begin{aligned}
\mathrm{spf}(\mathbf{P}) = \{ q_0 \alpha_1 \cdots \alpha_n q_n \mid & \forall i \in \{0, \cdots, n-1\} : (q_i, \alpha_{i+1}, q_{i+1}) \in \mathbf{E}, \\
& n > 0, q_0 \in \mathrm{dom}(\mathbf{P}), q_n \in \mathrm{dom}(\mathbf{P}) \\
& \forall i \in \{1, \cdots, n-1\} : q_i \notin \mathrm{dom}(\mathbf{P}) \}
\end{aligned}
$$

EXAMPLE 3.19: The short path fragments for Example 3.14 are

$$
\begin{aligned}
& q_{\rhd} \quad \mathtt{y} := 1 \quad q_1 \\
& q_1 \quad \mathtt{x} > 0 \quad \mathtt{y} := \mathtt{x} * \mathtt{y} \quad \mathtt{x} := \mathtt{x} - 1 \quad q_1 \\
& q_1 \quad \neg(\mathtt{x} > 0) \quad q_{\blacktriangleleft}
\end{aligned}
$$

EXERCISE 3.20: Determine the short path fragments for the partial predicate assignment of Example 3.15. □

ESSENTIAL EXERCISE 3.21: Argue that $\mathrm{spf}(\mathbf{P})$ is finite whenever the partial predicate assignment $\mathbf{P}$ covers the program graph.

We can construct an algorithm for computing the short path fragments $\mathrm{spf}(\mathbf{P})$ for a partial predicate assignment $\mathbf{P}$ that covers the program graph. It performs a

INPUT	a program graph with $\mathbf{Q}$, $\mathbf{Act}$, $\mathbf{E}$ as in Definition 1.2
	a partial predicate assignment $\mathbf{P}$ as in Definition 3.13
OUTPUT	$\mathbf{S}$: a set of short path fragments
DATA	$\mathbf{S} \subseteq \mathbf{Q} \times \mathbf{Act}^* \times \mathbf{Q}$: the fragments constructed so far
ALGORITHM	$\mathbf{S} := \{\ \}$;
	for all $q \in \mathrm{dom}(\mathbf{P})$ do BUILD($q \epsilon q$)
PROCEDURE	BUILD($q_\circ \omega q_\bullet$) is defined by
	for all edges $(q, \alpha, q_\circ) \in \mathbf{E}$
	do if $q \in \mathrm{dom}(\mathbf{P})$
	then $\mathbf{S} := \mathbf{S} \cup \{q \alpha \omega q_\bullet\}$
	else BUILD($q \alpha \omega q_\bullet$);

Figure 3.3: Computing short path fragments.

backward search from each node in $\mathrm{dom}(\mathbf{P})$, collecting a partial short path fragment along the way, and stopping when a node in $\mathrm{dom}(\mathbf{P})$ is encountered, in which case the partial short path fragment is emitted as a short path fragment. The details are in Figure 3.3.

TRY IT OUT 3.22: Use the algorithm of Figure 3.3 to construct the short path fragments for Example 3.14.   □

EXERCISE 3.23: Use the algorithm of Figure 3.3 to construct the short path fragments for Example 3.15.   □

PROPOSITION 3.24: The algorithm of Figure 3.3 correctly produces the set $\mathrm{spf}(\mathbf{P})$ whenever the partial predicate assignment $\mathbf{P}$ covers the program graph.

SKETCH OF PROOF: Let us say that $q_\circ \alpha_1 \cdots \alpha_n q_\bullet$ is *realised by* a sequence $q_0, \cdots, q_n$ of nodes whenever $q_0 = q_\circ$, $q_n = q_\bullet$, $q_n \in \mathrm{dom}(\mathbf{P})$, $q_1, \cdots, q_{n-1} \notin \mathrm{dom}(\mathbf{P})$, and all (q_{i-1}, α_i, q_i) are edges in the program graph (for $1 \leq i \leq n$).

Note that whenever there is a call BUILD($q_\circ \omega q_\bullet$) then $q_\circ \omega q_\bullet$ is realised by some sequence $q_0, \cdots, q_n$ such that $q_\circ = q_\bullet$ when $n = 0$ and $q_\circ \notin \mathrm{dom}(\mathbf{P})$ when $n > 0$. It follows that all $q \alpha \omega q_\bullet$ added to $\mathbf{S}$ are short path fragments and hence that $\mathbf{S} \subseteq \mathrm{spf}(\mathbf{P})$ is an invariant of the algorithm.

For a short path fragment $q_\circ \alpha_1 \cdots \alpha_n q_\bullet$ being realised by $q_0, \cdots, q_n$ we know that $n > 0$. We know that we perform the call BUILD($q_n \epsilon q_n$) and can prove by induction that we eventually perform the call BUILD($q_1 \alpha_2 \cdots \alpha_n q_n$). In the body of this call we add $q_\circ \alpha_1 \cdots \alpha_n q_\bullet$ to $\mathbf{S}$ and this shows that $\mathrm{spf}(\mathbf{P}) \subseteq \mathbf{S}$ upon termination of the algorithm.

From Essential Exercise 3.21 we know that $\mathrm{spf}(\mathbf{P})$ is finite, and each short path fragment can only be realised by a finite number of node sequences. It follows that we only perform finitely many calls to BUILD and hence that the algorithm terminates. □

The short path fragments give rise to proof obligations: whenever $q_\circ \alpha_1 \cdots \alpha_n q_\bullet$ is in $\mathrm{spf}(\mathbf{P})$ we obtain a *proof obligation* of the form

$$[\mathbf{P}(q_\circ)] \; \alpha_1 \cdots \alpha_n \; [\mathbf{P}(q_\bullet)]$$

which intuitively expresses that if the predicate $\mathbf{P}(q_\circ)$ holds in a memory and we execute the actions $\alpha_1 \cdots \alpha_n$ then the predicate $\mathbf{P}(q_\bullet)$ will hold in the resulting memory. To make this clear we need the following notation.

Let us write $\sigma_n = S[\![\alpha_1 \cdots \alpha_n]\!](\sigma_0)$ to mean that there exists $\sigma_1 \cdots \sigma_{n-1}$ such that $\sigma_i = S[\![\alpha_i]\!](\sigma_{i-1})$ for all $i \in \{1, \cdots, n\}$.

DEFINITION 3.25: A partial predicate assignment $\mathbf{P}$ is *correct* with respect to a semantics $S[\![\cdot]\!]$ whenever

$$\left(\; (\sigma, \underline{\sigma}) \vDash \mathbf{P}(q_\circ) \wedge \sigma' = S[\![\alpha_1 \cdots \alpha_n]\!](\sigma) \; \right) \Rightarrow (\sigma', \underline{\sigma}) \vDash \mathbf{P}(q_\bullet)$$

holds for each $(q_\circ \alpha_1 \cdots \alpha_n q_\bullet) \in \mathrm{spf}(\mathbf{P})$ and for all suitable pairs of memories $(\sigma, \underline{\sigma})$.

TRY IT OUT 3.26: Show that the partial predicate assignment of Example 3.14 is correct for the program graph of Figure 3.1: first identify the proof obligations and then argue for their correctness. □

EXERCISE 3.27: Show that the partial predicate assignment of Example 3.15 is correct for the program graph of Figure 3.2: first identify the proof obligations and then argue for their correctness. □

The following proposition shows that *partial correctness* can be established by providing a partial predicate assignment that is correct. This is a key and practical technique for proving programs correct.

PROPOSITION 3.28: Let $\mathbf{P}$ denote a correct partial predicate assignment. Whenever $q_\circ \in \mathrm{dom}(\mathbf{P})$, $(\sigma, \underline{\sigma}) \vDash \mathbf{P}(q_\circ)$, $\langle q_\circ; \sigma \rangle \overset{\omega}{\Longrightarrow}{}^* \langle q_\bullet; \sigma' \rangle$, and $q_\bullet \in \mathrm{dom}(\mathbf{P})$ we have that $(\sigma', \underline{\sigma}) \vDash \mathbf{P}(q_\bullet)$.

PROOF: As illustrated in Figure 3.4, we shall write $\langle q_\circ; \sigma \rangle \overset{\omega}{\Longrightarrow}{}^* \langle q_\bullet; \sigma' \rangle$ as

$$\langle q_\circ; \sigma \rangle = \langle q_0; \sigma_0 \rangle \overset{\omega_1}{\Longrightarrow}{}^* \langle q_1; \sigma_1 \rangle \overset{\omega_2}{\Longrightarrow}{}^* \cdots \overset{\omega_n}{\Longrightarrow}{}^* \langle q_n; \sigma_n \rangle = \langle q_\bullet; \sigma' \rangle$$

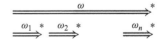

Figure 3.4: Splitting an execution sequence into smaller execution sequences.

such that $\omega = \omega_1\omega_2\cdots\omega_n$ and all $q_{i-1}\omega_i q_i$ are short path fragments (for $i \in \{1,\cdots,n\}$).

We shall perform mathematical induction on $n \geq 0$.

If $n = 0$ we know that $|\omega| = 0$ and the result is immediate (as in the proof of Proposition 3.11).

If $n = n' + 1$ for some number $n' \geq 0$ then from $(\sigma, \underline{\sigma}) \vDash \mathbf{P}(q_\circ)$ we get $(\sigma_1, \underline{\sigma}) \vDash \mathbf{P}(q_1)$ by the assumption that $\mathbf{P}$ is a correct partial predicate assignment, and then $(\sigma', \underline{\sigma}) \vDash \mathbf{P}(q_\bullet)$ by the induction hypothesis. $\square$

TEASER 3.29: Establish the correctness of your bubble sort algorithm from Exercise 1.18 by defining a partial predicate assignment, showing that it covers the program graph, and then argue for the correctness of the proof obligations. $\square$

3.4   Guarded Commands with Predicates

One way to find a set of nodes that covers the program graph is to do so when constructing the program graph. For most so-called structured programming languages it is easy to indicate in the programs themselves where the nodes will originate. If one then extends the syntax so as to explicitly mention the predicates holding at those program points one can directly construct a program graph together with a partial predicate assignment that covers it.

In this section we show how to do so for a version of the Guarded Commands language of Chapter 2. We shall write AP for an annotated program, AC for an annotated command, and AG for an annotated guarded command, and use x, A, a and b as before.

> DEFINITION 3.30: The syntax of *Guarded Commands with Predicates* is given by
>
> $$AP ::= \mathrm{begin}[\phi_\triangleright] \, AC \, \mathrm{end}[\phi_\blacktriangleleft]$$
> $$AC ::= x := a \mid A[a_1] := a_2 \mid \mathrm{skip} \mid AC_1\,;AC_2 \mid \mathrm{if}\ AG\ \mathrm{fi} \mid \mathrm{do}[\phi]\ AG\ \mathrm{od}$$
> $$AG ::= b \to AC \mid AG_1\,[]\,AG_2$$

An annotated version of the factorial program is shown in Figure 3.5.

Next we redefine the function $\mathbf{edges}(\cdot \rightsquigarrow \cdot)[\![\cdot]\!]$, which operated on commands and guarded commands, to a new function $\mathbf{edges}_\mathsf{v}(\cdot \rightsquigarrow \cdot)[\![\cdot]\!]$, which operates on annotated programs, annotated commands and annotated guarded commands. In Section 2.2 the result of $\mathbf{edges}(q_\circ \rightsquigarrow q_\bullet)[\![C]\!]$ for a command C was the set E of edges of a program graph with initial node $q_\circ$ and final node $q_\bullet$. Here we should like the result of $\mathbf{edges}_\mathsf{v}(q_\circ \rightsquigarrow q_\bullet)[\![AC]\!]$ for an annotated command to be a pair (E, P): the set E is

```
begin[x = n ∧ n ≥ 0]
y := 1;
do [n ≥ x ∧ x ≥ 0 ∧
      y · fac(x) = fac(n)]
   x > 0 → y := x ∗ y;
            x := x − 1
od
end[y = fac(n)]
```

Figure 3.5: Example program for the factorial function.

the set of edges of the program graph as before, and the partial predicate assignment P is such that $\text{dom}(P) \cup \{q_\circ, q_\bullet\}$ covers the program graph. Similar remarks apply to the result $\textbf{edges}_\text{v}(q_\circ \leadsto q_\bullet)[\![AG]\!]$ for an annotated guarded command AG, whereas the result $\textbf{edges}_\text{v}(q_\triangleright \leadsto q_\blacktriangleleft)[\![AP]\!]$ for an annotated program AP is to be such that $\text{dom}(P)$ covers the program graph.

DEFINITION 3.31: For annotated programs we have

$$\begin{aligned}
\textbf{edges}_\text{v}(q_\triangleright \leadsto q_\blacktriangleleft)&[\![\texttt{begin}[\phi_\triangleright]\ AC\ \texttt{end}[\phi_\blacktriangleleft]]\!] = \\
&\text{let } q_\circ, q_\bullet \text{ be fresh} \\
&\quad (E_1, P_1) = \textbf{edges}_\text{v}(q_\circ \leadsto q_\bullet)[\![AC]\!] \\
&\quad E_2 = \{(q_\triangleright, \texttt{skip}, q_\circ), (q_\bullet, \texttt{skip}, q_\blacktriangleleft)\} \\
&\quad P_2 = [q_\triangleright \mapsto \phi_\triangleright][q_\blacktriangleleft \mapsto \phi_\blacktriangleleft] \\
&\text{in } (E_1, P_1) \oplus (E_2, P_2)
\end{aligned}$$

During the construction of the program graphs we create fresh nodes as before. We use $\oplus$ to combine the pairs produced:

$$(E_1, P_1) \oplus (E_2, P_2) = (E_1 \cup E_2, P_1[P_2])$$

Here $(P_1[P_2])(q) = P_1(q)$ if $q \in \text{dom}(P_1) \setminus \text{dom}(P_2)$ and $(P_1[P_2])(q) = P_2(q)$ if $q \in \text{dom}(P_2)$. (Whenever we use the notation below it will be the case that $\text{dom}(P_1) \cap \text{dom}(P_2) = \{\ \}$ so that $P_1[P_2] = P_2[P_1]$.) Furthermore, we write $[\,]$ for the partial predicate assignment whose domain is empty.

DEFINITION 3.32: For annotated commands we have

$$\textbf{edges}_\text{v}(q_\circ \leadsto q_\bullet)[\![x := a]\!] = (\{(q_\circ, x := a, q_\bullet)\}, [\,])$$

$$\textbf{edges}_\text{v}(q_\circ \leadsto q_\bullet)[\![A[a_1] := a_2]\!] = (\{(q_\circ, A[a_1] := a_2, q_\bullet)\}, [\,])$$

$$\textbf{edges}_\text{v}(q_\circ \leadsto q_\bullet)[\![\texttt{skip}]\!] = (\{(q_\circ, \texttt{skip}, q_\bullet)\}, [\,])$$

$$\begin{aligned}
\textbf{edges}_\text{v}(q_\circ \leadsto q_\bullet)[\![AC_1; AC_2]\!] = \ &\text{let } q \text{ be fresh} \\
&\quad (E_1, P_1) = \textbf{edges}_\text{v}(q_\circ \leadsto q)[\![AC_1]\!] \\
&\quad (E_2, P_2) = \textbf{edges}_\text{v}(q \leadsto q_\bullet)[\![AC_2]\!] \\
&\text{in } (E_1, P_1) \oplus (E_2, P_2)
\end{aligned}$$

$$\textbf{edges}_\text{v}(q_\circ \leadsto q_\bullet)[\![\texttt{if}\ AG\ \texttt{fi}]\!] = \textbf{edges}_\text{v}(q_\circ \leadsto q_\bullet)[\![AG]\!]$$

$$\begin{aligned}
\textbf{edges}_\text{v}(q_\circ \leadsto q_\bullet)[\![\texttt{do}[\phi]\ AG\ \texttt{od}]\!] = \ &\text{let } b = \texttt{done}[\![AG]\!] \\
&\quad (E, P) = \textbf{edges}_\text{v}(q_\circ \leadsto q_\circ)[\![AG]\!] \\
&\text{in } (E, P) \oplus (\{(q_\circ, b, q_\bullet)\}, [q_\circ \mapsto \phi])
\end{aligned}$$

The auxiliary function done$[\![\cdot]\!]$ is defined much as before:

$$\text{done}[\![b \to AC]\!] = \neg b$$

$$\text{done}[\![AG_1 \,[]\, AG_2]\!] = \text{done}[\![AG_1]\!] \wedge \text{done}[\![AG_2]\!]$$

DEFINITION 3.33: For annotated guarded commands we have

$$
\begin{aligned}
\textbf{edges}_\vee(q_\circ \rightsquigarrow q_\bullet)[\![b \to AC]\!] \;=\; & \text{let } q \text{ be fresh} \\
& (E, P) = \textbf{edges}_\vee(q \rightsquigarrow q_\bullet)[\![C]\!] \\
& \text{in } (\{(q_\circ, b, q)\}, [\,]) \oplus (E, P)
\end{aligned}
$$

$$
\begin{aligned}
\textbf{edges}_\vee(q_\circ \rightsquigarrow q_\bullet)[\![AG_1 \,[]\, AG_2]\!] \;=\; & \text{let } (E_1, P_1) = \textbf{edges}_\vee(q_\circ \rightsquigarrow q_\bullet)[\![AG_1]\!] \\
& (E_2, P_2) = \textbf{edges}_\vee(q_\circ \rightsquigarrow q_\bullet)[\![AG_2]\!] \\
& \text{in } (E_1, P_1) \oplus (E_2, P_2)
\end{aligned}
$$

We construct the program graph **PG** for an annotated program AP as follows. The edges **E** come from $(\textbf{E}, \textbf{P}) = \textbf{edges}_\vee(q_\triangleright \rightsquigarrow q_\blacktriangleleft)[\![AP]\!]$ (where we ensure that $q_\triangleright \neq q_\blacktriangleleft$). The actions **Act** consist of the four kinds of actions: $x := a$, $A[a_1] := a_2$, skip and b. The nodes **Q** consist of all the nodes occurring as first or third components of tuples in **E**. The partial predicate assignment **P** also comes from $(\textbf{E}, \textbf{P}) = \textbf{edges}_\vee(q_\triangleright \rightsquigarrow q_\blacktriangleleft)[\![AP]\!]$.

EXAMPLE 3.34: Let us apply the function $\textbf{edges}_\vee(q_\triangleright \rightsquigarrow q_\blacktriangleleft)[\![\cdot]\!]$ to the program of Figure 3.5 and let $(\textbf{E}, \textbf{P})$ be the result produced. The set **E** of edges produced is shown in Figure 3.6 and the partial predicate assignment **P** is as in Example 3.14. The set dom(**P**) equals $\{q_\triangleright, q_1, q_\blacktriangleleft\}$ and covers the program graph.

EXERCISE 3.35: Rewrite the insertion sort algorithm of Examples 1.16, 3.2 and 3.3 with the appropriate predicates in Guarded Commands with Predicates.

How would you compare the resulting program graph and partial predicate assignment to the program graph of Figure 3.2 and the partial predicate assignment of Example 3.15? □

PROPOSITION 3.36: Given an annotated program AP and the result $(\textbf{E}, \textbf{P})$ of $\textbf{edges}_\vee(q_\triangleright \rightsquigarrow q_\blacktriangleleft)[\![AP]\!]$ where we ensure that $q_\triangleright \neq q_\blacktriangleleft$. The set of nodes dom(**P**) covers the program graph obtained from **E**.

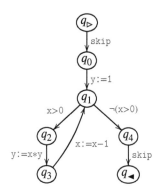

Figure 3.6: The program graph for the factorial function obtained using $\textbf{edges}_\vee(q_\triangleright \rightsquigarrow q_\blacktriangleleft)[\![\cdot]\!]$.

SKETCH OF PROOF: We will expand on the proof of Proposition 2.12. We shall prove for each recursive call $(E, P) = \textbf{edges}_\vee(q_\circ \rightsquigarrow q_\bullet)[\![AC]\!]$ that all nodes in E are reachable from $q_\circ$, that all nodes in E can reach $q_\bullet$, that if $q_\circ \neq q_\bullet$ then no edge in E has $q_\bullet$ as a first component, and that dom(P) $\cup \{q_\circ, q_\bullet\}$ covers E.

The key part of the proof is to show that dom(P) $\cup \{q_\circ, q_\bullet\}$ covers E. This is straightforward in most cases. As an example we consider $(E, P) = \textbf{edges}_\vee(q_\circ \rightsquigarrow q_\bullet)[\![AC_1; AC_2]\!]$ where for $(E_1, P_1) = \textbf{edges}_\vee(q_\circ \rightsquigarrow q)[\![AC_1]\!]$ and $(E_2, P_2) = \textbf{edges}_\vee(q \rightsquigarrow$

$q_\bullet)[\![AC_2]\!]$ we have $E = E_1 \cup E_2$ and $P = P_1[P_2]$. Any loop in $E_1 \cup E_2$ must be entirely within E_1 or E_2 and the result follows from the induction hypothesis.

The interesting case is $(E, P) = \mathbf{edges}_\mathsf{v}(q_\circ \rightsquigarrow q_\bullet)[\![\mathtt{do}[\phi]\ AG\ \mathtt{od}]\!]$, which expands to

$$(E, P) = \mathbf{edges}_\mathsf{v}(q_\circ \rightsquigarrow q_\bullet)[\![\mathtt{do}[\phi]\ b_1 \rightarrow AC_1\ []\ \cdots\ []\ b_n \rightarrow AC_n\ \mathtt{od}]\!]$$

and where $q_\circ \in \mathrm{dom}(\mathbf{P})$. Any loop in E is either entirely within some $\mathbf{edges}_\mathsf{v}(q_\circ \rightsquigarrow q_\bullet)[\![b_i \rightarrow C_i]\!]$ or not. In the former case the result follows from the induction hypothesis. In the latter case the loop must involve the node $q_\circ$ and the result follows. □

EXERCISE 3.37: Extend the development of the present section to the extended Guarded Commands language of Section 2.5. First include the loop control commands `break` and `continue` and then extend the development with the commands `try` C `catch` HC `yrt` and `throw` e for defining and throwing exceptions together with the handler commands HC. Do you need to annotate the new constructs with additional predicates? □

3.5 Reverse Postorder (Bonus Material)

If we are merely given a program graph and want to find a set of nodes that covers it we can construct a depth-first spanning tree and use the reverse postorder defined by it to find the set of nodes that covers the program graph.

> In this section we shall only be interested in the part of the program graph that is reachable from the start node $q_\triangleright$ and we ignore the remaining nodes.

We provide in Figure 3.7 the algorithm for producing a depth-first spanning tree and its associated reverse postorder. It takes as input a program graph with nodes **Q**, edges **E** and initial node $q_\triangleright$. It produces a *depth-first spanning tree* **T** (initially empty) and a so-called *reverse postorder numbering* **rP**. It makes use of a current number k (initially the number of nodes) and a set **V** of visited nodes (initially empty). The key part of the algorithm is the procedure DFS(q), which traverses all outgoing edges (to nodes that have not previously been traversed) in a depth-first manner while building the tree along the way. It assigns each node its reverse postorder number just before returning.

TRY IT OUT 3.38: Show that the algorithm of Figure 3.7 applied to the factorial program graph of Figure 3.1 may give rise to the depth-first spanning tree of Figure 3.8. Is it possible to construct other depth-first spanning trees? What are the possible reverse postorders? □

EXERCISE 3.39: Use the algorithm of Figure 3.7 to construct a depth-first spanning tree for the insertion sort program graph of Figure 3.2. How many different reverse postorders may arise from different ways of running the algorithm? □

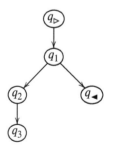

Figure 3.8: Depth-first spanning tree for the program graph of Figure 3.1.

INPUT	a program graph with $\mathbf{Q}$, $q_\triangleright$, $\mathbf{E}$ as in Definition 1.2
OUTPUT	$\mathbf{T}$: a set of edges in a depth-first spanning tree
	$\mathbf{rP}$: a reverse postorder numbering of the nodes in $\mathbf{Q}$
DATA	$\mathbf{T} \subseteq \mathbf{Q} \times \mathbf{Q}$: the tree constructed so far
	$\mathbf{V} \subseteq \mathbf{Q}$: the nodes visited so far
	$k \in \mathbf{Int}$: the current number
	$\mathbf{rP} : \mathbf{Q} \to \mathbf{Int}$: the reverse postorder numbering
ALGORITHM	$\mathbf{T} := \{\ \}$;
	$\mathbf{V} := \{\ \}$;
	$k := |\mathbf{Q}|$;
	DFS($q_\triangleright$)
PROCEDURE	DFS($q_\circ$) is defined by
	$\quad\mathbf{V} := \mathbf{V} \cup \{q_\circ\}$;
	$\quad$while there exists an edge $(q_\circ, \alpha, q_\bullet) \in \mathbf{E}$
	$\quad\quad$such that $q_\bullet \notin \mathbf{V}$
	$\quad\quad$do $\mathbf{T} := \mathbf{T} \cup \{(q_\circ, q_\bullet)\}$; DFS($q_\bullet$);
	$\quad\mathbf{rP}[q_\circ] := k$; $k := k{-}1$;

Figure 3.7: Depth-First Spanning Tree and Reverse Postorder.

We shall be writing $\mathbf{T}^*$ for the reflexive transitive closure of $\mathbf{T}$ (following zero or more edges in $\mathbf{T}$), $\mathbf{T}^+$ for the transitive closure of $\mathbf{T}$ (following one or more edges in $\mathbf{T}$) and $\mathbf{T}^{++}$ for $\mathbf{T}^+ \setminus \mathbf{T}$ (following two or more edges in $\mathbf{T}$).

DEFINITION 3.40: The edges in $\mathbf{E}$ can be classified with respect to $\mathbf{T}$ into one of four types:

- a *tree edge* is an edge $(q, \alpha, q') \in \mathbf{E}$ where $(q, q') \in \mathbf{T}$,

- a *forward edge* is an edge $(q, \alpha, q') \in \mathbf{E}$ where $(q, q') \in \mathbf{T}^{++}$, meaning that it points further down in the tree,

- a *back edge* is an edge $(q, \alpha, q') \in \mathbf{E}$ where $(q', q) \in \mathbf{T}^*$ (including $q = q'$), meaning that it points back up in the tree,

- a *cross edge* is an edge $(q, \alpha, q') \in \mathbf{E}$ where neither (q, q') nor (q', q) is in $\mathbf{T}^*$, meaning that neither q nor q' is an ancestor of the other.

EXAMPLE 3.41: The edges of the program graph of Figure 3.1 can be classified with respect to the depth-first spanning tree of Figure 3.8: all edges except $(q_3, \text{x} := \text{x} - 1, q_1)$ are tree edges while $(q_3, \text{x} := \text{x} - 1, q_1)$ is a back edge.

In general a program graph may have many different depth-first spanning trees and therefore the notions of tree edges, forward edges, back edges and cross edges are not uniquely determined but are always relative to the depth-first spanning tree of interest. However, for a large class of so-called *reducible program graphs* the notion of back edge will be the same regardless of the depth-first spanning tree considered. Most program graphs constructed from 'structured programming languages' will indeed produce reducible program graphs (and the Guarded Commands language is an example of this). A non-reducible program graph is shown in Figure 3.9.

Figure 3.9: A non-reducible program graph.

EXERCISE 3.42: Returning to Exercise 3.39, determine whether or not the different reverse postorders give rise to the same back edges.   □

PROPOSITION 3.43: The edge $(q, \alpha, q') \in \mathbf{E}$ is a *back edge* if and only if $\mathbf{rP}[q] \geq \mathbf{rP}[q']$.

PROOF: We first assume that $(q, \alpha, q') \in \mathbf{E}$ is a back edge and show that $\mathbf{rP}[q] \geq \mathbf{rP}[q']$. If (q, α, q') is additionally a self loop, i.e. $q = q'$, we have $\mathbf{rP}[q] = \mathbf{rP}[q']$ and the result is immediate. Otherwise q' is a proper ancestor of q in the depth-first spanning tree $\mathbf{T}$. Hence q' is visited before q in the depth-first traversal and the call $\mathrm{DFS}(q')$ is pending throughout the entire call of $\mathrm{DFS}(q)$, meaning that $\mathbf{rP}[q] > \mathbf{rP}[q']$ and the result is immediate.

We next assume that $\mathbf{rP}[q] \geq \mathbf{rP}[q']$ and show that $(q, \alpha, q') \in \mathbf{E}$ is a back edge. If $\mathbf{rP}[q] = \mathbf{rP}[q']$ we have $q = q'$ and hence we have a self loop, which is clearly a back edge. Otherwise $\mathbf{rP}[q] > \mathbf{rP}[q']$, which shows that the call of $\mathrm{DFS}(q)$ is left before that of $\mathrm{DFS}(q')$. This means that the call of $\mathrm{DFS}(q')$ must either be pending during the call of $\mathrm{DFS}(q)$ or has not yet been initiated. In the former case q' is a proper ancestor of q in $\mathbf{T}$ and the edge is a back edge. In the latter case the node q' has not yet been marked as visited and the algorithm would have initiated $\mathrm{DFS}(q')$, which would have ensured that $\mathbf{rP}[q] < \mathbf{rP}[q']$, which is impossible due to our assumption.   □

PROPOSITION 3.44: Any loop in $\mathbf{E}$ will involve at least one back edge.

PROOF: We prove this by contradiction. For this we shall suppose that there is a loop $(q_0, \alpha_1, q_1), \cdots, (q_{n-1}, \alpha_n, q_n)$ with $n > 0$ and $q_0 = q_n$ and that it involves no back edges. It then follows from Proposition 3.43 that $\mathbf{rP}[q_0] < \mathbf{rP}[q_n]$ but this is a contradiction since $\mathbf{rP}[q_0] = \mathbf{rP}[q_n]$.   □

The set of nodes that are targets of back edges is useful for identifying the set of nodes that cover the program graph.

PROPOSITION 3.45: The set $\{q_{\triangleright}, q_{\blacktriangleleft}\} \cup \{q' \mid \exists q, \alpha : (q, \alpha, q') \in \mathbf{E} \wedge \mathbf{rP}[q] \geq \mathbf{rP}[q']\}$ covers the program graph.

PROOF: This is a consequence of Propositions 3.43 and 3.44 (because we assumed in this section that all nodes in $\mathbf{Q}$ are reachable from $q_{\triangleright}$).   □

EXERCISE 3.46: Would we still obtain a set of nodes that covers the program graph if we used the sources of the back edges instead of the targets?   □

Chapter 4

Program Analysis

Program analysis is an approach to finding properties of programs and it can be fully automated unlike program verification. The price to pay is that we can only express approximate behaviours of programs and in general we need to admit more behaviours than are really possible. The gain is that everything is fully automatic and often very efficient.

4.1 Abstract Properties

The aim of this chapter is to introduce static techniques for obtaining useful information about programs. The techniques are called *static* in contrast to *dynamic* because we obtain the information without executing the programs.

> EXAMPLE 4.1: Consider the program graph of Figure 4.1. It is intended to compute the average of the non-negative elements of an array A of length n; it is assumed that the variables x, y and i are initialised to 0 and that $n > 0$. The expression x/y performs integer division and it fails if y is zero. We may want to ensure that this will never be the case. Using a program analysis called *detection of signs* analysis we can show that
>
> - if A only contains non-negative elements then we never divide by zero,
> - if all the elements of A are negative then we will indeed divide by zero,
> - in all other cases we may or may not divide by zero.
>
> So unless we know for sure that A does not contain any negative elements we should improve the program graph by inserting a test on the value of y before performing the division.

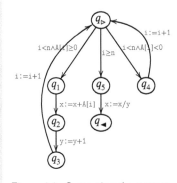

Figure 4.1: Computing the average of some of the elements of an array.

In program analysis we compute with abstractions of the memories rather than the

© Springer Nature Switzerland AG 2019
F. Nielson, H. Riis Nielson, *Formal Methods*, https://doi.org/10.1007/978-3-030-05156-3_4

memories themselves. Often the abstraction will capture some property of the values. For the *detection of signs* analysis mentioned in Example 4.1 we are interested in the signs of the values.

Suppose that we have variables as well as arrays as in Example 4.1. Following Section 1.3 it is natural to let a memory be a mapping

$$\sigma \in \textbf{Mem} = \left(\ \textbf{Var} \ \cup \ \{A[i] \mid A \in \textbf{Arr}, 0 \le i < \text{size}(A)\} \ \right) \to \textbf{Int}$$

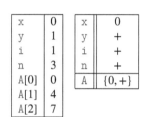

Figure 4.2: A memory and its abstraction.

associating a value with each variable and with each entry in the arrays; we shall sometimes call this a *concrete memory*. In the *abstract memory* the values are replaced by *properties*, in our case signs. For each variable we will record the sign of its value. It does not make much sense to record the sign of each entry in an array – our analysis will give us information about the sign of the index but not its actual value. Instead for each array we record a *set* of signs, namely the ones possessed by the entries of the array. So it is natural to let an abstract memory consist of two mappings, one for the variables and one for the arrays:

$$(\hat{\sigma}_1, \hat{\sigma}_2) \in \widehat{\textbf{Mem}} = (\textbf{Var} \to \textbf{Sign}) \times (\textbf{Arr} \to \text{PowerSet}(\textbf{Sign}))$$

where we write **Sign** for the set $\{-, 0, +\}$ of signs. Figure 4.2 gives an example of a memory and its abstraction and Figure 4.3 depicts PowerSet(**Sign**).

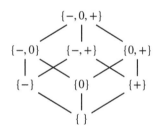

Figure 4.3: Diagram of PowerSet(**Sign**).

DEFINITION 4.2: Consider a semantics using a concrete memory **Mem** and an analysis using an abstract memory $\widehat{\textbf{Mem}}$. The relationship between memories and abstract memories is provided by an *extraction function*

$$\eta : \textbf{Mem} \to \widehat{\textbf{Mem}}$$

that associates an abstract memory with each memory.

In our scenario we define $\eta(\sigma) = (\hat{\sigma}_1, \hat{\sigma}_2)$ where

$$\begin{aligned} \hat{\sigma}_1(x) &= \textbf{sign}(\sigma(x)) &&\text{for } x \in \textbf{Var} \\ \hat{\sigma}_2(A) &= \{\textbf{sign}(\sigma(A[i])) \mid 0 \le i < \text{length}(A)\} &&\text{for } A \in \textbf{Arr} \end{aligned}$$

and where the function **sign** : **Int** $\to$ **Sign** returns the *sign* of its argument (so $\textbf{sign}(n) = +$ if $n > 0$, $\textbf{sign}(n) = -$ if $n < 0$ and $\textbf{sign}(n) = 0$ if $n = 0$).

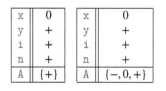

Figure 4.4: Two abstract memories.

The abstract memory (in the right part) of Figure 4.2 is obtained by applying the function η to the concrete memory (in the left part) of the figure – it is an abstraction of the concrete memory. The two abstract memories of Figure 4.4 are *not* abstractions of the memory of Figure 4.2; the leftmost one is excluded because the array contains the element 0 and the rightmost one is excluded because the array does not contain any negative number.

TRY IT OUT 4.3: Provide concrete memories corresponding to the abstract memories of Figure 4.4.   □

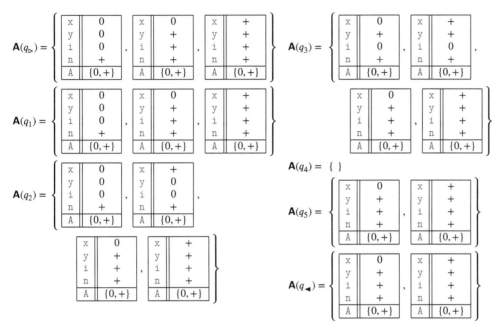

Figure 4.5: An analysis assignment **A** for the program graph of Figure 4.1.

EXERCISE 4.4: Specify an extraction function mapping concrete memories to abstract memories of the form

$$\widehat{\textbf{Mem}}_p = (\textbf{Var} \rightarrow \textbf{Parity}) \times (\textbf{Arr} \rightarrow \text{PowerSet}(\textbf{Parity}))$$

where **Parity** is the set {even, odd} (and an integer is even when it is a multiple of 2 and odd otherwise). □

4.2 Analysis Assignments

The result of a program analysis will be an analysis assignment associating a *collection of abstract memories* with each node in the program graph – Figure 4.5 is an example of such an assignment for the program graph of Figure 4.1.

DEFINITION 4.5: An *analysis assignment* of a program graph with nodes **Q** is a mapping

$$\textbf{A} : \textbf{Q} \rightarrow \text{PowerSet}(\widehat{\textbf{Mem}})$$

where the analysis domain $\text{PowerSet}(\widehat{\textbf{Mem}})$ is the set of collections of abstract memories.

The collection of abstract memories associated with a node should be an over-approximation of the set of memories that could occur at that node in an execution sequence. That it is an over-approximation means that if the memory σ arises at some node q at some point during an execution sequence then the collection of abstract memories at q must contain the corresponding abstract memory $\eta(\sigma)$ – but it may contain additional abstract memories as well.

DEFINITION 4.6: The analysis assignment $\mathbf{A} : \mathbf{Q} \rightarrow \mathrm{PowerSet}(\widehat{\mathbf{Mem}})$ is *semantically correct* (or just *correct*) with respect to a semantics with $S[\![\cdot]\!]$ as in Definition 2.17, a set of initial memories $\mathbf{Mem}_\triangleright$ and an extraction function η when it satisfies the following two conditions:

- whenever we have an edge $(q_\circ, \alpha, q_\bullet) \in \mathbf{E}$ we have for all memories σ that

$$\left(\ \eta(\sigma) \in \mathbf{A}(q_\circ) \wedge \sigma' = S[\![\alpha]\!]\sigma \ \right) \Rightarrow \eta(\sigma') \in \mathbf{A}(q_\bullet)$$

where $\sigma' = S[\![\alpha]\!]\sigma$ means that S is defined on σ and gives σ', and

- whenever $\sigma \in \mathbf{Mem}_\triangleright$ we have $\eta(\sigma) \in \mathbf{A}(q_\triangleright)$.

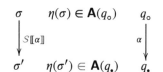

Figure 4.6: Semantic correctness.

This is illustrated in Figure 4.6.

EXAMPLE 4.7: Let us consider the program graph of Figure 4.1 and the edge from q_1 to q_2, which is labelled with the action $\mathtt{x := x + A[i]}$. Let $(\hat{\sigma}_1, \hat{\sigma}_2)$ be the abstract memory in the right part of Figure 4.2 and note that it is an element of the collection associated with q_1 in Figure 4.5.

We need to reason about every concrete memory σ having $\eta(\sigma) = (\hat{\sigma}_1, \hat{\sigma}_2)$, and writing $\sigma' = S[\![\mathtt{x := x + A[i]}]\!]\sigma$ we need to argue that $\eta(\sigma')$ is an element of the collection associated with q_2 in Figure 4.5.

In this case $\eta(\sigma')$ either amounts to $(\hat{\sigma}_1, \hat{\sigma}_2)$ or to the abstract memory in the right part of Figure 4.7. We observe that both are members of the collection associated with q_2 in Figure 4.5.

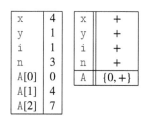

Figure 4.7: Another memory and its abstraction.

EXERCISE 4.8: Perform some of the remaining checks required to show that the analysis assignment of Figure 4.5 is indeed a semantically correct analysis assignment with respect to the set of initial memories $\mathbf{Mem}_\triangleright$ where $\mathtt{x}$, $\mathtt{y}$ and $\mathtt{i}$ are initially zero, $\mathtt{n}$ is positive and the entries of the array $\mathtt{A}$ are non-negative. $\square$

PROPOSITION 4.9: Let $\mathbf{A}$ be a semantically correct analysis assignment. Whenever $\eta(\sigma) \in \mathbf{A}(q_\circ)$ and $\langle q_\circ; \sigma \rangle \overset{\omega}{\Longrightarrow}{}^* \langle q_\bullet; \sigma' \rangle$ we have that $\eta(\sigma') \in \mathbf{A}(q_\bullet)$.

PROOF: We prove the result by mathematical induction on the length $|\omega|$ of ω.

If $|\omega| = 0$ then $q_\circ = q_\bullet$ and $\sigma = \sigma'$ and the result is trivial.

If $|\omega| = n + 1$ for some n then we can write $\langle q_\circ; \sigma \rangle \overset{\omega}{\Longrightarrow}{}^* \langle q_\bullet; \sigma' \rangle$ as $\langle q_\circ; \sigma \rangle \overset{\omega'}{\Longrightarrow}{}^*$ $\langle q''; \sigma'' \rangle \overset{\alpha}{\Longrightarrow} \langle q_\bullet; \sigma' \rangle$ so that $\omega = \omega' \alpha$ and hence $|\omega'| = n$. From $\eta(\sigma) \in \mathbf{A}(q_\circ)$ and the induction hypothesis we get that $\eta(\sigma'') \in \mathbf{A}(q'')$. From $\langle q''; \sigma'' \rangle \overset{\alpha}{\Longrightarrow} \langle q_\bullet; \sigma' \rangle$ we get that $\mathcal{S}[\![\alpha]\!]\sigma'' = \sigma'$ and using the definition of a semantically correct analysis assignment (Definition 4.6) it follows that $\eta(\sigma') \in \mathbf{A}(q_\bullet)$ as required. $\qquad\square$

EXAMPLE 4.10: Let us assume that our initial memory σ maps x, y and i to zero and that the array A has positive length (so n is positive) and only contains non-negative elements. Then $\eta(\sigma)$ equals the first abstract memory in the set $\mathbf{A}(q_\rhd)$ in Figure 4.5 – also displayed in Figure 4.8.

Now consider an execution sequence for the program graph starting in the configuration $\langle q_\rhd; \sigma \rangle$ and ending in $\langle q_5; \sigma' \rangle$ for some σ'. Since the analysis assignment of Figure 4.5 is semantically correct, Proposition 4.9 gives us that $\eta(\sigma')$ is in the set $\mathbf{A}(q_5)$. So in particular $\eta(\sigma')$ will map y to $+$ and this means that it must be the case that $\sigma'(\text{y}) > 0$. Hence we will never run the risk of dividing by zero in the action taking us from q_5 to $q_\blacktriangleleft$.

Thus we have proved that if the non-empty array A only contains non-negative elements then we will never divide by zero, as was claimed in Example 4.1.

x	0
y	0
i	0
n	+
A	$\{0, +\}$

Figure 4.8: The initial abstract memory of Figure 4.5.

EXERCISE 4.11: Assume now that the initial memory σ maps x, y and i to zero and that the array A has positive length (so n is positive) but only contains negative elements. This gives rise to the abstract memory shown in Figure 4.9. Suggest a semantically correct analysis assignment $\mathbf{A}'$ for the program graph in this scenario; it should satisfy that the abstract memory of Figure 4.9 belongs to $\mathbf{A}'(q_\rhd)$ as well as the remaining requirements of Definition 4.6. Does your analysis assignment allow you to conclude that it is always the case that we will attempt to divide by zero in the action from q_5 to $q_\blacktriangleleft$? $\qquad\square$

x	0
y	0
i	0
n	+
A	$\{-\}$

Figure 4.9: An abstract memory.

For simplicity we shall assume throughout this chapter that the set $\widehat{\mathbf{Mem}}$ of abstract memories is a finite set so that the set of *collections of abstract memories* PowerSet($\widehat{\mathbf{Mem}}$) is also finite. In a more general set-up the set of collections of abstract memories needs neither to be finite nor to be a powerset.

4.3 Analysis Functions

Let us assume that we have three kinds of actions, namely assignments to variables $x := a$, tests b and assignments to array entries $A[a_1] := a_2$. The arithmetic and boolean expressions are given by the syntax

$$a \quad ::= \quad n \mid x \mid a_1 + a_2 \mid a_1 - a_2 \mid a_1 * a_2 \mid a_1 / a_2 \mid a_1 \char`\^ a_2 \mid A[a]$$

$$b \quad ::= \quad \texttt{true} \mid a_1 = a_2 \mid a_1 > a_2 \mid a_1 \geq a_2 \mid b_1 \wedge b_2 \mid b_1 \,\&\&\, b_2 \mid \neg b$$

much as in Chapter 2 and Example 4.1. We now define the corresponding analysis functions.

TRY IT OUT 4.12: Argue that `skip` should be analysed the same way as `true`.☐

The detection of signs analysis for expressions   As a first step we shall specify how to compute the potential signs of an arithmetic expression from an abstract memory. To do this we shall replace the semantic function $\mathcal{A}[\![a]\!]$, taking a memory as argument and returning an integer (or being undefined), with an *analysis function* $\widehat{\mathcal{A}}[\![a]\!]$, taking an abstract memory as argument and returning a set of signs. It is defined by

$$\widehat{\mathcal{A}}[\![n]\!](\hat{\sigma}_1, \hat{\sigma}_2) = \{\mathbf{sign}(n)\}$$

$$\widehat{\mathcal{A}}[\![x]\!](\hat{\sigma}_1, \hat{\sigma}_2) = \{\hat{\sigma}_1(x)\}$$

$$\widehat{\mathcal{A}}[\![a_1 \ op \ a_2]\!](\hat{\sigma}_1, \hat{\sigma}_2) = \widehat{\mathcal{A}}[\![a_1]\!](\hat{\sigma}_1, \hat{\sigma}_2) \ \widehat{op} \ \widehat{\mathcal{A}}[\![a_2]\!](\hat{\sigma}_1, \hat{\sigma}_2)$$

$$\widehat{\mathcal{A}}[\![A[a]]\!](\hat{\sigma}_1, \hat{\sigma}_2) = \begin{cases} \hat{\sigma}_2(A) & \text{if } \widehat{\mathcal{A}}[\![a]\!](\hat{\sigma}_1, \hat{\sigma}_2) \cap \{0, +\} \neq \{\,\} \\ \{\,\} & \text{otherwise} \end{cases}$$

where $op \in \{+, *, -, /, \char`\^\}$ and $\widehat{op}$ is the analogue of op operating on sets of signs. The operator $\widehat{op}$ is defined using an auxiliary operator $\tilde{op}$ working on signs:

$\tilde{+}$	$-$	0	$+$
$-$	$\{-\}$	$\{-\}$	$\{-, 0, +\}$
0	$\{-\}$	$\{0\}$	$\{+\}$
$+$	$\{-, 0, +\}$	$\{+\}$	$\{+\}$

Figure 4.10: Addition of individual signs (with the left argument in the first column and the right argument in the first row).

$$S_1 \ \widehat{op} \ S_2 = \bigcup_{s_1 \in S_1, s_2 \in S_2} s_1 \ \tilde{op} \ s_2$$

Figure 4.10 defines $\tilde{+}$ and thus shows how to add signs; it follows that

$$\{0, +\} \ \tilde{+} \ \{0, +\} = (0 \ \tilde{+} \ 0) \cup (0 \ \tilde{+} \ +) \cup (+ \ \tilde{+} \ 0) \cup (+ \ \tilde{+} \ +) = \{0, +\}$$

For indexing into the array we check that $\widehat{\mathcal{A}}[\![a]\!](\hat{\sigma}_1, \hat{\sigma}_2) \cap \{0, +\} \neq \{\,\}$ as otherwise the index is negative or undefined and hence out of bounds.

TRY IT OUT 4.13: Specify tables corresponding to Figure 4.10 for $\tilde{-}$, $\tilde{*}$, $\tilde{/}$ and $\tilde{\char`\^}$. Calculate $\{\,\} \ \widehat{+} \ \{0, +\}$, $\{0, +\} \ \widehat{-} \ \{0, +\}$, $\{0, +\} \ \widehat{*} \ \{0, +\}$ and $\{0, +\} \ \widehat{/} \ \{0, +\}$.   ☐

EXERCISE 4.14: Prove that the analysis function defined above satisfies the following property:

$$\mathbf{sign}(\mathcal{A}[\![a]\!]\sigma) \in \widehat{\mathcal{A}}[\![a]\!](\eta(\sigma))$$

whenever $\mathcal{A}[\![a]\!]\sigma$ is defined. The property expresses that the sign of the value obtained by evaluating the expression in the semantics is included in the result obtained by analysing the expression based on the abstraction of the memory. □

TEASER 4.15: Suppose that the semantics uses a memory where mathematical integers are replaced by *signed bytes* as considered in Section 1.5. What consequences does that have for the definition of $\hat{+}$, $\hat{-}$, $\hat{*}$, $\hat{/}$ and $\hat{\char`\^}$? □

For boolean expressions the semantic function $\mathcal{B}[\![b]\!]$ takes a memory and returns either true or false (or is undefined). The *analysis function* $\widehat{\mathcal{B}}[\![b]\!]$ will take an abstract memory as argument and return a *set* of truth values – as we may not be able to determine whether the expression evaluates to true or false, as illustrated in Figure 4.11.

$\tilde{\geq}$	$-$	0	$+$
$-$	$\{$tt, ff$\}$	$\{$ff$\}$	$\{$ff$\}$
0	$\{$tt$\}$	$\{$tt$\}$	$\{$ff$\}$
$+$	$\{$tt$\}$	$\{$tt$\}$	$\{$tt, ff$\}$

Figure 4.11: Comparison of individual signs (with the left argument in the first column and the right argument in the first row).

The analysis function $\widehat{\mathcal{B}}[\![b]\!]$ is specified as follows:

$$
\begin{aligned}
\widehat{\mathcal{B}}[\![\texttt{true}]\!](\hat{\sigma}_1, \hat{\sigma}_2) &= \{\text{tt}\} \\
\widehat{\mathcal{B}}[\![a_1 = a_2]\!](\hat{\sigma}_1, \hat{\sigma}_2) &= \widehat{\mathcal{A}}[\![a_1]\!](\hat{\sigma}_1, \hat{\sigma}_2) \mathbin{\hat{=}} \widehat{\mathcal{A}}[\![a_2]\!](\hat{\sigma}_1, \hat{\sigma}_2) \\
\widehat{\mathcal{B}}[\![a_1 > a_2]\!](\hat{\sigma}_1, \hat{\sigma}_2) &= \widehat{\mathcal{A}}[\![a_1]\!](\hat{\sigma}_1, \hat{\sigma}_2) \mathbin{\hat{>}} \widehat{\mathcal{A}}[\![a_2]\!](\hat{\sigma}_1, \hat{\sigma}_2) \\
\widehat{\mathcal{B}}[\![a_1 \geq a_2]\!](\hat{\sigma}_1, \hat{\sigma}_2) &= \widehat{\mathcal{A}}[\![a_1]\!](\hat{\sigma}_1, \hat{\sigma}_2) \mathbin{\hat{\geq}} \widehat{\mathcal{A}}[\![a_2]\!](\hat{\sigma}_1, \hat{\sigma}_2) \\
\widehat{\mathcal{B}}[\![b_1 \wedge b_2]\!](\hat{\sigma}_1, \hat{\sigma}_2) &= \widehat{\mathcal{B}}[\![b_1]\!](\hat{\sigma}_1, \hat{\sigma}_2) \mathbin{\hat{\wedge}} \widehat{\mathcal{B}}[\![b_2]\!](\hat{\sigma}_1, \hat{\sigma}_2) \\
\widehat{\mathcal{B}}[\![b_1 \texttt{ \&\& } b_2]\!](\hat{\sigma}_1, \hat{\sigma}_2) &= \widehat{\mathcal{B}}[\![b_1]\!](\hat{\sigma}_1, \hat{\sigma}_2) \mathbin{\widehat{\&\&}} \widehat{\mathcal{B}}[\![b_2]\!](\hat{\sigma}_1, \hat{\sigma}_2) \\
\widehat{\mathcal{B}}[\![\texttt{¬b}]\!](\hat{\sigma}_1, \hat{\sigma}_2) &= \hat{\neg} \, \widehat{\mathcal{B}}[\![b]\!](\hat{\sigma}_1, \hat{\sigma}_2)
\end{aligned}
$$

Here $S_1 \mathbin{\hat{\geq}} S_2 = \bigcup_{s_1 \in S_1, s_2 \in S_2} s_1 \mathbin{\tilde{\geq}} s_2$ where $\tilde{\geq}$ is specified in Figure 4.11, and similarly $S_1 \mathbin{\hat{\wedge}} S_2 = \bigcup_{s_1 \in S_1, s_2 \in S_2} s_1 \mathbin{\tilde{\wedge}} s_2$ where $\tilde{\wedge}$ is specified in Figure 4.12. The case of short-circuit conjunction is more complex and is given by

$\tilde{\wedge}$	tt	ff
tt	$\{$tt$\}$	$\{$ff$\}$
ff	$\{$ff$\}$	$\{$ff$\}$

Figure 4.12: Conjunction of individual truth values (with the left argument in the first column and the right argument in the first row).

$$
S_1 \mathbin{\widehat{\&\&}} S_2 = \left(S_1 \cap \{\text{ff}\} \right) \cup \left(S_1 \mathbin{\hat{\wedge}} S_2 \right)
$$

since it does not require both arguments to be evaluated.

EXERCISE 4.16: Complete this specification by providing figures like the ones in Figures 4.11 and 4.12 for the remaining operators. Then prove that the specification satisfies that

$$
\mathcal{B}[\![b]\!]\sigma \in \widehat{\mathcal{B}}[\![b]\!](\eta(\sigma))
$$

whenever $\mathcal{B}[\![b]\!]\sigma$ is defined. This means that the actual truth value is included in the analysis result and you will need the result of Exercise 4.14 to establish this. □

EXERCISE 4.17: Continuing Exercise 4.4, specify how to compute the potential parities of an arithmetic expression from an abstract memory. This should result in a function $\widehat{\mathcal{A}}_{\mathsf{p}}[\![a]\!]$ that takes an abstract memory as argument and returns a set of parities. For boolean expressions specify a function $\widehat{\mathcal{B}}_{\mathsf{p}}[\![b]\!]$ that takes an abstract memory as argument and returns a set of truth values.   □

The detection of signs analysis for actions   We are now ready to specify the *analysis function* $\widehat{\mathcal{S}}[\![\cdot]\!]$ for the actions; it will take a collection M of abstract memories as argument and it will return a collection of abstract memories. Let us first consider the clause for the test b; here the idea is that we consider each of the abstract memories individually and return those for which b might be true as captured by the analysis function $\widehat{\mathcal{B}}[\![b]\!]$:

$$\widehat{\mathcal{S}}[\![b]\!](M) = \{(\hat{\sigma}_1, \hat{\sigma}_2) \mid (\hat{\sigma}_1, \hat{\sigma}_2) \in M \ \wedge \ \mathsf{tt} \in \widehat{\mathcal{B}}[\![b]\!](\hat{\sigma}_1, \hat{\sigma}_2)\}$$

TRY IT OUT 4.18: Preparing for Example 4.28 below, you should consider each of the three tests $(q_\circ, b, q_\bullet)$ in the program graph of Figure 4.1, and the analysis assignment **A** in Figure 4.5. Show that each test satisfies the constraint $\widehat{\mathcal{S}}[\![b]\!](\mathbf{A}(q_\circ)) \subseteq \mathbf{A}(q_\bullet)$.   □

In the clause for an assignment $x := a$ we also consider each of the abstract memories of M and determine the possible signs of a using the analysis function $\widehat{\mathcal{A}}[\![a]\!]$; for each of those we then construct a new abstract memory that will be part of the result:

$$\widehat{\mathcal{S}}[\![x := a]\!](M) = \{(\hat{\sigma}_1[x \mapsto s], \hat{\sigma}_2) \mid (\hat{\sigma}_1, \hat{\sigma}_2) \in M \ \wedge \ s \in \widehat{\mathcal{A}}[\![a]\!](\hat{\sigma}_1, \hat{\sigma}_2)\}$$

TRY IT OUT 4.19: Preparing for Example 4.28 below, you should consider each of the five assignments $(q_\circ, x := a, q_\bullet)$ in the program graph of Figure 4.1, and the analysis assignment in Figure 4.5. Show that each assignment satisfies the constraint $\widehat{\mathcal{S}}[\![x := a]\!](\mathbf{A}(q_\circ)) \subseteq \mathbf{A}(q_\bullet)$.   □

The clause for an array assignment $A[a_1] := a_2$ is somewhat more complex. Again we consider the abstract memories $(\hat{\sigma}_1, \hat{\sigma}_2)$ of M individually. The first observation is that the assignment only has a chance of being successful if the sign of a_1 is either 0 or positive, that is, if $\widehat{\mathcal{A}}[\![a_1]\!](\hat{\sigma}_1, \hat{\sigma}_2) \cap \{0, +\} \neq \{\ \}$. Only in this case we will modify the abstract memory to record the potential new signs of the entries of the array and include it in the overall result. Before the assignment the signs of the entries in A are collected in the set $\hat{\sigma}_2(A)$. The assignment may modify one of the entries of A to have a sign from the set $\widehat{\mathcal{A}}[\![a_2]\!](\hat{\sigma}_1, \hat{\sigma}_2)$. This may result in removing one of the existing signs (if there was only one entry with that sign) and adding a new sign. This is captured by

$$\widehat{S}[\![A[a_1] := a_2]\!](M) = \{(\hat{\sigma}_1, \hat{\sigma}_2[A \mapsto S]) \mid \\ (\hat{\sigma}_1, \hat{\sigma}_2) \in M \ \wedge\ \widehat{\mathcal{A}}[\![a_1]\!](\hat{\sigma}_1, \hat{\sigma}_2) \cap \{0, +\} \neq \{\ \} \ \wedge \\ \exists s' \in \hat{\sigma}_2(A) : \exists s'' \in \widehat{\mathcal{A}}[\![a_2]\!](\hat{\sigma}_1, \hat{\sigma}_2) : \\ (\hat{\sigma}_2(A) \setminus \{s'\}) \cup \{s''\} \subseteq S \subseteq \hat{\sigma}_2(A) \cup \{s''\}\}$$

If the array only has one entry with the sign s' it will be removed and replaced by the sign s'' of the updated entry; if there are more entries with the sign s' then we just include the sign s''. Our definition caters for both possibilities.

EXERCISE 4.20: Continuing Exercises 4.4 and 4.17 on parity analysis, specify the analysis functions $\widehat{S}_p[\![\cdot]\!]$ for actions. As before, each function should take a collection of abstract memories as argument and return a collection of abstract memories. □

4.4 Analysis Specification

In program analysis we construct the analysis assignments by computing with the abstract properties. For our detection of signs analysis this amounts to computing with signs. The analysis specification tells us how to do this and it has a form that is very similar to that of the semantics – the semantic domain is replaced by an analysis domain and the semantic functions are replaced by analysis functions. We provided an example development in Section 4.3 and this motivates the following definition.

DEFINITION 4.21: A *specification of a program analysis* requires

- a powerset $(\text{PowerSet}(\widehat{\textbf{Mem}}), \subseteq)$ called the *analysis domain* and consisting of the collections of abstract memories,

- an *analysis function* $\widehat{S}[\![\cdot]\!] : \textbf{Act} \rightarrow (\text{PowerSet}(\widehat{\textbf{Mem}}) \rightarrow_m \text{PowerSet}(\widehat{\textbf{Mem}}))$, and

- a collection $\widehat{\textbf{Mem}}_\triangleright$ of abstract memories holding initially,

where $\text{PowerSet}(\widehat{\textbf{Mem}}) \rightarrow_m \text{PowerSet}(\widehat{\textbf{Mem}})$ is the space of *monotonic* functions.

Recall that a function $f : \text{PowerSet}(\widehat{\textbf{Mem}}) \rightarrow \text{PowerSet}(\widehat{\textbf{Mem}})$ is a *monotonic function* if whenever we have two collections M_1 and M_2 of abstract memories satisfying $M_1 \subseteq M_2$ then it follows that $f(M_1) \subseteq f(M_2)$.

It is natural to impose that our analysis functions are monotonic because this reflects the fact that if the set of input memories potentially get larger then so does the set of output memories.

TRY IT OUT 4.22: Show that the analysis functions of Section 4.3 are monotonic.

Together with choosing $\widehat{\mathbf{Mem}}_\rhd$ to be the singleton set consisting of the abstract memory of Figure 4.8 this constitutes a specification of a program analysis which we shall call the *detection of signs* analysis. □

Semantic soundness The analysis functions should capture the essence of the semantics as recorded through the extraction function. This gives rise to the following definition of soundness.

DEFINITION 4.23: A specification of a program analysis is *semantically sound* (or just *sound*) with respect to a semantics with $\mathcal{S}[\![\cdot]\!]$ as in Definition 2.17, an initial set of memories $\mathbf{Mem}_\rhd$ and an extraction function $\eta : \mathbf{Mem} \to \widehat{\mathbf{Mem}}$ provided the following conditions hold:

- whenever $\sigma' = \mathcal{S}[\![\alpha]\!](\sigma)$ (meaning that $\mathcal{S}[\![\alpha]\!]$ is defined on σ and gives σ') and $\eta(\sigma) \in M$ for some set M of abstract memories then it follows that $\eta(\sigma') \in \widehat{\mathcal{S}}[\![\alpha]\!](M)$, and

- whenever $\sigma \in \mathbf{Mem}_\rhd$ we have $\eta(\sigma) \in \widehat{\mathbf{Mem}}_\rhd$.

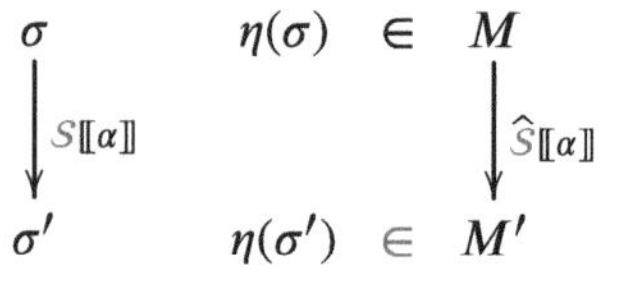

$$\begin{array}{ccc} \sigma & \eta(\sigma) & \in \quad M \\ \downarrow{\scriptstyle \mathcal{S}[\![\alpha]\!]} & & \downarrow{\scriptstyle \widehat{\mathcal{S}}[\![\alpha]\!]} \\ \sigma' & \eta(\sigma') & \in \quad M' \end{array}$$

Figure 4.13: Semantic soundness.

This is illustrated in Figure 4.13.

EXERCISE 4.24: An alternative formulation of the first bullet in Definition 4.23 would be that
$$\{\eta(\mathcal{S}[\![\alpha]\!](\sigma))\} \subseteq \widehat{\mathcal{S}}[\![\alpha]\!](\{\eta(\sigma)\})$$
for all $\sigma \in \mathbf{Mem}$. (You should take $\{\eta(\mathcal{S}[\![\alpha]\!](\sigma))\} = \{\}$ whenever $\mathcal{S}[\![\alpha]\!](\sigma)$ is not defined.) Determine whether or not Definition 4.23 is equivalent to the alternative definition suggested here. □

PROPOSITION 4.25: The *detection of signs* analysis specification is *semantically sound* with respect to the semantics of Chapters 1 and 2, assuming that $\eta(\sigma) \in \widehat{\mathbf{Mem}}_\rhd$ whenever $\sigma \in \mathbf{Mem}_\rhd$.

PROOF: We shall consider two of the cases in the proof – leaving the remaining case to Exercise 4.26 below.

For tests we consider an arbitrary memory $\sigma' = \mathcal{S}[\![b]\!]\sigma$ satisfying $\eta(\sigma) \in M$ and we need to show that $\eta(\sigma') \in \widehat{\mathcal{S}}[\![b]\!](M)$. From $\sigma' = \mathcal{S}[\![b]\!]\sigma$ we get that $\mathcal{B}[\![b]\!]\sigma = \mathrm{tt}$ and hence $\sigma' = \sigma$. From Exercise 4.16 we get $\mathrm{tt} \in \widehat{\mathcal{B}}[\![b]\!](\eta(\sigma))$ and hence $\eta(\sigma) \in \widehat{\mathcal{S}}[\![b]\!](M)$, as required.

For assignments we consider an arbitrary memory σ satisfying $\eta(\sigma) \in M$ and let $\sigma' = \mathcal{S}[\![x := a]\!]\sigma$; we then want to show that $\eta(\sigma') \in \widehat{\mathcal{S}}[\![x := a]\!](M)$. From the semantics it follows that $\mathcal{A}[\![a]\!]\sigma$ is defined and that $\sigma' = \sigma[x \mapsto \mathcal{A}[\![a]\!]\sigma]$. From

Exercise 4.14 we get that $s \in \widehat{\mathcal{A}}[\![a]\!](\eta(\sigma))$ for $s = \mathbf{sign}(\mathcal{A}[\![a]\!]\sigma)$. From the definition of η we can show that if we write $(\hat{\sigma}_1, \hat{\sigma}_2)$ for $\eta(\sigma)$ then $\eta(\sigma') = (\hat{\sigma}_1[x \mapsto s], \hat{\sigma}_2)$. We have assumed that $\eta(\sigma) \in M$ and from the definition of $\widehat{S}[\![x := a]\!](M)$ it follows that $\eta(\sigma') \in \widehat{S}[\![x := a]\!](M)$, as required. $\qquad\square$

EXERCISE 4.26: Complete the proof of Proposition 4.25: Consider a memory σ with $\eta(\sigma) \in M$ and let $\sigma' = S[\![A[a_1] := a_2]\!]\sigma$; argue that it will be the case that $\eta(\sigma') \in \widehat{S}[\![A[a_1] := a_2]\!](M)$. You may assume that the semantics of the array assignment is such that if $\sigma' = S[\![A[a_1] := a_2]\!]\sigma$ then $i = \mathcal{A}[\![a_1]\!]\sigma$ is defined and furthermore $0 \le i < \text{length}(A)$ and $\sigma' = \sigma[A[i] \mapsto \mathcal{A}[\![a_2]\!]\sigma]$. $\qquad\square$

TEASER 4.27: Let us return to the parity analysis developed in Exercises 4.4, 4.17 and 4.20. State and prove a soundness result along the lines of Proposition 4.25. $\square$

Solutions Given a program graph, an analysis specification gives rise to a number of constraints on analysis assignments, as illustrated by the following example.

EXAMPLE 4.28: For the program graph of Figure 4.1 the analysis specification gives rise to the following constraints:

$$\widehat{S}[\![i < n \wedge A[i] \ge 0]\!](\mathbf{A}(q_\rhd)) \subseteq \mathbf{A}(q_1)$$
$$\widehat{S}[\![i < n \wedge A[i] < 0]\!](\mathbf{A}(q_\rhd)) \subseteq \mathbf{A}(q_4)$$
$$\widehat{S}[\![i \ge n]\!](\mathbf{A}(q_\rhd)) \subseteq \mathbf{A}(q_5)$$
$$\widehat{S}[\![x := x + A[i]]\!](\mathbf{A}(q_1)) \subseteq \mathbf{A}(q_2)$$
$$\widehat{S}[\![y := y + 1]\!](\mathbf{A}(q_2)) \subseteq \mathbf{A}(q_3)$$
$$\widehat{S}[\![i := i + 1]\!](\mathbf{A}(q_3)) \subseteq \mathbf{A}(q_\rhd)$$
$$\widehat{S}[\![i := i + 1]\!](\mathbf{A}(q_4)) \subseteq \mathbf{A}(q_\rhd)$$
$$\widehat{S}[\![x := x/y]\!](\mathbf{A}(q_5)) \subseteq \mathbf{A}(q_\blacktriangleleft)$$

We verified in Try It Out 4.18 and 4.19 that these constrains are true for the analysis assignment $\mathbf{A}$ in Figure 4.5.

We now extend the constraints from Example 4.28 with a constraint $\widehat{\mathbf{Mem}}_\rhd \subseteq \mathbf{A}(q_\rhd)$ expressing that the analysis assignment takes care of the collection of abstract memories holding initially.

DEFINITION 4.29: An analysis assignment $\mathbf{A} : \mathbf{Q} \to \text{PowerSet}(\widehat{\mathbf{Mem}})$ is *computationally valid* (or just *valid*) for the analysis problem for a program graph with respect to a specification of a program analysis whenever it satisfies the following two conditions:

- whenever we have an edge $(q_\circ, \alpha, q_\bullet) \in \mathbf{E}$ we have $\widehat{S}[\![\alpha]\!](\mathbf{A}(q_\circ)) \subseteq \mathbf{A}(q_\bullet)$, and

- $\widehat{\mathbf{Mem}}_{\triangleright} \subseteq \mathbf{A}(q_{\triangleright})$.

A computationally valid analysis assignment is also called a *solution*.

x	0
y	0
i	0
n	+
A	{+}

Figure 4.14: An abstract memory.

EXERCISE 4.30: Assume now that $\widehat{\mathbf{Mem}}_{\triangleright}$ is the singleton set with the abstract memory of Figure 4.14. Propose an analysis assignment that is *computationally valid*.   □

Solutions are correct   So far we have talked about three conditions:

- An analysis assignment can be *semantically correct* as in Definition 4.6.

- An analysis specification can be *semantically sound* as in Definition 4.23.

- An analysis assignment can be *computationally valid* as in Definition 4.29.

Their relationship is clarified in the following result giving us a simple way of checking the correctness of an analysis assignment.

PROPOSITION 4.31: Assume that we have a *semantically sound* analysis specification and a *computationally valid* analysis assignment. Then the analysis assignment is *semantically correct*.

PROOF: Assume that $\mathbf{A}$ is a computationally valid analysis assignment and let us show that $\mathbf{A}$ is semantically correct. For this we consider an edge $(q_\circ, \alpha, q_\bullet)$ and assume that $\eta(\sigma) \in \mathbf{A}(q_\circ)$ and that $\sigma' = \mathcal{S}[\![\alpha]\!]\sigma$; we then have to show that $\eta(\sigma') \in \mathbf{A}(q_\bullet)$. From the semantic soundness of the analysis specification it follows that $\eta(\sigma') \in \widehat{\mathcal{S}}[\![\alpha]\!](\mathbf{A}(q_\circ))$. Since $\mathbf{A}$ is computationally valid we get that $\widehat{\mathcal{S}}[\![\alpha]\!](\mathbf{A}(q_\circ)) \subseteq \mathbf{A}(q_\bullet)$. Thus it follows that $\eta(\sigma') \in \mathbf{A}(q_\bullet)$, as required.   □

4.5   Computing Solutions (Bonus Material)

We are now ready to specify an algorithm that given an analysis specification and a program graph will compute an analysis assignment solving the problem. The algorithm consists of an initialisation step and an iteration step and is shown in Figure 4.15.

The algorithm is non-deterministic in that it does not prescribe an order in which to select an edge in the iteration step. To obtain a good running time one should organise the selection of edges in an appropriate manner and we consider this shortly.

PROPOSITION 4.32: The algorithm of Figure 4.15 always terminates and upon termination it has computed a solution to the analysis problem.

PROOF: We have assumed that $\widehat{\text{Mem}}$ is a finite set and hence the analysis domain PowerSet($\widehat{\text{Mem}}$) will also be finite. In the iteration step one of the sets $\mathbf{A}(q)$ will increase in size but this can only happen a finite number of times. Thus the iteration will eventually stop.

When the algorithm terminates it will be the case that $\widehat{\mathcal{S}}[\![\alpha]\!](\mathbf{A}(q_\circ)) \subseteq \mathbf{A}(q_\bullet)$ for all edges $(q_\circ, \alpha, q_\bullet)$ of the program graph and furthermore $\widehat{\text{Mem}}_\triangleright \subseteq \mathbf{A}(q_\triangleright)$. Hence $\mathbf{A}$ is a solution to the analysis problem.   □

EXERCISE 4.33: Use the algorithm to solve the analysis problems considered in Exercises 4.11 and 4.30.   □

INPUT	a program graph with $\mathbf{Q}$, $q_\triangleright$, $\mathbf{E}$ as in Defn. 1.2
	an analysis specification with $\widehat{\mathcal{S}}[\![\cdot]\!]$, $\widehat{\text{Mem}}_\triangleright$ as in Defn. 4.21
OUTPUT	$\mathbf{A}$: an analysis assignment as in Defn. 4.5
	that is a solution to the analysis specification
	in the sense of Defn. 4.29
ALGORITHM	forall $q \in \mathbf{Q} \setminus \{q_\triangleright\}$ do $\mathbf{A}(q) := \{\ \}$;
	$\mathbf{A}(q_\triangleright) := \widehat{\text{Mem}}_\triangleright$;
	while there exists an edge $(q_\circ, \alpha, q_\bullet) \in \mathbf{E}$
	such that $\widehat{\mathcal{S}}[\![\alpha]\!](\mathbf{A}(q_\circ)) \nsubseteq \mathbf{A}(q_\bullet)$
	do $\mathbf{A}(q_\bullet) := \mathbf{A}(q_\bullet) \cup \widehat{\mathcal{S}}[\![\alpha]\!](\mathbf{A}(q_\circ))$

Figure 4.15: Chaotic iteration towards the solution.

Properties of solutions It is interesting to observe that we can always find an analysis assignment that is a solution for a program graph: simply take $\mathbf{A}(q) = \widehat{\text{Mem}}$ for all nodes q. This satisfies the conditions of Definition 4.29 as any collection of abstract memories M satisfies $M \subseteq \widehat{\text{Mem}}$. However, this analysis assignment does not provide any useful information about the program graph.

TRY IT OUT 4.34: Consider the analysis assignment with $\mathbf{A}(q) = \{\ \}$ for all $q \in \mathbf{Q}$; determine whether or not this can be a solution in the sense of Definition 4.29. □

Another interesting property is that if we have two different analysis assignments $\mathbf{A}_1$ and $\mathbf{A}_2$ that are both solutions, then we can construct an even better analysis assignment $\mathbf{A}$ that is also a solution – merely take $\mathbf{A}(q) = \mathbf{A}_1(q) \cap \mathbf{A}_2(q)$ for all nodes q. We say that $\mathbf{A}$ is the *pointwise intersection* of $\mathbf{A}_1$ and $\mathbf{A}_2$.

INPUT   a program graph with $\mathbf{Q}$, $q_{\triangleright}$, $\mathbf{E}$ as in Defn. 1.2
                        an analysis specification with $\widehat{S}[\![\cdot]\!]$, $\widehat{\mathbf{Mem}}_{\triangleright}$ as in Defn. 4.21

OUTPUT $\mathbf{A}$: an analysis assignment as in Defn. 4.5
                        that is a solution to the analysis specification
                        in the sense of Defn. 4.29

DATA $\mathbf{W} \subseteq \mathbf{Q}$: a worklist of nodes

ALGORITHM   forall $q \in \mathbf{Q} \setminus \{q_{\triangleright}\}$ do $\mathbf{A}(q) := \{\ \}$;
                    $\mathbf{A}(q_{\triangleright}) := \widehat{\mathbf{Mem}}_{\triangleright}$;
                    $\mathbf{W} := \{q_{\triangleright}\}$;

                    while $\mathbf{W} \neq \{\ \}$ do
                      choose $q \in \mathbf{W}$;
                      $\mathbf{W} := \mathbf{W} \setminus \{q\}$;
                      for all edges $(q_{\circ}, \alpha, q_{\bullet}) \in \mathbf{E}$ with $q_{\circ} = q$ do
                         if $\widehat{S}[\![\alpha]\!](\mathbf{A}(q_{\circ})) \not\subseteq \mathbf{A}(q_{\bullet})$
                         then $\mathbf{A}(q_{\bullet}) := \mathbf{A}(q_{\bullet}) \cup \widehat{S}[\![\alpha]\!](\mathbf{A}(q_{\circ}))$; $\mathbf{W} := \mathbf{W} \cup \{q_{\bullet}\}$;

Figure 4.16: Worklist algorithm for iterating towards the solution.

EXERCISE 4.35: Show that if $\mathbf{A}_1$ and $\mathbf{A}_2$ are solutions in the sense of Definition 4.29 then this also holds for $\mathbf{A}$ as constructed above. □

It follows that any program graph has a unique analysis assignment that is smallest among all the solutions. To see this, note that there is at least one solution and that there are only finitely many solutions. We can then iteratively take their pointwise intersection to obtain a solution and by construction it is the smallest one. It is possible to extend the proof of Proposition 4.32 to show that this is the solution computed by the algorithm in Figure 4.15.

Refining the algorithm   The algorithm displayed in Figure 4.15 is highly non-deterministic and to get an efficient solution we need to find a way of resolving some of the non-determinism. The worklist algorithm of Figure 4.16 gives one approach to this. Here there is a worklist $\mathbf{W}$ that keeps track of those nodes that need to be reconsidered before we can be sure that a solution has been found. There is still a bit of non-determinism left concerning how to organise the worklist and how to find the edges. As for the organisation of the worklist there are at least two obvious choices: considering it to be a stack (adding and removing from the front) or considering it to be queue (adding to the rear and removing from the front). Fine-tuning of these details may depend on the analysis problem and are key to obtaining an efficient solution. The correctness of the algorithm should be unaffected by this.

TEASER 4.36: Argue that the algorithm of Figure 4.16 produces the same result as that of Figure 4.15 whenever $\widehat{S}[\![\alpha]\!](\{\ \}) = \{\ \}$ holds for all actions α. □

Chapter 5

Language-Based Security

Security is becoming increasingly important and formal methods offer powerful techniques for ensuring it. There are three important components in security: *Confidentiality*, meaning that private data is not made public data; *Integrity*, meaning that trusted data is not influenced by dubious data; *Availability*, meaning that data is not inaccessible when needed. In this chapter we show how formal methods can be used to ensure that programs preserve confidentiality and integrity.

5.1   Information Flow

The key approach to ensure security is to limit the *information flow* allowed by programs. To do so we first discuss what confidentiality and integrity is, and then we explain how information flow can be used to ensure confidentiality and integrity.

Confidentiality   What does it mean for a program to maintain *confidentiality* of data? The basic idea is pretty simple: we have a notion of which data is *private* and which data is *public*, and we want to prevent private data x from finding its way into public data y.

One component of this is that there should be no *explicit* (sometimes called direct) flow of information from x to y. In particular, an assignment $y := x$ would constitute an explicit flow violating the confidentiality of x with respect to y.

Another component of this is that there should be no *implicit* (sometimes called indirect) flow of information from x to y. In particular, a conditional assignment of the form shown in Figure 5.1 would constitute an implicit flow where the sign of x is made visible in y.

```
if   x < 0 → y := −1
[]   x = 0 → y := 0
[]   x > 0 → y := 1
fi
```

Figure 5.1: Example of implicit flow for confidentiality.

© Springer Nature Switzerland AG 2019
F. Nielson, H. Riis Nielson, *Formal Methods*, https://doi.org/10.1007/978-3-030-05156-3_5

Integrity   What does it mean for a program to maintain *integrity* of data? The basic idea is pretty simple: we have a notion of which data is *trusted* and which data is *dubious*, and we want to prevent trusted data x from being influenced by dubious data y.

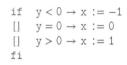

```
if   y < 0 → x := −1
[]   y = 0 → x := 0
[]   y > 0 → x := 1
fi
```

Figure 5.2: Example of implicit flow for integrity.

One component of this is that there should be no *explicit* flow of information from y to x. In particular, an assignment x := y would constitute an explicit flow violating the integrity of x with respect to y.

Another component of this is that there should be no *implicit* flow of information from y to x. In particular, a conditional assignment of the form shown in Figure 5.2 would constitute an implicit flow where the value of x can no longer be trusted if y is dubious.

Information Flow   What is common between our descriptions of confidentiality and integrity is that data of a certain security classification should not find its way into data of another security classification.

To formalise this we shall assume that there is a reflexive and transitive *flow relation* → between variables indicating which flows are permissible. Recall that reflexivity means that $x \rightarrow x$ holds for all variables x, and that transitivity means that if $x \rightarrow y$ and $y \rightarrow z$ then also $x \rightarrow z$.

In the confidentiality example of Figure 5.1, if x is private and y is public we have y → x but x ↛ y (meaning that x → y does not hold). More generally we define $x \rightarrow y$ whenever x is public or y is private.

In the integrity example of Figure 5.2, if x is trusted and y is dubious we have x → y but y ↛ x. More generally we define $x \rightarrow y$ whenever x is trusted or y is dubious.

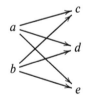

Figure 5.3: $\{a,b\} \rightrightarrows \{c,d,e\}$.

It is useful to extend the flow relation to work on sets of variables. So if X and Y are two sets of variables we shall define $X \rightrightarrows Y$ to mean that each and every variable in X is allowed to flow to each and every variable in Y – see Figure 5.3 for an example. We summarise our notation in the following definition.

DEFINITION 5.1: A *flow relation* is a reflexive and transitive relation → between variables and array names; it is intended to indicate those flows that are permissible, meaning that flows not in the flow relation are not permissible.

It is extended to work on sets of variables and array names by defining $X \rightrightarrows Y$ to mean that

$$\forall x \in X : \forall y \in Y : x \rightarrow y$$

EXERCISE 5.2: Show that $\rightrightarrows$ is not necessarily reflexive, nor symmetric (that is, $X \rightrightarrows Y$ implies $Y \rightrightarrows X$), nor transitive. Next let us restrict our attention to non-empty sets of variables; determine whether or not $\rightrightarrows$ is reflexive, symmetric or transitive.   □

EXAMPLE 5.3: Imagine that we have a database with an array A of length n and an array B of length m. To increase each entry of A by 27 we may use the program of Figure 5.4; similarly the program of Figure 5.5 increases each entry of B by 12.

```
i := 0;
do i < n → A[i] := A[i] + 27;
          i := i + 1
od
```

Figure 5.4: Incrementation of A.

In a proper database the execution of these programs might be interleaved, as illustrated by the program

```
i := 0;
j := 0;
do (i < n) ∧ (j = m ∨ b)  →  A[i] := A[i] + 27;
                             i := i + 1
[] (j < m) ∧ (i = n ∨ ¬b) →  B[j] := B[j] + 12;
                             j := j + 1
od
```

```
j := 0;
do j < m → B[j] := B[j] + 12;
          j := j + 1
od
```

Figure 5.5: Incrementation of B.

where b indicates an interleaving condition such as $i < j$ or $(n - i) > (m - j)$.

To ensure that the operations on A are entirely independent of the operations on B we need to specify a flow relation $\rightarrow$ such that $\{i, j, n, m\} \rightrightarrows \{i, j, A, B\}$ but $A \not\rightarrow B$ and $B \not\rightarrow A$.

From a confidentiality point of view this says that the information in each of the arrays A and B remains confidential from the other. From an integrity point of view this says that the information in each of the arrays A and B remains unaffected by the other. From an isolation point of view this says that the operations on arrays A and B are completely independent – as indeed they are in the programs of Figures 5.4 and 5.5.

5.2 Reference-Monitor Semantics

One way to enforce a security policy, whether for confidentiality or integrity, is to do so dynamically (meaning at runtime). The mechanism that enforces the security policy is often called a *reference monitor* because it monitors the execution and brings it to a halt whenever the security policy is violated.

It would be fairly easy to extend our semantics for Guarded Commands from Definition 2.17 in Section 2.3 to deal with *explicit* flows. Instead of setting

$$\mathcal{S}[\![x := a]\!]\sigma \;=\; \begin{cases} \sigma[x \mapsto \mathcal{A}[\![a]\!]\sigma] & \text{if } \mathcal{A}[\![a]\!]\sigma \text{ is defined} \\ \text{undefined} & \text{otherwise} \end{cases}$$

we could use

$$\mathcal{S}[\![x := a]\!]\sigma \;=\; \begin{cases} \sigma[x \mapsto \mathcal{A}[\![a]\!]\sigma] & \text{if } \mathcal{A}[\![a]\!]\sigma \text{ is defined} \\ & \text{and } \mathsf{fv}(a) \rightrightarrows \{x\} \\ \text{undefined} & \text{otherwise} \end{cases}$$

so that progress is halted whenever we attempt an assignment that violates the explicit flows admitted by the flow relation – that is whenever there is a variable or array name in a that is not allowed to flow to x.

The set $\mathsf{fv}(a)$ consists of the (free) variables and array names occurring in a, and $\mathsf{fv}(b)$ consists of the (free) variables and array names occurring in b.

To also deal with *implicit* flows we would need to know the set X of variables that constitute an implicit dependency and then we could attempt the following definition:

$$
\mathcal{S}[\![x := a\{X\}]\!]\sigma \;=\; \begin{cases} \sigma[x \mapsto \mathcal{A}[\![a]\!]\sigma] & \text{if } \mathcal{A}[\![a]\!]\sigma \text{ is defined} \\ & \quad \text{and } X \cup \mathsf{fv}(a) \rightrightarrows \{x\} \\ \text{undefined} & \text{otherwise} \end{cases}
$$

For this to work we need to slightly modify the construction of program graphs from Definitions 2.7 and 2.8 in Section 2.2 so as to record the set X of implicit dependencies in each assignment.

For reasons to be discussed towards the end of Section 5.3 we shall restrict our attention to deterministic programs in the Guarded Commands language. We do so by modifying the construction of program graphs using the ideas from Section 2.4.

Following the approach of Section 2.4 we define a function $\mathbf{edges}_s$, which works on commands and guarded commands and produces the set of edges of a program graph – but with the assignment actions indicating the implicit flows.

DEFINITION 5.4: *Instrumented program graphs* for commands are constructed as follows:

$$
\mathbf{edges}_s(q_\circ \rightsquigarrow q_\bullet)[\![x := a]\!](X) \;=\; \{(q_\circ, x := a\{X\}, q_\bullet)\}
$$

$$
\mathbf{edges}_s(q_\circ \rightsquigarrow q_\bullet)[\![A[a_1] := a_2]\!](X) \;=\; \{(q_\circ, A[a_1] := a_2\{X\}, q_\bullet)\}
$$

$$
\mathbf{edges}_s(q_\circ \rightsquigarrow q_\bullet)[\![\texttt{skip}]\!](X) \;=\; \{(q_\circ, \texttt{skip}, q_\bullet)\}
$$

$$
\begin{aligned}
\mathbf{edges}_s(q_\circ \rightsquigarrow q_\bullet)[\![C_1; C_2]\!](X) \;=\; & \text{let } q \text{ be fresh} \\
& \quad E_1 = \mathbf{edges}_s(q_\circ \rightsquigarrow q)[\![C_1]\!](X) \\
& \quad E_2 = \mathbf{edges}_s(q \rightsquigarrow q_\bullet)[\![C_2]\!](X) \\
& \text{in } E_1 \cup E_2
\end{aligned}
$$

$$\textbf{edges}_s(q_\circ \rightsquigarrow q_\bullet)[\![\texttt{if } GC \texttt{ fi}]\!](X) \;=$$
$$\text{let } (E, d) = \textbf{edges}_{s2}(q_\circ \rightsquigarrow q_\bullet)[\![GC]\!](\text{false}, X)$$
$$\text{in } E$$

$$\textbf{edges}_s(q_\circ \rightsquigarrow q_\bullet)[\![\texttt{do } GC \texttt{ od}]\!](X) \;=$$
$$\text{let } (E, d) = \textbf{edges}_{s2}(q_\circ \rightsquigarrow q_\circ)[\![GC]\!](\text{false}, X)$$
$$\text{in } E \cup \{(q_\circ, \neg d, q_\bullet)\}$$

As in Section 2.4, for a guarded command GC the function $\textbf{edges}_s$ is supplied with an additional parameter indicating which tests have been attempted previously and it returns an updated version of this information together with a set of edges.

DEFINITION 5.5: *Instrumented program graphs* for guarded commands are constructed as follows:

$$\textbf{edges}_{s2}(q_\circ \rightsquigarrow q_\bullet)[\![b \to C]\!](d, X) =$$
$$\text{let } q \text{ be fresh}$$
$$E = \textbf{edges}_s(q \rightsquigarrow q_\bullet)[\![C]\!](X \cup \mathsf{fv}(b) \cup \mathsf{fv}(d))$$
$$\text{in } (\{(q_\circ, b \wedge \neg d, q)\} \cup E, b \vee d)$$

$$\textbf{edges}_{s2}(q_\circ \rightsquigarrow q_\bullet)[\![GC_1 \, [] \, GC_2]\!](d, X) =$$
$$\text{let } (E_1, d_1) = \textbf{edges}_{s2}(q_\circ \rightsquigarrow q_\bullet)[\![GC_1]\!](d, X)$$
$$(E_2, d_2) = \textbf{edges}_{s2}(q_\circ \rightsquigarrow q_\bullet)[\![GC_2]\!](d_1, X)$$
$$\text{in } (E_1 \cup E_2, d_2)$$

Note the way in which the set X of implicit dependencies is updated as we pass through a test.

TRY IT OUT 5.6: Use the algorithm of Definitions 5.4 and 5.5 to construct the program graph for the program of Figure 5.1. $\square$

EXERCISE 5.7: Use the algorithm of Definitions 5.4 and 5.5 to construct program graphs for the programs of Exercise 2.6. $\square$

We will define two versions of the semantics given in Definition 2.17 (together with Definitions 1.11 and 1.13); one that enforces the reference monitor (denoted by subscript 1) and one that does not (denoted by subscript 0).

DEFINITION 5.8: We define the semantics S_0 and *reference-monitor semantics* S_1 for Guarded Commands using the semantic domain

$$\textbf{Mem} = \big(\textbf{Var} \cup \{A[i] \mid A \in \textbf{Arr}, 0 \leq i < \mathsf{length}(A)\} \big) \to \textbf{Int}$$

They have functionality $S_i[\![\cdot]\!] : \textbf{Act} \to (\textbf{Mem} \hookrightarrow \textbf{Mem})$ and are given by

$$S_i[\![\texttt{skip}]\!]\sigma = \sigma$$

$$S_i[\![x := a\{X\}]\!]\sigma = \begin{cases} \sigma[x \mapsto \mathcal{A}[\![a]\!]\sigma] & \text{if} \quad \mathcal{A}[\![a]\!]\sigma \text{ is defined and} \\ & \qquad i = 0 \; \vee \; X \cup \mathsf{fv}(a) \rightrightarrows \{x\} \\ \text{undefined} & \text{otherwise} \end{cases}$$

$$S_i[\![A[a_1] := a_2\{X\}]\!]\sigma = \begin{cases} \sigma[A[j] \mapsto \mathcal{A}[\![a_2]\!]\sigma] & \text{if} \quad j = \mathcal{A}[\![a_1]\!]\sigma \text{ is defined,} \\ & \qquad 0 \le j < \mathsf{length}(A), \\ & \qquad \mathcal{A}[\![a_2]\!]\sigma \text{ is defined and} \\ & \qquad i = 0 \; \vee \\ & \qquad\qquad X \cup \mathsf{fv}(a_1 a_2) \rightrightarrows \{A\} \\ \text{undefined} & \text{otherwise} \end{cases}$$

$$S_i[\![b]\!]\sigma = \begin{cases} \sigma & \text{if } \mathcal{B}[\![b]\!]\sigma \text{ is defined and holds} \\ \text{undefined} & \text{otherwise} \end{cases}$$

Whenever $(q_\circ, \alpha, q_\bullet) \in \mathbf{E}$ we have an *execution step*

$$\langle q_\circ ; \sigma \rangle \overset{\alpha}{\Longrightarrow}_i \langle q_\bullet ; \sigma' \rangle \quad \text{if } S_i[\![\alpha]\!]\sigma = \sigma'$$

and we write $\langle q_\circ ; \sigma \rangle \overset{\omega}{\Longrightarrow}{}^*_i \langle q_\bullet ; \sigma' \rangle$ for the reflexive and transitive closure of the transition relation (and sometimes dispense with actually writing the ω).

The definitions for $\texttt{skip}$ and b are independent of i and are as in Chapter 2. We already motivated the definition for $x := a\{X\}$ in the case where $i = 1$ and it is as in Chapter 2 in the case $i = 0$. To motivate the definition for $A[a_1] := a_2\{X\}$ note that $A[a_1] := a_2$ can be viewed as a shorthand for a command of the form

$$\texttt{if } a_1 = 0 \to A[0] := a_2 \; [] \cdots [] \; a_1 = n-1 \to A[n-1] := a_2 \texttt{ fi}$$

where n is the length of the array A, and hence that we need to record also the implicit flow from a_1 to A (and for succinctness we write $\mathsf{fv}(a_1 a_2)$ for $\mathsf{fv}(a_1) \cup \mathsf{fv}(a_2)$).

TRY IT OUT 5.9: Show that the execution of the program of Figure 5.1 is halted by the reference-monitor semantics $\Longrightarrow_1$ in the case $\texttt{x} \not\to \texttt{y}$ and that it is allowed to progress in the case $\texttt{x} \to \texttt{y}$.   □

Note that the semantics $\Longrightarrow$ obtained using the definitions in Sections 1.2, 2.2 and 2.3 behaves in the same way as the semantics $\Longrightarrow_0$ obtained using the definitions in the present section.

ESSENTIAL EXERCISE 5.10: Prove that if $\langle q_\circ; \sigma \rangle \Rightarrow_1^* \langle q_\bullet; \sigma' \rangle$ then we also have $\langle q_\circ; \sigma \rangle \Rightarrow_0^* \langle q_\bullet; \sigma' \rangle$.

Provide an example where $\langle q_\circ; \sigma \rangle \Rightarrow_0^* \langle q_\bullet; \sigma' \rangle$ but $\langle q_\circ; \sigma \rangle \not\Rightarrow_1^* \langle q_\bullet; \sigma' \rangle$.

EXERCISE 5.11: Suppose that $\Rightarrow_0$ gives rise to an *evolving system* in the sense of Definition 1.24; determine whether $\Rightarrow_1$ also gives rise to an evolving system. What about the other direction?   □

5.3 Security Analysis

Consider the program of Figure 5.6, where there is an explicit flow from z to y and an implicit flow from x to y. The reference-monitor semantics of the previous section will enforce this by checking that $\{z\} \Rrightarrow \{y\}$ and $\{x\} \Rrightarrow \{y\}$ and halt the program in case of violations.

```
if   x < 0 → y := -1 * z * z
[]   x = 0 → y := 0
[]   x > 0 → y := z * z
fi
```

Figure 5.6: Example with implicit and explicit flows.

Should we be happy about this way of enforcing the security policy? There are at least two reasons for wanting to avoid the program halting when executed. One is that it is never pleasant when our programs stop working. The other is that we might be able to learn a bit about the sign of x if we are told the program point where the program is halted.

To rectify the situation we shall enforce the security policy statically (meaning at compile-time). We do so by a functional specification using the functions $\mathbf{sec}[\![\cdot]\!](X)$ and $\mathbf{sec}_2[\![\cdot]\!](d, X)$ defined in Definitions 5.12 and 5.13 below; the idea is that when $\mathbf{sec}[\![C]\!](X) = \text{true}$ it will never be the case that the reference-monitor semantics halts the execution unless the ordinary semantics does the same.

DEFINITION 5.12: The security analysis for commands is specified as follows:

$$
\begin{aligned}
\mathbf{sec}[\![x := a]\!](X) &= X \cup \mathsf{fv}(a) \Rrightarrow \{x\} \\
\mathbf{sec}[\![A[a_1] := a_2]\!](X) &= X \cup \mathsf{fv}(a_1) \cup \mathsf{fv}(a_2) \Rrightarrow \{A\} \\
\mathbf{sec}[\![\text{skip}]\!](X) &= \text{true} \\
\mathbf{sec}[\![C_1; C_2]\!](X) &= \mathbf{sec}[\![C_1]\!](X) \wedge \mathbf{sec}[\![C_2]\!](X) \\
\mathbf{sec}[\![\text{if } GC \text{ fi}]\!](X) &= \begin{aligned}&\text{let} \quad (w, d) = \mathbf{sec}_2[\![GC]\!](\text{false}, X) \\ &\text{in} \quad w\end{aligned} \\
\mathbf{sec}[\![\text{do } GC \text{ od}]\!](X) &= \begin{aligned}&\text{let} \quad (w, d) = \mathbf{sec}_2[\![GC]\!](\text{false}, X) \\ &\text{in} \quad w\end{aligned}
\end{aligned}
$$

For an assignment $x := a$ giving rise to an edge in the instrumented program graph with the action $x := a\{X\}$ we check that $X \cup \mathsf{fv}(a) \Rrightarrow \{x\}$, meaning that the implicit and explicit flows are permitted according to the flow relation. In a similar way, for an assignment $A[a_1] := a_2$ giving rise to an edge in the instrumented program graph with the action $A[a_1] := a_2\{X\}$ we check that $X \cup \mathsf{fv}(a_1) \cup \mathsf{fv}(a_2) \Rrightarrow \{A\}$. A skip is always permitted and for sequencing, conditional and iteration it suffices that the constituent (guarded) commands are permitted.

DEFINITION 5.13: The security analysis for guarded commands is specified as follows:

$$
\begin{aligned}
\mathbf{sec}_2[\![b \to C]\!](d, X) \;&=\; \begin{aligned}[t]&\text{let}\;\; w = \mathbf{sec}[\![C]\!](X \cup \mathsf{fv}(b) \cup \mathsf{fv}(d))\\ &\text{in}\;\; (w, b \vee d)\end{aligned}\\[2ex]
\mathbf{sec}_2[\![GC_1 [] GC_2]\!](d, X) \;&=\; \begin{aligned}[t]&\text{let}\;\; (w_1, d_1) = \mathbf{sec}_2[\![GC_1]\!](d, X)\\ &\text{let}\;\; (w_2, d_2) = \mathbf{sec}_2[\![GC_2]\!](d_1, X)\\ &\text{in}\;\; (w_1 \wedge w_2, d_2)\end{aligned}
\end{aligned}
$$

For a guarded command $b \to C$ we check that the constituent command C is permitted assuming that the implicit dependencies now come not only from the variables in X but also those in $\mathsf{fv}(b)$ and $\mathsf{fv}(d)$. For a choice $GC_1 [] GC_2$ between guarded commands GC_1 and GC_2 we check that both are permitted.

TRY IT OUT 5.14: Consider again the program of Figure 5.6 and check that it is permitted according to the security analysis (of Definitions 5.12 and 5.13) exactly when $\{x, z\} \Rrightarrow \{y\}$.   □

EXERCISE 5.15: In the manner of Try It Out 5.14 consider the program of Example 5.3 and use the security analysis (of Definitions 5.12 and 5.13) to determine the flows that need to be admitted for the program to be permitted.   □

EXERCISE 5.16: In the manner of Try It Out 5.14 consider the programs of Exercise 2.6 and use the security analysis (of Definitions 5.12 and 5.13) to determine the flows that need to be admitted for the programs to be permitted.   □

The security analysis allows us to complement the insights from Essential Exercise 5.10. It says that for permissible programs the reference monitor never halts the program due to a violation of the security policy. In preparation for this result we need to dig into the interplay between the security analysis and the construction of the instrumented program graph.

ESSENTIAL EXERCISE 5.17: Prove the following results

If $\mathbf{sec}[\![C]\!](X)$, $q_\circ \neq q_\bullet$, and
$\quad (q, x := a\{X'\}, q') \in \mathbf{edges}_s(q_\circ \rightsquigarrow q_\bullet)[\![C]\!](X)$
then $X' \cup \mathsf{fv}(a) \Rrightarrow \{x\}$ and $X \subseteq X'$.

If $\mathbf{sec}[\![C]\!](X)$, $q_\circ \neq q_\bullet$, and
$\quad (q, A[a_1] := a_2\{X'\}, q') \in \mathbf{edges}_s(q_\circ \rightsquigarrow q_\bullet)[\![C]\!](X)$
then $X' \cup \mathsf{fv}(a_1) \cup \mathsf{fv}(a_2) \Rrightarrow \{A\}$ and $X \subseteq X'$.

by induction on the size of C (which you may take to be the number of nodes in the abstract syntax tree for C).

PROPOSITION 5.18: Suppose that $\mathbf{sec}[\![C]\!](X)$ and that $\Longrightarrow_0$ and $\Longrightarrow_1$ are the ordinary semantics and reference-monitor semantics obtained from the instrumented program graph $\mathbf{edges}_s(q_\circ \rightsquigarrow q_\bullet)[\![C]\!](X)$ (for $q_\circ \neq q_\bullet$) in Section 5.2.

If $\langle q; \sigma \rangle \Longrightarrow_0^* \langle q'; \sigma' \rangle$ then also $\langle q; \sigma \rangle \Longrightarrow_1^* \langle q'; \sigma' \rangle$.

PROOF: Suppose by way of contradiction that $\langle q; \sigma \rangle \overset{\alpha}{\Longrightarrow}_0 \langle q'; \sigma' \rangle$ but $\langle q; \sigma \rangle \not\Longrightarrow_1 \langle q'; \sigma' \rangle$. By inspection of Definition 5.8 it is immediate that α must be of the form $x := a\{X'\}$ or $A[a_1] := a_2\{X'\}$. In the first case, $(q, x := a\{X'\}, q') \in \mathbf{edges}_s(q_\circ \rightsquigarrow q_\bullet)[\![C]\!](X)$ and from Essential Exercise 5.17 we get that $X' \cup \mathrm{fv}(a) \rightrightarrows \{x\}$; in the second case, $(q, A[a_1] := a_2\{X'\}, q') \in \mathbf{edges}_s(q_\circ \rightsquigarrow q_\bullet)[\![C]\!](X)$ and from Essential Exercise 5.17 we get that $X' \cup \mathrm{fv}(a_1) \cup \mathrm{fv}(a_2) \rightrightarrows \{A\}$. This provides the required contradiction. $\square$

Our development concentrates on preventing information flow due to *explicit flows*, as illustrated by $\mathrm{y} := \mathrm{x}$, as well as *implicit flows*, as illustrated by $\mathrm{if}\ \mathrm{x} > 7 \rightarrow \mathrm{y} := 1\ []\ \mathrm{x} < 8 \rightarrow \mathrm{y} := 2\ \mathrm{fi}$.

However, there are other and more subtle ways in which information may flow that are not prevented by our security analysis. The name *covert channel* is used to describe such phenomena.

As an example, the program

$$\mathrm{y} := 0; \mathrm{x}' := \mathrm{x}; \mathrm{do}\ \mathrm{x}' > 0 \rightarrow \mathrm{x}' := \mathrm{x}' - 1\ []\ \mathrm{x}' < 0 \rightarrow \mathrm{x}' := \mathrm{x}' + 1\ \mathrm{od}$$

always terminates. It has no explicit or implicit flow from x to y but if we can observe the *execution time* it reveals some information about the absolute value of x.

Similar examples can be constructed where the computation on x will only terminate successfully for some values of x and otherwise will enter a loop or a stuck configuration. If we can observe the *non-termination* it also reveals some information about the value of x.

For another example, allow programs to be non-deterministic and consider the program

$$\mathrm{y} := 0; \mathrm{if}\ \mathrm{true} \rightarrow \mathrm{y} := 1\ []\ \mathrm{x} = 0 \rightarrow \mathrm{skip}\ \mathrm{fi}$$

which may terminate with the final value of y being 0 or 1 if $\mathrm{x} = 0$, but only with the final value of 1 if $x \neq 0$. If we can observe the *non-determinism* (by running the program several times) it once again reveals some information about the value of x.

5.4 Multi-Level Security

So far we described the permissible flows by directly defining a flow relation between variables and array names and then extending it to sets of variables and array names in Definition 5.1. In the *multi-level security* approach to information flow it is customary to define the flow relation by means of a security classification of the variables.

private
|
public

Figure 5.7: A simple lattice for confidentiality.

dubious
|
trusted

Figure 5.8: A simple lattice for integrity.

Security lattices   For this we shall need two components. One is a *partially ordered set* $(L, \sqsubseteq)$ that describes the security classes and how information may flow. That $(L, \sqsubseteq)$ is a *partially ordered set* merely means that the relation $\sqsubseteq$ between elements of L is *reflexive* ($\forall l \in L : l \sqsubseteq l$) and *transitive* ($\forall l_1, l_2, l_3 \in L : l_1 \sqsubseteq l_2 \wedge l_2 \sqsubseteq l_3 \Rightarrow l_1 \sqsubseteq l_3$) and *antisymmetric* ($\forall l_1, l_2 \in L : l_1 \sqsubseteq l_2 \wedge l_2 \sqsubseteq l_1 \Rightarrow l_1 = l_2$). We shall write $l_1 \sqsubset l_2$ whenever $l_1 \sqsubseteq l_2$ and $l_1 \neq l_2$. For our confidentiality example we would have $L = \{\text{private}, \text{public}\}$ with public $\sqsubset$ private and for our integrity example we would have $L = \{\text{trusted}, \text{dubious}\}$ with trusted $\sqsubset$ dubious, as illustrated in Figures 5.7 and 5.8, respectively.

One way to present a partially ordered set is by means of a *directed acyclic graph* (DAG). So suppose that $(L, \rightarrow)$ is a directed acyclic graph and let $\rightarrow^*$ be the reflexive and transitive closure of $\rightarrow$ (following zero or more edges in $\rightarrow$). Defining $\sqsubseteq$ to be $\rightarrow^*$ then gives rise to a partially ordered set $(L, \sqsubseteq)$: reflexivity and transitivity are immediate and antisymmetry follows from acyclicity. When L is finite we can draw $(L, \rightarrow)$ in such a way that edges always slant upwards; in particular, no edges slant downwards and no edges are horizontal. When omitting the arrow heads on the edges this is said to be a Hasse diagram for $(L, \sqsubseteq)$. We saw an example of this already in Figure 4.3; other examples are given in Figures 5.7 and 5.8.

The other is a *security classification* $\mathbf{L} : (\mathbf{Var} \cup \mathbf{Arr}) \rightarrow L$ providing the security levels of variables and arrays. Our flow relation $x \rightarrow y$ would then be defined by $\mathbf{L}(x) \sqsubseteq \mathbf{L}(y)$ and our flow relation $X \rightrightarrows Y$ would then be equivalent to $\forall x \in X : \forall y \in Y : \mathbf{L}(x) \sqsubseteq \mathbf{L}(y)$. This definition makes it clear that information is permitted to flow from smaller (lower) security classes to larger (higher) ones.

TRY IT OUT 5.19: Argue that this way of defining the flow relation lives up to the demands of Definition 5.1.   □

Often the partially ordered set $(L, \sqsubseteq)$ has some extra structure. If for every two elements l_1 and l_2 of L we can find an element l_3 of L such that

$$\forall l \in L : (l_1 \sqsubseteq l \wedge l_2 \sqsubseteq l \Leftrightarrow l_3 \sqsubseteq l)$$

then L is a $\sqcup$-semilattice and we write $l_1 \sqcup l_2$ for l_3. (The symbol $\sqcup$ is pronounced *join*.) Similarly, if for every two elements l_1 and l_2 of L we can find an element l_3 of L such that

$$\forall l \in L : (l \sqsubseteq l_1 \wedge l \sqsubseteq l_2 \Leftrightarrow l \sqsubseteq l_3)$$

then L is a $\sqcap$-semilattice and we write $l_1 \sqcap l_2$ for l_3. (The symbol $\sqcap$ is pronounced *meet*.) When the partially ordered set L is both a $\sqcup$-semilattice and a $\sqcap$-semilattice it is a *lattice*. For this reason $(L, \sqsubseteq)$ is traditionally called a *security lattice*.

TRY IT OUT 5.20: Consider our confidentiality example where $L = \{\text{private}, \text{public}\}$ with public $\sqsubseteq$ private; determine private $\sqcup$ public and private $\sqcap$ public. ☐

EXERCISE 5.21: Suppose that $(L, \sqsubseteq)$ is a lattice. Show that the operation $\sqcup$ is commutative (that is, $l_1 \sqcup l_2 = l_2 \sqcup l_1$) and associative (that is, $l_1 \sqcup (l_2 \sqcup l_3) = (l_1 \sqcup l_2) \sqcup l_3$). Similarly show that the operation $\sqcap$ is commutative and associate. ☐

TEASER 5.22: A partially ordered set $(L, \sqsubseteq)$ is a *complete lattice* when it satisfies the following two properties:

- for all subsets $L' \subseteq L$ we can find an element l' of L such that $\forall l \in L : (\forall l'' \in L' : l'' \sqsubseteq l) \Leftrightarrow l' \sqsubseteq l$ and we then write $\sqcup L'$ for l';

- for all subsets $L' \subseteq L$ we can find an element l' of L such that $\forall l \in L : (\forall l'' \in L' : l \sqsubseteq l'') \Leftrightarrow l \sqsubseteq l'$ and we then write $\sqcap L'$ for l'.

First argue that a complete lattice is also a lattice.

Next show that a *finite* and *non-empty* lattice is also a complete lattice. (Hint: $\sqcup\{\ \} = \sqcap L$ and $\sqcap\{\ \} = \sqcup L$.)

Finally show that $X \Rrightarrow Y$ is equivalent to $\sqcup\{\boldsymbol{L}(x) \mid x \in X\} \sqsubseteq \sqcap\{\boldsymbol{L}(y) \mid y \in Y\}$. (In case you wonder why we perform this development: the above formulation is the one usually found in research papers on multi-level security and information flow.) ☐

Confidentiality reconsidered We already said that our treatment of *confidentiality* so far corresponds to having a security lattice with the following ordering between elements: public $\sqsubset$ private. This is depicted in Figure 5.7.

There are many variations on this theme. A standard textbook example is that of

$$\text{unclassified} \sqsubset \text{classified} \sqsubset \text{secret} \sqsubset \text{top secret}$$

intended to mimic the confidentiality levels of Western military forces. This is depicted in Figure 5.9.

It is not required that the partially ordered set is totally ordered as has been the case so far. For an example of this consider the security lattice $\text{PowerSet}(\{\text{financial}, \text{medical}\})$ under the subset ordering

$$\{\ \} \sqsubset \{\text{financial}\} \sqsubset \{\text{financial}, \text{medical}\} \qquad \{\ \} \sqsubset \{\text{medical}\} \sqsubset \{\text{financial}, \text{medical}\}$$

top secret

|

secret

|

classified

|

unclassified

Figure 5.9: Another lattice for confidentiality.

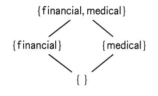

Figure 5.10: Yet another lattice for confidentiality.

as illustrated in Figure 5.10. It describes a scenario where access to data may be restricted to those who are permitted to see financial data, or medical data or both.

EXERCISE 5.23: Suppose there are three users of a system: Alice, Bob and Charlie. Define a security lattice PowerSet({Alice, Bob, Charlie}) for modelling readership rights: as information flows it is permitted to remove readers but never to add readers.   □

Integrity reconsidered We already said that our treatment of *integrity* so far corresponds to having a security lattice with the following ordering between elements: trusted ⊑ dubious. This is illustrated in Figure 5.8.

Figure 5.11: Another lattice for integrity.

Once again there are many variations on this theme. As an example,

$$\text{known fact} \sqsubseteq \text{conjecture} \sqsubseteq \text{alternative fact}$$

is intended to record the trustworthiness of information in a scenario where uncorroborated and fake information is abundant. This is depicted in Figure 5.11.

For an example where the partially ordered set is not totally ordered, consider the security lattice PowerSet({host, client}) under the subset ordering

$$\{\,\} \sqsubseteq \{\text{host}\} \sqsubseteq \{\text{host}, \text{client}\} \qquad \{\,\} \sqsubseteq \{\text{client}\} \sqsubseteq \{\text{host}, \text{client}\}$$

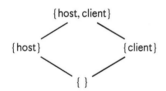

Figure 5.12: Yet another lattice for integrity.

as illustrated in Figure 5.12. It describes a scenario where the trustworthiness of data may depend on whether the host has not been tampered with, the client has not been tampered with, or both. It is useful for controlling the design of client-server systems so that malicious modification of the (Java or JavaScript) client cannot jeopardise the overall security of the system.

An interesting example, spanning both confidentiality and integrity, is to use a partially ordered set {clean, Microsoft, Google, Facebook} where the partial order is given by

$$\text{clean} \sqsubseteq \text{Microsoft} \qquad \text{clean} \sqsubseteq \text{Google} \qquad \text{clean} \sqsubseteq \text{Facebook}$$

as depicted in Figure 5.13. This is useful for ensuring that data belonging to different companies is kept in *isolation* (as regards both explicit and implicit flow). It is possible to turn it into a security lattice by adding an element (called confused) at the top.

Figure 5.13: A partial order for isolation.

EXAMPLE 5.24: Returning to Example 5.3 we might set $L(\text{i}) = \text{clean}$, $L(\text{j}) = \text{clean}$, $L(\text{n}) = \text{clean}$, $L(\text{m}) = \text{clean}$, $L(\text{A}) = \text{Microsoft}$ and $L(\text{B}) = \text{Google}$. This would be a more natural way to ensure that $\text{A} \not\rightarrow \text{B}$ and $\text{B} \not\rightarrow \text{A}$ than that used there.

5.5   Non-Interference (Bonus Material)

Experience shows that it is very hard to get security analyses correct. As an example, it would be very easy to overlook the complications arising if programs were not ensured to be deterministic. In this section we show how we can scrutinise a security analysis so as ensure that there are no remaining flaws concerning explicit and implicit flows.

We begin by studying some properties of instrumented program graphs.

> ESSENTIAL EXERCISE 5.25: Show that we can never leave the final node. Formally, prove that if $(q', \alpha, q'') \in \textbf{edges}_s(q_\circ \rightsquigarrow q_\bullet)[\![C]\!](X)$ (for $q_\circ \neq q_\bullet$) then $q' \neq q_\bullet$.
>
> Show that if a node is left by two edges and the action on one of them is not a boolean condition then in fact the two edges are the same. Formally, prove that if $(q', \alpha_1, q_1), (q', \alpha_2, q_2) \in \textbf{edges}_s(q_\circ \rightsquigarrow q_\bullet)[\![C]\!](X)$ (for $q_\circ \neq q_\bullet$) and $(q', \alpha_1, q_1) \neq (q', \alpha_2, q_2)$ then $\alpha_1 = b_1$ and $\alpha_2 = b_2$ for some b_1 and b_2.
>
> Show that boolean conditions only arise due to the if construct or the do construct. Formally, prove that if $(q', \alpha_1, q_1), (q', \alpha_2, q_2) \in \textbf{edges}_s(q_\circ \rightsquigarrow q_\bullet)[\![C]\!](X)$ (for $q_\circ \neq q_\bullet$) and $(q', \alpha_1, q_1) \neq (q', \alpha_2, q_2)$ then one of the following cases applies:
>
> - C contains a subprogram if GC fi such that $(q', \alpha_1, q_1), (q', \alpha_2, q_2) \in \textbf{edges}_s(q' \rightsquigarrow q'')[\![\text{if } GC \text{ fi}]\!](X') \subseteq \textbf{edges}_s(q_\circ \rightsquigarrow q_\bullet)[\![C]\!](X)$, or
> - C contains a subprogram do GC od such that $(q', \alpha_1, q_1), (q', \alpha_2, q_2) \in \textbf{edges}_s(q' \rightsquigarrow q'')[\![\text{do } GC \text{ od}]\!](X') \subseteq \textbf{edges}_s(q_\circ \rightsquigarrow q_\bullet)[\![C]\!](X)$
>
> for suitable q'' and X' (satisfying $X \subseteq X'$).

We can then establish a so-called *non-interference* result that basically says that, if we perform two executions on memories that agree on all variables and arrays that may flow into some designated variable or array, then the two executions produce final values of the designated variable or array that agree.

> To express this it is useful to write $\uparrow x = \{y \in \textbf{Var} \cup \textbf{Arr} \mid y \rightarrow x\}$ for $x \in \textbf{Var} \cup \textbf{Arr}$ and to observe that $x \in \uparrow x$.
>
> Furthermore, for $A \in \textbf{Arr}$ we shall write $\sigma(A) = (\sigma(A[0]), \cdots, \sigma(A[\text{length}(A) - 1]))$.

> PROPOSITION 5.26: Suppose that $\textbf{sec}[\![C]\!](X)$ and that $\Longrightarrow_0$ and $\Longrightarrow_1$ are the ordinary semantics and reference-monitor semantics obtained from the instrumented program graph $\textbf{edges}_s(q_\circ \rightsquigarrow q_\bullet)[\![C]\!](X)$ (for $q_\circ \neq q_\bullet$) as in Section 5.2.

If $\langle q; \sigma_1 \rangle \Longrightarrow_0^* \langle q_\bullet; \sigma_1' \rangle$ and $\langle q; \sigma_2 \rangle \Longrightarrow_0^* \langle q_\bullet; \sigma_2' \rangle$ and $\forall y \in \,\uparrow x : \sigma_1(y) = \sigma_2(y)$ then $\sigma_1'(x) = \sigma_2'(x)$.

PROOF: Using Proposition 5.18 it suffices to prove that

$$\text{if } \langle q; \sigma_1 \rangle \Longrightarrow_1^{k_1} \langle q_\bullet; \sigma_1' \rangle \text{ and } \langle q; \sigma_2 \rangle \Longrightarrow_1^{k_2} \langle q_\bullet; \sigma_2' \rangle$$
$$\text{and } \forall y \in \,\uparrow x : \sigma_1(y) = \sigma_2(y)$$
$$\text{then } \sigma_1'(x) = \sigma_2'(x).$$

We prove by induction on n that the result holds if $k_1 + k_2 \le n$.

The base case is when $k_1 + k_2 = 0$ in which case $q = q_\bullet$ and $\sigma_1' = \sigma_1$ and $\sigma_2' = \sigma_2$ and the result is immediate.

For the induction step we assume that $k_1 + k_2 = n + 1$ and that the induction hypothesis applies to shorter sequences of length k_1' and k_2' such that $k_1' + k_2' \le n$. Since $k_1 + k_2 > 0$ we have that both $k_1 > 0$ and $k_2 > 0$ as otherwise $q = q_\bullet$ in which case $k_1 = k_2 = 0$ by Essential Exercise 5.25. This means that we can rewrite our assumptions $\langle q; \sigma_1 \rangle \Longrightarrow_1^{k_1} \langle q_\bullet; \sigma_1' \rangle$ and $\langle q; \sigma_2 \rangle \Longrightarrow_1^{k_2} \langle q_\bullet; \sigma_2' \rangle$ to

$$\langle q; \sigma_1 \rangle \overset{\alpha_1}{\Longrightarrow}_1 \langle q_1; \sigma_1'' \rangle \Longrightarrow_1^{k_1-1} \langle q_\bullet; \sigma_1' \rangle$$
$$\langle q; \sigma_2 \rangle \overset{\alpha_2}{\Longrightarrow}_1 \langle q_2; \sigma_2'' \rangle \Longrightarrow_1^{k_2-1} \langle q_\bullet; \sigma_2' \rangle$$

We now proceed by cases on α_1.

If α_1 is skip it follows from Essential Exercise 5.25 that also α_2 is skip and that $q_1 = q_2$. It follows from Definition 5.8 that $\sigma_1 = \sigma_1''$ and $\sigma_2 = \sigma_2''$. Hence we can apply the induction hypothesis to $\langle q_1; \sigma_1'' \rangle \Longrightarrow_1^{k_1-1} \langle q_\bullet; \sigma_1' \rangle$ and $\langle q_2; \sigma_2'' \rangle \Longrightarrow_1^{k_2-1} \langle q_\bullet; \sigma_2' \rangle$ since $k_1 - 1 + k_2 - 1 \le n$.

If α_1 is $z := a\{X\}$ it follows from Essential Exercise 5.25 that also α_2 is $z := a\{X\}$ and that $q_1 = q_2$. It follows from Definition 5.8 that $\sigma_1'' = \sigma_1[z \mapsto \mathcal{A}[\![a]\!]\sigma_1]$ and that $\sigma_2'' = \sigma_2[z \mapsto \mathcal{A}[\![a]\!]\sigma_2]$ and that $\mathsf{fv}(a) \rightrightarrows \{z\}$. If $z \not\rightarrow x$ it is immediate that $\forall y \in \,\uparrow x : \sigma_1''(y) = \sigma_2''(y)$; if $z \rightarrow x$ we have that $\mathsf{fv}(a) \rightrightarrows \{x\}$ and $\mathcal{A}[\![a]\!]\sigma_1 = \mathcal{A}[\![a]\!]\sigma_2$ so that also in this case $\forall y \in \,\uparrow x : \sigma_1''(y) = \sigma_2''(y)$. Hence we can apply the induction hypothesis to $\langle q_1; \sigma_1'' \rangle \Longrightarrow_1^{k_1-1} \langle q_\bullet; \sigma_1' \rangle$ and $\langle q_2; \sigma_2'' \rangle \Longrightarrow_1^{k_2-1} \langle q_\bullet; \sigma_2' \rangle$ since $k_1 - 1 + k_2 - 1 \le n$.

If α_1 is $A[a_1] := a_2\{X\}$ it follows from Essential Exercise 5.25 that also α_2 is $A[a_1] := a_2\{X\}$ and that $q_1 = q_2$. It follows from Definition 5.8 that $\sigma_1'' = \sigma_1[A[\mathcal{A}[\![a_1]\!]\sigma_1] \mapsto \mathcal{A}[\![a_2]\!]\sigma_1]$ and that $\sigma_2'' = \sigma_2[A[\mathcal{A}[\![a_1]\!]\sigma_2] \mapsto \mathcal{A}[\![a_2]\!]\sigma_2]$ and that $\mathsf{fv}(a_1) \cup \mathsf{fv}(a_2) \rightrightarrows \{A\}$. If $A \not\rightarrow x$ it is immediate that $\forall y \in \,\uparrow x : \sigma_1''(y) = \sigma_2''(y)$; if $A \rightarrow x$ we have that $\mathsf{fv}(a_1) \cup \mathsf{fv}(a_2) \rightrightarrows \{x\}$ and $\mathcal{A}[\![a_1]\!]\sigma_1 = \mathcal{A}[\![a_1]\!]\sigma_2$ and $\mathcal{A}[\![a_2]\!]\sigma_1 = \mathcal{A}[\![a_2]\!]\sigma_2$ so that also in this case $\forall y \in \,\uparrow x : \sigma_1''(y) = \sigma_2''(y)$. Hence we can apply the induction hypothesis to $\langle q_1; \sigma_1'' \rangle \Longrightarrow_1^{k_1-1} \langle q_\bullet; \sigma_1' \rangle$ and $\langle q_2; \sigma_2'' \rangle \Longrightarrow_1^{k_2-1} \langle q_\bullet; \sigma_2' \rangle$ since $k_1 - 1 + k_2 - 1 \le n$.

If α_1 is b_1 it follows from Essential Exercise 5.25 that also α_2 is some b_2 but we do not know that b_1 and b_2 are the same nor that q_1 and q_2 are the same. We proceed by subcases.

The first subcase is when $b_1 = b_2$ and $q_1 = q_2$. It then follows from Definition 5.8 that $\sigma_1 = \sigma_1''$ and $\sigma_2 = \sigma_2''$. Hence we can apply the induction hypothesis to $\langle q_1; \sigma_1'' \rangle \Longrightarrow_1^{k_1-1} \langle q_\bullet; \sigma_1' \rangle$ and $\langle q_2; \sigma_2'' \rangle \Longrightarrow_1^{k_2-1} \langle q_\bullet; \sigma_2' \rangle$ since $k_1 - 1 + k_2 - 1 \leq n$.

The second subcase is when $(q, b_1, q_1) \neq (q, b_2, q_2)$ and by Essential Exercise 5.25 $(q, b_1, q_1), (q, b_2, q_2) \in \mathbf{edges}_s(q \rightsquigarrow q')[\![\texttt{if } GC \texttt{ fi}]\!](X') \subseteq \mathbf{edges}_s(q_\circ \rightsquigarrow q_\bullet)[\![C]\!](X)$. We can then rewrite our assumptions $\langle q; \sigma_1 \rangle \Longrightarrow_1^{k_1} \langle q_\bullet; \sigma_1' \rangle$ and $\langle q; \sigma_2 \rangle \Longrightarrow_1^{k_2} \langle q_\bullet; \sigma_2' \rangle$ to

$$\langle q; \sigma_1 \rangle \overset{\alpha_1}{\Longrightarrow}_1 \langle q_1; \sigma_1 \rangle \overset{\omega_1}{\Longrightarrow}_1^{k_1'} \langle q'; \sigma_1'' \rangle \Longrightarrow_1^{k_1-k_1'-1} \langle q_\bullet; \sigma_1' \rangle$$
$$\langle q; \sigma_2 \rangle \overset{\alpha_2}{\Longrightarrow}_1 \langle q_2; \sigma_2 \rangle \overset{\omega_2}{\Longrightarrow}_1^{k_2'} \langle q'; \sigma_2'' \rangle \Longrightarrow_1^{k_2-k_2'-1} \langle q_\bullet; \sigma_2' \rangle$$

for $k_1' \geq 0$ and $k_2' \geq 0$. We will argue that $\forall y \in {\uparrow}x : \sigma_1''(y) = \sigma_1(y)$ by induction on the length of ω_1. There will be at least one variable y' in $\mathsf{fv}(b_1)$ such that $y' \not\rightarrow x$ as otherwise $\mathcal{B}[\![b_1]\!]\sigma_1 = \mathcal{B}[\![b_1]\!]\sigma_2$, which violates that the language is deterministic. Since all assignments $z' := a'\{X'\}$ in ω_1 will have $y' \in X'$ this ensures that $z' \not\rightarrow x$ and it follows that $\forall y \in {\uparrow}x : \sigma_1''(y) = \sigma_1(y)$. In a similar way we get that $\forall y \in {\uparrow}x : \sigma_2''(y) = \sigma_2(y)$. Hence we have that $\forall y \in {\uparrow}x : \sigma_1''(y) = \sigma_2''(y)$ and this allows us to apply the induction hypothesis to $\langle q'; \sigma_1'' \rangle \Longrightarrow_1^{k_1-k_1'-1} \langle q_\bullet; \sigma_1' \rangle$ and $\langle q'; \sigma_2' \rangle \Longrightarrow_1^{k_2-k_2'-1} \langle q_\bullet; \sigma_2' \rangle$.

The third subcase is when $(q, b_1, q_1) \neq (q, b_2, q_2)$ and by Essential Exercise 5.25 $(q, b_1, q_1), (q, b_2, q_2) \in \mathbf{edges}_s(q \rightsquigarrow q')[\![\texttt{do } GC \texttt{ od}]\!](X') \subseteq \mathbf{edges}_s(q_\circ \rightsquigarrow q_\bullet)[\![C]\!](X)$. It follows from Definition 5.4 that at least one of q_1 and q_2 will not be equal to q'; let us, without loss of generality, assume it is q_1. We can then rewrite our assumptions $\langle q; \sigma_1 \rangle \Longrightarrow_1^{k_1} \langle q_\bullet; \sigma_1' \rangle$ and $\langle q; \sigma_2 \rangle \Longrightarrow_1^{k_2} \langle q_\bullet; \sigma_2' \rangle$ to

$$\langle q; \sigma_1 \rangle \overset{\alpha_1}{\Longrightarrow}_1 \langle q_1; \sigma_1 \rangle \overset{\omega_1}{\Longrightarrow}_1^{k_1'} \langle q; \sigma_1'' \rangle \Longrightarrow_1^{k_1-k_1'-1} \langle q_\bullet; \sigma_1' \rangle$$
$$\langle q; \sigma_2 \rangle \Longrightarrow_1^{k_2} \langle q_\bullet; \sigma_2' \rangle$$

for $k_1' \geq 0$. Arguing as in the previous subcase we have that $\forall y \in {\uparrow}x : \sigma_1''(y) = \sigma_1(y)$ and hence that $\forall y \in {\uparrow}x : \sigma_1''(y) = \sigma_2(y)$. This allows us to apply the induction hypothesis to $\langle q; \sigma_1'' \rangle \Longrightarrow_1^{k_1-k_1'-1} \langle q_\bullet; \sigma_1' \rangle$ and $\langle q; \sigma_2 \rangle \Longrightarrow_1^{k_2} \langle q_\bullet; \sigma_2' \rangle$.

This completes the proof.   □

EXERCISE 5.27: Point out the place in the proof where we use that the security analysis only admits deterministic programs.   □

Sometimes there is a need to let properly *sanitised* data flow in the opposite direction to the flow relation. In this case careful analysis is needed to ensure that this flow should be permitted and one can no longer rely on the security analysis for guidance. In the case of confidentiality this is often called *declassification* and in the case of integrity it is often called *endorsement*.

Chapter 6

Model Checking

Model checking is an approach to finding properties of programs. It can be fully automated but its efficiency is usually not as good as that of program analysis. The gain is that the precision is closer to that of program verification.

6.1 Transition Systems

Program graphs are intended to represent the *control structure* of programs and systems whereas memories are intended to represent the *data structure* over which they operate. Sometimes it is convenient not to distinguish so clearly between control and data. This leads us to define transition systems as directed graphs where the nodes are *states* and the edges are *transitions*.

> DEFINITION 6.1: A *transition system* **TS** consists of the following:
>
> - **S**: a non-empty set of *states*
> - **I** $\subseteq$ **S**: a non-empty set of *initial states*
> - $\longrightarrow$ $\subseteq$ **S** $\times$ **S**: the *transition relation*
> - **AP**: a set of *atomic propositions*
> - **L** : **S** $\rightarrow$ PowerSet(**AP**): a *labelling function* for states
>
> It is standard notation to write $\varsigma \longrightarrow \varsigma'$ for $(\varsigma, \varsigma') \in \longrightarrow$.

Even though both program graphs and transition systems are directed graphs it is important to remember that program graphs only represent the control structure whereas transition systems represent a mixture of control structure and data; we

© Springer Nature Switzerland AG 2019
F. Nielson, H. Riis Nielson, *Formal Methods*, https://doi.org/10.1007/978-3-030-05156-3_6

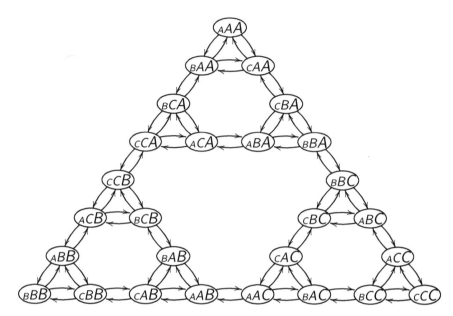

Figure 6.2: Transition System for Towers of Hanoi.

shall return to this in Section 6.4.

EXAMPLE 6.2: As an example of a transition system we shall consider the game called Towers of Hanoi. It consists of three rods (A, B and C) and a number of disks of different sizes which can slide onto any rod. However, disks only fit on top of larger disks or empty rods. The puzzle starts with the disks in a neat conical stack on one rod (say A) and the objective of the game is to move the disks one by one so that they end up in a similar neat conical stack on one of the other rods (say C). Clearly we can only move a disk from the top of one rod and place it at the top of another rod.

Let us model the version of the game with just three disks. The set **S** of states will be sequences of three letters chosen among the names of the rods; the first letter tells us the rod where the smallest disk is placed, the next letter tells us the rod where the middle disk is placed, and the last letter tells us where the largest disk is placed – as illustrated in Figure 6.1. The set of initial states **I** = {$_{A}AA$} consists of a single state $_{A}AA$ (where for ease of understanding we have used different sizes of the names of the rods). The transition relation is depicted in the diagram of Figure 6.2. In this example it is natural to choose the set of atomic propositions to be the same as the set of states, **AP = S**, so that the labelling function is trivially defined by $\mathbf{L}(\varsigma) = \{\varsigma\}$.

Figure 6.1: Towers of Hanoi configuration $_{B}AA$.

TRY IT OUT 6.3: Perform a similar modelling of the game of Towers of Hanoi where there are just two disks (but still three rods).   □

INPUT   a transition system as in Definition 6.1
                    a set S_0 of states

OUTPUT   **R**: the set $\mathbf{Reach}_1(S_0)$

ALGORITHM   **R** := { };

                    for each transition $\varsigma \longrightarrow \varsigma'$
                    do if $\varsigma \in S_0$ then **R** := **R** $\cup \{\varsigma'\}$

Figure 6.3: Algorithm for $\mathbf{Reach}_1(S_0)$.

INPUT   a transition system as in Definition 6.1
                    a set S_0 of states

OUTPUT   **R**: the set $\mathbf{Reach}(S_0)$

ALGORITHM   **R** := S_0;

                    while there exists a transition $\varsigma \longrightarrow \varsigma'$
                      with $\varsigma \in$ **R** and $\varsigma' \notin$ **R**
                    do **R** := **R** $\cup \{\varsigma'\}$

Figure 6.4: Algorithm for $\mathbf{Reach}(S_0)$.

A state is *stuck* whenever it has no transitions leaving it. A *path* in a transition system is a sequence of states $\varsigma_0 \varsigma_1 \cdots \varsigma_{n-1} \varsigma_n \cdots$ where each state arises from the previous one according to the transition relation, $\forall n > 0 : \varsigma_{n-1} \longrightarrow \varsigma_n$, and where the path is as long as possible. We write $\mathbf{Path}(\varsigma_0)$ for the set of paths $\pi = \varsigma_0 \varsigma_1 \cdots \varsigma_{n-1} \varsigma_n \cdots$ starting in ς_0.

A path in a transition system will be infinitely long unless it ends in a stuck state. If the state ς is stuck we have $\mathbf{Path}(\varsigma) = \{\varsigma\}$. A *path fragment* does not have to be as long as possible.

TRY IT OUT 6.4: Consider Example 6.2. Are there any stuck states? Are there any infinite paths? Are there any finite paths? Trace the shortest path fragment from $_AA A$ to $_cC C$.   □

We write $\mathbf{Reach}_1(S_0) = \{\varsigma_1 \mid \varsigma_0 \varsigma_1 \cdots \varsigma_n \cdots \in \mathbf{Path}(\varsigma_0) \wedge \varsigma_0 \in S_0\}$ for the set of states in **S** reachable from some state in S_0 in exactly one step.

We write $\mathbf{Reach}(S_0) = \{\varsigma_n \mid \varsigma_0 \varsigma_1 \cdots \varsigma_n \cdots \in \mathbf{Path}(\varsigma_0) \wedge \varsigma_0 \in S_0 \wedge n \geq 0\}$ for the set of states in **S** reachable from some state in S_0 in zero or more steps. States in $\mathbf{Reach}(\mathbf{I})$ are said to be *reachable*.

TRY IT OUT 6.5: Which states in Example 6.2 are reachable? Which states are not reachable? What is $\mathbf{Reach}_1(_ABC)$? What is $\mathbf{Reach}(_ABC)$?   □

EXERCISE 6.6: Assume that the set **S** is finite. First argue that the algorithm in Figure 6.3 correctly computes **Reach**$_1(S_0)$. Next argue that the algorithm in Figure 6.4 correctly computes **Reach**(S_0).   □

6.2 Computation Tree Logic – CTL

We shall be concerned with expressing properties of paths in transition systems and for this we make use of a logic called *Computation Tree Logic* (abbreviated *CTL*). We introduce most of it by example in this section and we will give its formal syntax and semantics in the next section.

Figure 6.5: A transition system.

In this section we concentrate on a transition system that has four states, **S** = $\{a, e, g, h\}$, one initial state, **I** = $\{a\}$, the transition relation as illustrated in Figure 6.5, two atomic propositions, **AP** = $\{c, v\}$ (with c meaning consonant and v meaning vowel) and the labelling function defined by **L**$(a) = \{v\}$, **L**$(e) = \{v\}$, **L**$(g) = \{c\}$ and **L**$(h) = \{c\}$.

Atomic propositions   We shall write

$$\varsigma \vDash \Phi$$

to indicate that the state ς satisfies the CTL formula Φ. The simplest CTL formulae are the atomic propositions and in this case we have $\varsigma \vDash$ ap whenever ap $\in$ **L**(ς). As an example, we have $g \vDash c$ but $a \nvDash c$ (meaning that $a \vDash c$ is false).

Reachability in one step   Another CTL formula is

$$\mathsf{EX}\,\Phi$$

which says that it is possible to reach a state in one step such that the state satisfies Φ. Looking at Figure 6.5 it is clear that we can get from e to a state satisfying c in one step and we write $e \vDash \mathsf{EX}\,c$ to indicate this; on the other hand, $a \nvDash \mathsf{EX}\,c$. In general, $\varsigma \vDash \mathsf{EX}\,\Phi$ whenever $\exists \varsigma' \in$ **Reach**$_1(\{\varsigma\}) : \varsigma' \vDash \Phi$.

A related CTL formula is

$$\mathsf{AX}\,\Phi$$

which says the next state is certain to satisfy Φ. Looking at Figure 6.5 we have $a \vDash \mathsf{AX}\,v$ but $e \nvDash \mathsf{AX}\,v$. In general, $\varsigma \vDash \mathsf{AX}\,\Phi$ whenever $\forall \varsigma' \in$ **Reach**$_1(\{\varsigma\}) \neq \{\,\} : \varsigma' \vDash \Phi$.

TRY IT OUT 6.7: Consider the transition system in Example 6.2. Consider each of the formulae

$$(1) \quad \text{EX} \quad {}_cA\mathcal{A}$$
$$(2) \quad \text{AX} \quad {}_cA\mathcal{A}$$

and determine whether or not they hold in the state ${}_AA\mathcal{A}$.   □

Reachability   A CTL formula for reachability is

$$\text{EF}\,\Phi$$

which says that it is possible to reach a state (possibly without moving at all) such that the state satisfies Φ. Looking at Figure 6.5 it is clear that we can get from a to a state satisfying c and we write $a \vDash \text{EF}\,c$ to indicate this; on the other hand, $g \nvDash \text{EF}\,v$. In general, $\varsigma \vDash \text{EF}\,\Phi$ whenever $\exists \varsigma' \in \textbf{Reach}(\{\varsigma\}) : \varsigma' \vDash \Phi$.

A related CTL formula is

$$\text{AF}\,\Phi$$

which says it is impossible not to eventually reach a state (including without moving at all) such that the state satisfies Φ. Looking at Figure 6.5 we have $a \nvDash \text{AF}\,c$ but $g \vDash \text{AF}\,c$.

TRY IT OUT 6.8: Consider the transition system in Example 6.2. Consider each of the formulae

$$(1) \quad \text{EF} \quad {}_cC\mathcal{C}$$
$$(2) \quad \text{AF} \quad {}_cC\mathcal{C}$$

and determine whether or not they hold in the state ${}_AA\mathcal{A}$.   □

Unavoidability   A CTL formula for unavoidability is

$$\text{AG}\,\Phi$$

which says there is no way to escape states satisfying Φ as you move along. Looking at Figure 6.5 we have $g \vDash \text{AG}\,c$ to indicate this; on the other hand, $a \nvDash \text{AG}\,v$. In general, $\varsigma \vDash \text{AG}\,\Phi$ whenever $\forall \varsigma' \in \textbf{Reach}(\{\varsigma\}) : \varsigma' \vDash \Phi$.

A related CTL formula is

$$\text{EG}\,\Phi$$

which says that it is possible to continue only to move to states satisfying Φ. Looking at Figure 6.5 we have $a \vDash \text{EG}\,v$ but $g \nvDash \text{EG}\,v$.

Try It Out 6.9: Consider the transition system in Example 6.2. Consider each of the formulae

$$(1) \quad \mathsf{EG} \ \neg cCC$$
$$(2) \quad \mathsf{AG} \ \neg cCC$$

and determine whether or not they hold in the state aAA. □

Summary We may summarise our explanation of *CTL* as follows:

formula	meaning of formula
Φ	Φ holds right now
$\mathsf{EX}\,\Phi$	it is possible in one step to go to Φ
$\mathsf{AX}\,\Phi$	in the next step we are at Φ
$\mathsf{EF}\,\Phi$	it is possible to go to Φ
$\mathsf{AF}\,\Phi$	it is not possible to escape Φ forever
$\mathsf{EG}\,\Phi$	it is possible to continue to enjoy Φ forever
$\mathsf{AG}\,\Phi$	you cannot escape Φ

On top of the operators explained so far we also use CTL formulae of the form $\neg\Phi$, $\Phi_1 \wedge \Phi_2$ etc.

6.3   Syntax and Semantics of CTL

Computation Tree Logic distinguishes between so-called state formulae, providing information about states, and so-called path formulae, providing information about paths.

DEFINITION 6.10: The syntax of the *state formulae* Φ and *path formulae* Ψ of *Computation Tree Logic* (*CTL*) are mutually recursively defined using the following BNF notation:

$$\Phi \ ::= \ \mathsf{tt} \mid \mathsf{ap} \mid \Phi_1 \wedge \Phi_2 \mid \neg\Phi \mid \mathsf{E}\Psi \mid \mathsf{A}\Psi$$
$$\Psi \ ::= \ \mathsf{X}\Phi \mid \mathsf{F}\Phi \mid \mathsf{G}\Phi \mid \Phi_1 \,\mathsf{U}\,\Phi_2$$

where ap denotes an atomic proposition.

We shall write ff for $\neg\mathsf{tt}$, $\Phi_1 \vee \Phi_2$ for $\neg((\neg\Phi_1) \wedge (\neg\Phi_2))$ and $\Phi_1 \Rightarrow \Phi_2$ for $(\neg\Phi_1) \vee \Phi_2$ without explicitly incorporating them in the above syntax. The meanings of state formulae and path formulae depend on each other and are defined below.

DEFINITION 6.11: The *semantics* of the *state formulae* Φ is given by:

$\varsigma \vDash \text{tt}$	iff	true
$\varsigma \vDash \text{ap}$	iff	$\text{ap} \in \mathbf{L}(\varsigma)$
$\varsigma \vDash \Phi_1 \wedge \Phi_2$	iff	$(\varsigma \vDash \Phi_1) \wedge (\varsigma \vDash \Phi_2)$
$\varsigma \vDash \neg\Phi$	iff	$\varsigma \nvDash \Phi$
$\varsigma \vDash \text{E}\Psi$	iff	$\exists \pi : \pi \in \mathbf{Path}(\varsigma) \wedge \pi \vDash \Psi$
$\varsigma \vDash \text{A}\Psi$	iff	$\forall \pi : \pi \in \mathbf{Path}(\varsigma) \Rightarrow \pi \vDash \Psi$

The atomic proposition ap holds in a state whenever it is one of the atomic formulae labelling that state. The quantifiers have much the same meaning as in predicate logic but they range over paths rather than states; the first ensures the existence of a path $(\pi = \varsigma_0\varsigma_1 \cdots \varsigma_n \cdots)$ with a certain property, whereas the other ensures that all paths must have a certain property (and recall that $\mathbf{Path}(\varsigma)$ is never empty).

DEFINITION 6.12: The *semantics* of the *path formulae* Ψ is given by:

$\varsigma_0\varsigma_1 \cdots \varsigma_n \cdots \vDash \text{X}\,\Phi$	iff	$\varsigma_1 \vDash \Phi \wedge n > 0$
$\varsigma_0\varsigma_1 \cdots \varsigma_n \cdots \vDash \text{F}\,\Phi$	iff	$\varsigma_n \vDash \Phi \wedge n \geq 0$
$\varsigma_0\varsigma_1 \cdots \varsigma_n \cdots \vDash \text{G}\,\Phi$	iff	$\forall m : \varsigma_m \vDash \Phi$
$\varsigma_0\varsigma_1 \cdots \varsigma_n \cdots \vDash \Phi_1 \,\text{U}\, \Phi_2$	iff	$(\varsigma_n \vDash \Phi_2) \wedge n \geq 0 \wedge$
		$\forall m \in \{0, \cdots, n-1\} : (\varsigma_m \vDash \Phi_1)$

The path formula $\text{X}\,\Phi$ holds on a path $\varsigma_0\varsigma_1 \cdots \varsigma_n \cdots$ whenever Φ holds in the state that is next in the path and there indeed is a next state. The path formula $\text{F}\,\Phi$ holds on a path whenever Φ holds in some state on the path – possibly the one we are in right now (that is ς_0). The path formula $\text{G}\,\Phi$ holds on a path whenever Φ holds in all states on the path – including the one we are in right now (that is ς_0). Finally, the path formula $\Phi_1 \,\text{U}\, \Phi_2$ not only requires $\text{F}\,\Phi_2$ but additionally that Φ_1 holds in all states up to (the first time) Φ_2 holds.

EXERCISE 6.13: We did not introduce $\Phi_1 \,\text{U}\, \Phi_2$ in Section 6.2. Explain the meaning of $\text{A}(\Phi_1 \,\text{U}\, \Phi_2)$ and $\text{E}(\Phi_1 \,\text{U}\, \Phi_2)$ in the same informal manner used in Section 6.2.□

EXERCISE 6.14: Check that the informal explanation of CTL in Section 6.2 is correct with respect to Definitions 6.11 and 6.12. □

DEFINITION 6.15: A state formula Φ *holds on a transition system* whenever it holds for all initial states: $\forall \varsigma \in \mathbf{I} : \varsigma \vDash \Phi$.

TRY IT OUT 6.16: Consider the transition system in Example 6.2. Consider each of the formulae

(1) EF $_cC\!C$
(2) $_aA\!A \wedge$ EF $_cC\!C$
(3) $_bB\!B \Rightarrow$ AG $_cC\!C$
(4) AF $_cC\!C$

and determine whether or not they hold for the transition system. □

6.4 From Program Graphs to Transition Systems

Recall that program graphs are intended to represent the *control structure* of programs and systems whereas memories are intended to represent the *data structure* over which they operate. When defining the semantics of program graphs we are working with *configurations* consisting of program points (nodes in the program graph) and memories and we are defining *execution steps* between configurations.

One way in which a program graph **PG** and a semantics may give rise to a transition system is to take the states **S** to be the configurations **Q** × **Mem**, the initial states **I** to be $\{\langle q_{\triangleright}; \sigma \rangle) \mid \sigma \in \mathbf{Mem}\}$, and the transition relation $\longrightarrow$ to be $\{(\varsigma, \varsigma') \mid \varsigma \Longrightarrow \varsigma'\}$ where $\Longrightarrow$ is as in Definition 1.11. We shall define $\mathbf{AP} = \{@_q \mid q \in \mathbf{Q}\} \cup \{\#_\sigma \mid \sigma \in \mathbf{Mem}\} \cup \{\triangleright, \blacktriangleleft\}$ and take

$$\mathbf{L}(\langle q; \sigma \rangle) = \{@_q, \#_\sigma\} \cup \{\triangleright \mid q = q_{\triangleright}\} \cup \{\blacktriangleleft \mid q = q_{\blacktriangleleft}\}$$

so that each state is labelled by the program point and the memory it consists of and we have explicit labels for the initial and final program points.

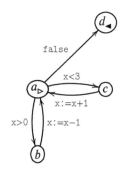

Figure 6.6: A program graph.

EXAMPLE 6.17: Let us consider the program graph depicted in Figure 6.6. It has four program points and operates on a variable that can take integer values among 0, 1, 2 and 3 only.

For readability we shall write the states $\langle q; n \rangle$ simply as qn where the first component gives a program point (chosen among a, b, c, d) and the second component gives the value of a variable (chosen among $0, 1, 2, 3$). Hence we obtain a transition system with states $\mathbf{S} = \{qn \mid q \in \{a, b, c, d\} \wedge n \in \{0, 1, 2, 3\}\}$ and the initial states $\mathbf{I} = \{a0, a1, a2, a3\}$ are the ones starting in program point a.

The set of atomic propositions $\mathbf{AP} = \{@_a, @_b, @_c, @_d, \#_0, \#_1, \#_2, \#_3, \triangleright, \blacktriangleleft\}$ are able to express the program point we are at, as well as the value of the variable.

We define the labelling function by setting (for $n \in \{0,1,2,3\}$)

$$
\begin{aligned}
\mathsf{L}(an) &= \{@_a, \#_n, \rhd\} \\
\mathsf{L}(bn) &= \{@_b, \#_n\} \\
\mathsf{L}(cn) &= \{@_c, \#_n\} \\
\mathsf{L}(dn) &= \{@_d, \#_n, \blacktriangleleft\}
\end{aligned}
$$

The transition relation $\longrightarrow$ is defined as follows:

$$
qn \longrightarrow q'n' \text{ iff }
\begin{pmatrix}
(n' = n \wedge q = a \wedge q' \in \{b,c\} \wedge \\
\quad (q' = b \Rightarrow n > 0) \wedge (q' = c \Rightarrow n < 3)) \vee \\
(n' = n+1 \wedge q = c \wedge q' = a) \vee \\
(n' = n-1 \wedge q = b \wedge q' = a)
\end{pmatrix}
$$

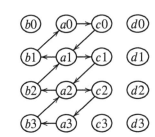

Figure 6.7: A transition system.

which is illustrated in Figure 6.7.

TRY IT OUT 6.18: How many states are there in the transition system of Example 6.17? How many of these are reachable? □

EXERCISE 6.19: Write a program in the Guarded Commands language of Chapter 2 so as to obtain the program graph of Figure 6.6. □

EXERCISE 6.20: Consider the transition system of Example 6.17 and the following state formulae:

(1) $@_a$
(2) $\#_2$
(3) $\mathsf{EF}(@_a \wedge \#_2)$
(4) $(@_c \wedge \#_2) \Rightarrow \mathsf{AX}(@_a \wedge \#_3)$
(5) $(@_c \wedge \#_3) \Rightarrow \mathsf{AX}@_d$
(6) $\mathsf{AG}(@_c \Rightarrow \mathsf{AX}@_a)$
(7) $\mathsf{AG}(@_c \Rightarrow \neg\#_3)$
(8) $\mathsf{AG}(\neg@_d)$

For each formula determine the set of states where it holds.

Next determine the set of reachable states (from Try It Out 6.18) where it holds.

Finally determine whether or not it holds of the transition system. □

For a transition system obtained from a program graph we may express the *termination* of the system in different ways. The formula

$$\rhd \Rightarrow \mathsf{EF}\,\blacktriangleleft$$

says that for all initial states it is possible to terminate. The formula

$$\rhd \Rightarrow \mathsf{AF}\,\blacktriangleleft$$

says that for all initial states we can be certain to terminate. These formulae have different meanings in general but their meanings coincide on transition systems obtained from deterministic systems (as defined in Definition 1.21 and considered in Proposition 1.22).

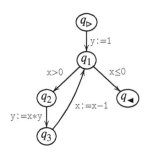

Figure 6.8: Program graph for the factorial function.

EXAMPLE 6.21: Let us return to the factorial program of Section 1.1, as displayed in Figure 6.8. Consider the transition system obtained from the program graph and the configurations and transitions of Section 1.2. Let us write $\#_{n\ m}$ to mean that the value of x is n and the value of y is m.

The formula $\triangleright \Rightarrow \mathsf{EF} \blacktriangleleft$ expresses that when we start running the factorial program there is a way for it to finish. The formula $\triangleright \Rightarrow \mathsf{AF} \blacktriangleleft$ expresses that when we start running the factorial program it will eventually finish. Since the program is deterministic the two formulae will have the same truth value.

The formula $(\triangleright \wedge \#_{7\ 0}) \Rightarrow \mathsf{AF}(\blacktriangleleft \wedge \#_{0\ 5040})$ expresses that the program will compute the factorial of 7 to be 5040. Note that neither of the more general formulae $(\triangleright \wedge \#_{n\ 0}) \Rightarrow \mathsf{AF}(\blacktriangleleft \wedge \#_{0\ n!})$ or $\forall n : (\triangleright \wedge \#_{n\ 0}) \Rightarrow \mathsf{AF}(\blacktriangleleft \wedge \#_{0\ n!})$ is permissible in CTL.

TRY IT OUT 6.22: Consider the program graph of Figure 6.8 and suppose that x takes values in the set $\{0, 1, 2, 3\}$ and that y takes values in the set $\{0, 1, 2, 3, 4, 5, 6\}$. Determine how many states there are in the transition system constructed as explained above.

Determine whether or not the formulae $\triangleright \Rightarrow \mathsf{EF} \blacktriangleleft$ and $\triangleright \Rightarrow \mathsf{AF} \blacktriangleleft$ hold for the transition system.   □

6.5 Towards an Algorithm (Bonus Material)

The main advantage of using a logic like CTL to express properties of transition systems is that there are fully automatic programs, called *model checkers*, that can determine whether or not the property holds of a system.

The best result that can be obtained is that model checking for CTL takes time $\mathcal{O}(|\mathbf{TS}| \cdot |\Phi|)$ where the size $|\mathbf{TS}|$ of the transition system is the number of states plus the number of transitions plus the sum over all states of the number of atomic propositions, and the size $|\Phi|$ of the formula is the number of symbols in it. However, when the transition system is constructed from a program graph as in Section 6.4 and the memory **Mem** represents m variables taking values among $\{0, \cdots, n-1\}$ this works out to $\mathcal{O}(n^m \cdot |\mathbf{Q}| \cdot |\Phi|)$, showing exponential growth in the number of variables; this is commonly called *state explosion*.

In this section we will cover some of the key ideas in the construction of a model checker for CTL but we will not go into the symbolic data structures or optimisations needed to achieve the best result.

> In model checking one sometimes assumes that there are transitions leaving all (reachable) states as this reduces the complexity of some of the developments. When this is the case we have some nice laws regarding negation, for example that $AX\,\Phi$ is the same as $\neg(EX\,(\neg\Phi))$. We shall be making this assumption in the remainder of this section; in order to meet this assumption we might add self loops on stuck states. Furthermore, we shall assume that the set S of states is finite.

We perform the model checking by defining a procedure $\mathbf{Sat}(\Phi)$ computing the set of states satisfying Φ; thus it is intended to satisfy the equation

$$\mathbf{Sat}(\Phi) = \{\varsigma \mid \varsigma \vDash \Phi\}$$

The procedure works by performing a recursive descent over the formula given as argument.

The straightforward cases We begin with the straightforward cases:

$$
\begin{aligned}
\mathbf{Sat}(\mathrm{tt}) &= S \\
\mathbf{Sat}(\mathrm{ap}) &= \{\varsigma \in S \mid \mathrm{ap} \in L(\varsigma)\} \\
\mathbf{Sat}(\Phi_1 \wedge \Phi_2) &= \mathbf{Sat}(\Phi_1) \cap \mathbf{Sat}(\Phi_2) \\
\mathbf{Sat}(\neg\Phi) &= S \setminus \mathbf{Sat}(\Phi) \\
\mathbf{Sat}(EX\,\Phi) &= \{\varsigma \mid \mathbf{Reach}_1(\{\varsigma\}) \cap \mathbf{Sat}(\Phi) \neq \{\,\}\} \\
\mathbf{Sat}(AX\,\Phi) &= \{\varsigma \mid \mathbf{Reach}_1(\{\varsigma\}) \subseteq \mathbf{Sat}(\Phi)\}
\end{aligned}
$$

For the last two equations we make use of the algorithm of Figure 6.3 computing the set of states reachable in exactly one step.

EXERCISE 6.23: Explain why the equations for tt, ap, $\Phi_1 \wedge \Phi_2$, $\neg\Phi$, $EX\,\Phi$ and $AX\,\Phi$ are in agreement with the explanations given in Section 6.2. In particular, explain where we are using the assumption that there are transitions leaving all (reachable) states. □

Two of the simpler cases We continue with two of the simpler cases:

$$
\begin{aligned}
\mathbf{Sat}(EF\,\Phi) &= \{\varsigma \mid \mathbf{Reach}(\{\varsigma\}) \cap \mathbf{Sat}(\Phi) \neq \{\,\}\} \\
\mathbf{Sat}(AG\,\Phi) &= \{\varsigma \mid \mathbf{Reach}(\{\varsigma\}) \subseteq \mathbf{Sat}(\Phi)\}
\end{aligned}
$$

Here we may recall the algorithm of Figure 6.4 for computing the reachable states although it may be preferable to develop more direct algorithms.

INPUT   a transition system as in Definition 6.1
                the set **Sat**(Φ)

OUTPUT   **R**: the set **Sat**(EF Φ)

ALGORITHM   **R** := **Sat**(Φ);

                while there exists a transition $\varsigma \longrightarrow \varsigma'$
                    with $\varsigma \notin$ **R** and $\varsigma' \in$ **R**
                do **R** := **R** $\cup \{\varsigma\}$

Figure 6.9: Algorithm for **Sat**(EF Φ).

EXERCISE 6.24: Argue that the algorithm of Figure 6.9 correctly computes the set **Sat**(EF Φ). How does the algorithm differ from that of Figure 6.4?   □

EXERCISE 6.25: Argue that AG Φ is the same as $\neg$(EF ($\neg\Phi$)) under the assumption that there are transitions leaving all states. Use this to modify the algorithm of Figure 6.9 to compute **Sat**(AG Φ). (Hint: it suffices to change the initialisation of **R** and to insert an additional assignment at the end of the algorithm.)   □

Two of the harder cases   We next consider the case of EG Φ, where we first display the definition and subsequently explain it.

$$\textbf{Sat}(\text{EG}\,\Phi) \quad = \quad \bigcap_n F^n(\textbf{Sat}(\Phi))$$
$$\text{where } F(S') = \{\varsigma \in S' \mid \textbf{Reach}_1(\{\varsigma\}) \cap S' \neq \{\,\}\}$$

The definition starts with **Sat**(Φ) = F^0(**Sat**(Φ)) and gradually removes states until each remaining state has a successor within the resulting set.

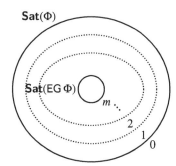

Figure 6.10: Calculating **Sat**(EG Φ).

EXERCISE 6.26: In this exercise we show that the calculation goes as follows

$$\textbf{Sat}(\Phi) \quad \supset \quad F^1(\textbf{Sat}(\Phi)) \supset \cdots \supset F^m(\textbf{Sat}(\Phi))$$
$$= \quad F^{m+1}(\textbf{Sat}(\Phi)) = \cdots = F^{m+p}(\textbf{Sat}(\Phi)) = \cdots = \bigcap_n F^n(\textbf{Sat}(\Phi))$$

as illustrated in Figure 6.10.

To see this, first show that F is reductive: $F(S') \subseteq S'$ for all S'.

Next show that F is monotonic: if $S_1 \subseteq S_2$ then $F(S_1) \subseteq F(S_2)$.

Then show that if $F^m(S') = F^{m+1}(S')$ then indeed $F^m(S') = F^{m+p}(S')$ for all $p \geq 0$.

Argue that it cannot be the case that $F^m(\textbf{Sat}(\Phi)) \supset F^{m+1}(\textbf{Sat}(\Phi))$ for all m and conclude that the calculation goes as displayed above.   □

INPUT   a transition system as in Definition 6.1
                  the set **Sat**(Φ)

OUTPUT   **R**: the set **Sat**(EG Φ)

ALGORITHM   **R** := **Sat**(Φ);

                  while there is $\varsigma \in$ **R**
                      with **Reach**$_1$($\{\varsigma\}$) $\cap$ **R** = { }
                  do **R** := **R** $\setminus \{\varsigma\}$

Figure 6.11: Algorithm for **Sat**(EG Φ).

TEASER 6.27: Show using mathematical induction on n that

$$F^n(\mathbf{Sat}(\Phi)) = \{\varsigma \mid \exists \varsigma_0 \varsigma_1 \cdots \varsigma_{n-1} \varsigma_n \cdots \in \mathbf{Path}(\varsigma) : \forall i \leq n : \varsigma_i \in \mathbf{Sat}(\Phi)\}$$

Further conclude that the result $\bigcap_n F^n(\mathbf{Sat}(\Phi))$ produced is the intended set of states. □

EXERCISE 6.28: Argue that the algorithm of Figure 6.11 correctly computes the set **Sat**(EG Φ). □

Next we consider the case AF Φ, where we first display the definition and subsequently explain it.

$$\mathbf{Sat}(\mathrm{AF}\,\Phi) \;=\; \mathbf{S} \setminus (\textstyle\bigcap_n F^n(\mathbf{S} \setminus \mathbf{Sat}(\Phi)))$$
$$\text{where } F(S') = \{\varsigma \in S' \mid \mathbf{Reach}_1(\{\varsigma\}) \cap S' \neq \{\,\}\}$$

EXERCISE 6.29: Argue that AF Φ is the same as $\neg$(EG ($\neg\Phi$)) under the assumption that there are transitions leaving all states. Conclude that **Sat**(AF Φ) = **Sat**($\neg$(EG ($\neg\Phi$))) and use this to argue for the correctness of the definition above. □

EXERCISE 6.30: In the manner of Exercise 6.25 use the previous exercise to modify the algorithm of Figure 6.11 to compute **Sat**(AF Φ). (Hint: it suffices to change the initialisation of **R** and to insert an additional assignment at the end of the algorithm.) □

The remaining cases There are several approaches to dealing with the remaining cases of E(Φ_1 U Φ_2) and A(Φ_1 U Φ_2). In the subsequent exercises we outline one way to do so.

EXERCISE 6.31: Observe that EF Φ is the same as E(tt U Φ) and that the algorithm of Figure 6.9 computes **Sat**(EF Φ). Use this to argue that the algorithm of Figure 6.12 computes **Sat**(E(Φ_1 U Φ_2)). □

INPUT   a transition system as in Definition 6.1
                      the set $\mathbf{Sat}(\Phi_1)$
                      the set $\mathbf{Sat}(\Phi_2)$

OUTPUT $\mathbf{R}$: the set $\mathbf{Sat}(E(\Phi_1 \cup \Phi_2))$

ALGORITHM $\mathbf{R} := \mathbf{Sat}(\Phi_2)$;

                      while there exists a transition $\varsigma \longrightarrow \varsigma'$
                           with $\varsigma \in \mathbf{Sat}(\Phi_1) \setminus \mathbf{R}$ and $\varsigma' \in \mathbf{R}$
                      do $\mathbf{R} := \mathbf{R} \cup \{\varsigma\}$

Figure 6.12: Algorithm for $\mathbf{Sat}(E(\Phi_1 \cup \Phi_2))$.

TEASER 6.32: Dealing with $A(\Phi_1 \cup \Phi_2)$ is considerably harder. First show that

$$\neg A(\Phi_1 \cup \Phi_2)$$

is equivalent to

$$EG(\neg \Phi_2) \vee E(\neg \Phi_2 \cup (\neg \Phi_1 \wedge \neg \Phi_2))$$

Deduce that

$$\mathbf{Sat}(A(\Phi_1 \cup \Phi_2)) = \mathbf{S} \setminus \left(\ \mathbf{Sat}(EG(\neg \Phi_2)) \cup \mathbf{Sat}(E(\neg \Phi_2 \cup (\neg \Phi_1 \wedge \neg \Phi_2))) \ \right)$$

and that this can be used to obtain an algorithm for computing $\mathbf{Sat}(A(\Phi_1 \cup \Phi_2))$.□

Chapter 7

Procedures

Procedures (or functions) are found in most programming languages and provide a means for reusing code in a number of programming tasks. In this chapter we will illustrate how to add procedures to the Guarded Commands language. Our focus will be on defining the semantics of procedures (as opposed to reasoning about them).

7.1   Declarations

So far we have taken the point of view that the memory needs to contain entries for all the variables and arrays used in the program. This is not appropriate for dealing with procedures and as a first step we introduce *declarations* that extend the memory with entries for variables and arrays.

Syntax   For this we assume that programs have the form $D\,;C$ so commands C are preceded by declarations D of variables and arrays:

$$D \quad ::= \quad \texttt{var } x \mid \texttt{array } A[n] \mid D_1\,;D_2$$

$$C \quad ::= \quad \cdots \text{as in Definition 2.3 (with arrays)} \cdots$$

$$GC \quad ::= \quad \cdots \text{as in Definition 2.3} \cdots$$

The integer n in the array declaration $\texttt{array } A[n]$ specifies the length of the array and is required to be positive.

> EXAMPLE 7.1: The function displayed in Figure 2.11 in Section 2.3 might more naturally be written using declarations of the auxiliary variables i and x as shown in Figure 7.1

```
var i;
var x;
do i < 10  →  x := x + A[i];
              B[i] := x;
              i := i + 1
od
```

Figure 7.1: Traversing an array.

© Springer Nature Switzerland AG 2019
F. Nielson, H. Riis Nielson, *Formal Methods*, https://doi.org/10.1007/978-3-030-05156-3_7

Program graphs   We next extend the generation of program graphs from Chapter 2. For this we introduce two new actions, var x and array $A[n]$, corresponding to the two basic types of declarations and we then define a function $\mathbf{edges}(q_{\circ} \leadsto q_{\bullet})[\![\cdot]\!]$ for dealing with declarations.

DEFINITION 7.2: For declarations the edges are constructed as follows:

$$\mathbf{edges}(q_{\circ} \leadsto q_{\bullet})[\![\text{var } x]\!] \quad = \quad \{(q_{\circ}, \text{var } x, q_{\bullet})\}$$

$$\mathbf{edges}(q_{\circ} \leadsto q_{\bullet})[\![\text{array } A[n]]\!] \quad = \quad \{(q_{\circ}, \text{array } A[n], q_{\bullet})\}$$

$$\mathbf{edges}(q_{\circ} \leadsto q_{\bullet})[\![D_1 \, ; D_2]\!] \quad = \quad \begin{array}{l} \text{let } q \text{ be fresh} \\ \quad E_1 = \mathbf{edges}(q_{\circ} \leadsto q)[\![D_1]\!] \\ \quad E_2 = \mathbf{edges}(q \leadsto q_{\bullet})[\![D_2]\!] \\ \text{in } E_1 \cup E_2 \end{array}$$

Note that in the case of sequencing we are creating a new node exactly as we did when dealing with sequencing of commands.

We also need a version of $\mathbf{edges}(q_{\circ} \leadsto q_{\bullet})[\![\cdot]\!]$ for dealing with programs of the form $D \, ; C$; for commands (and guarded commands) we can reuse the corresponding functions from Chapter 2. For programs the edges of the program graphs are constructed as follows:

$$\mathbf{edges}(q_{\circ} \leadsto q_{\bullet})[\![D \, ; C]\!] \quad = \quad \begin{array}{l} \text{let } q \text{ be fresh} \\ \quad E_1 = \mathbf{edges}(q_{\circ} \leadsto q)[\![D]\!] \\ \quad E_2 = \mathbf{edges}(q \leadsto q_{\bullet})[\![C]\!] \\ \text{in } E_1 \cup E_2 \end{array}$$

Semantics   Finally we must extend the semantic function $\mathcal{S}[\![\cdot]\!]$ from Chapter 2 to take care of the two new actions var x and array $A[n]$:

$$\mathcal{S}[\![\text{var } x]\!]\sigma \quad = \quad \sigma[x \mapsto 0]$$

$$\mathcal{S}[\![\text{array } A[n]]\!]\sigma \quad = \quad \sigma[A[0] \mapsto 0] \cdots [A[n-1] \mapsto 0]$$

Variables are initialised to 0 and all entries of an array are similarly initialised to 0. Note how $\mathcal{S}[\![\text{var } x]\!]\sigma$ differs from $\mathcal{S}[\![x := 0]\!]\sigma$ (defined in Definition 2.17): in the former we do not require that an entry for x is already present in the memory σ whereas this is the case for the latter.

TRY IT OUT 7.3: What happens if we make multiple declarations of the same variable (as in var u ; var u)? Is it equivalent to just a single declaration (as in var u)?   □

TRY IT OUT 7.4: What happens if we make multiple declarations of the same array but using different lengths (as in array A[7] ; array A[3])?   □

7.2 Blocks

Declarations are fine for introducing new variables and arrays but we would also like to 'get rid of them' when they are no longer needed. To this end we introduce *blocks* of the form $\{D\,;C\}$ where the declarations D before a command C are indeed *local* to that command. It is also customary to say that the *scope* of the variables and arrays introduced in the declarations D is restricted to the command C.

Syntax   We shall take blocks to be commands and a program will simply be a command.

DEFINITION 7.5: The syntax of *Guarded Commands with Blocks* is given by

$$
\begin{aligned}
D &\ ::=\ \ \text{var } x \mid \text{array } A[n] \mid D_1\,;D_2 \\
C &\ ::=\ \ \{D\,;C\} \mid \cdots \text{as in Definition 2.3 (with arrays)} \cdots \\
GC &\ ::=\ \ \cdots \text{as in Definition 2.3} \cdots
\end{aligned}
$$

The integer n in the array declaration array $A[n]$ is required to be positive.

EXAMPLE 7.6: As an example let us consider the program of Figure 7.2. The variable x occurring in the assignment y := x + 1 refers to the innermost declaration of x whereas the occurrence of x in x := x + y refers to the global variable x – just as the assignment x := 1 does. Therefore the value of y after the assignment y := x + 1 is intended to be 3 (and not 2) and the value of x after the assignment x := x + y is intended to be 4 (and not 5).

```
{   var y;
    y := 1;
    x := 1;
    { var x;
      x := 2;
      y := x + 1
    };
    x := x + y
}
```

Figure 7.2: Nested declarations.

Program graphs   To define program graphs for this language we need to extend Definition 2.7 from Chapter 2 to take care of blocks. Declarations are handled as in the previous section.

DEFINITION 7.7: For blocks the edges are constructed as follows:

$$
\begin{aligned}
\mathbf{edges}(q_\circ \rightsquigarrow q_\bullet)[\![\{D\,;C\}]\!] =\ & \\
\text{let } q_1,q_2,q_3 &\text{ be fresh} \\
E_1 &= \mathbf{edges}(q_1 \rightsquigarrow q_2)[\![D]\!] \\
E_2 &= \mathbf{edges}(q_2 \rightsquigarrow q_3)[\![C]\!] \\
\text{in } \{(q_\circ, \text{enter}, q_1)\} &\cup E_1 \cup E_2 \cup \{(q_3, \text{exit}, q_\bullet)\}
\end{aligned}
$$

The remaining cases for commands are as in Definition 2.7 (with arrays as in Definition 2.19) and the ones for declarations are as in Definition 7.2.

The main difference from the treatment in Section 7.1 is that we introduce two new actions enter and exit to mark the points where a new local *scope* begins

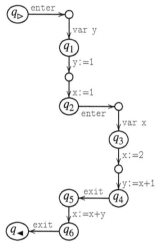

Figure 7.3: Program graph for Figure 7.2.

```
{ var z;
  var i;
  z := 1;
  y := 0;
  i := 0;
  do i < x → { var t;
               t := z;
               z := y;
               y := t + z;
               i := i + 1
             }
  od
}
```

Figure 7.4: Example program for the Fibonacci function.

and ends. The idea is that when meeting an `exit` we should be able to remove the entries in the memory that were added since the previous `enter`. The details will be made precise shortly when we provide the semantics of the actions `enter` and `exit`.

EXAMPLE 7.8: Returning to Example 7.6 and Figure 7.2, the resulting program graph is as displayed in Figure 7.3 where we have taken the liberty of naming only some of the nodes.

EXAMPLE 7.9: Figure 7.4 illustrates a program with nested blocks and where the innermost block is within a loop. This means that a new instance of the variable `t` is declared whenever the body of the loop is entered. The program is intended to compute in `y` the `x`'th Fibonacci number (from the familiar sequence 1, 1, 2, 3, 5, 8, ⋯) and taking non-positive Fibonacci numbers to be 0.

TRY IT OUT 7.10: Construct the program graph for the program of Figure 7.4.☐

Semantics   The main challenge is to find a way to let the new actions `enter` and `exit` do what we intend them to do: to create a 'marker' when a block is entered and to remove the entries added since the last 'marker' was placed when a block is exited. There are many ways to do so and one that interacts well with our approach so far is to redefine a *memory* to be a stack of frames where each *frame* is a partial mapping from variables and array entries to their values; it is partial because each frame is only intended to contain entries for some of the variables. Creating a 'marker' can then be performed by pushing a new frame on the top of the stack. Removing the entries since the last 'marker' was placed can be performed by popping the topmost frame on the stack.

This leads to taking $\mathbf{Mem_F} = \mathbf{Frame}^*$ (or equivalently $\mathbf{Mem_F} = \mathrm{List}(\mathbf{Frame})$) and

$$\mathbf{Frame} = \big(\ \mathbf{Var} \cup \{A[i] \mid A \in \mathbf{Arr}, \exists n : 0 \leq i < n\}\ \big) \hookrightarrow \mathbf{Int}$$

and pretending this is a stack. When a block is entered (by executing the `enter` action) we will push a new empty frame on the stack. The subsequent declarations contained in the block will add entries to the topmost frame. When leaving the block (by executing an `exit` action) we pop the topmost frame from the stack. When determining the value of a variable we will always search for the topmost frame giving a value to it and use that. Similarly, when updating a variable we will always find the topmost frame mentioning the variable and update its value.

EXAMPLE 7.11: Before embarking upon the formal development let us illustrate our approach by returning to the program of Figure 7.2. In doing so we will encounter the memories of Figure 7.5 and they are annotated with the nodes from the corresponding program graph of Figure 7.3. The initial memory corresponding to the node $q_{\triangleright}$ consists of a single frame recording that the value of the single global variable x is 0. A new frame is created when entering the outer block and after the declaration of y we have the memory labelled (q_1). The values of x and y are updated and just before entering the inner block we have the memory labelled (q_2). Yet another frame is introduced and we obtain the memory labelled (q_3) containing two frames defining the value of x. The topmost occurrence of x is first updated and next inspected in order to compute y so we arrive at the memory labelled (q_4). We are now ready to exit the inner block and the topmost frame is popped so we get the memory labelled (q_5). After the assignment to x we have the memory labelled (q_6) and when exiting the outer block we pop the topmost frame and the resulting memory contains the single frame labelled $(q_{\blacktriangleleft})$ in Figure 7.5.

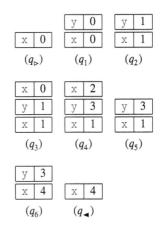

Figure 7.5: The memories for the program of Figures 7.2 and 7.3.

In the following we write σ for an element of **Frame** and $\vec{\sigma}$ for an element of **Mem**$_F$, that is, a stack of frames; an empty frame is written [ ] whereas an empty stack of frames is written ε. The top of the stack will be to the left so we shall write $\sigma::\vec{\sigma}$ for a stack of frames with σ as the topmost frame and $\vec{\sigma}$ being the stack of frames below it.

A frame specifies the values of a finite set of variables and array entries and we shall write dom(σ) for this set; as a special case we have dom([ ]) = { } for the empty frame. We extend this notation to memories by defining

$$\mathsf{dom}(\vec{\sigma}) = \begin{cases} \mathsf{dom}(\sigma) \cup \mathsf{dom}(\vec{\sigma}') & \text{if } \vec{\sigma} = \sigma::\vec{\sigma}' \\ \{\,\} & \text{otherwise} \end{cases}$$

One of the key operations on the memory is to determine the value of a variable. For a frame σ we write $\sigma(x)$ for the value of x provided that $x \in \mathsf{dom}(\sigma)$. We shall now extend this notation to memories and define $\vec{\sigma}(x)$:

$$\vec{\sigma}(x) = \begin{cases} \sigma(x) & \text{if } \vec{\sigma} = \sigma::\vec{\sigma}' \text{ and } x \in \mathsf{dom}(\sigma) \\ \vec{\sigma}'(x) & \text{if } \vec{\sigma} = \sigma::\vec{\sigma}' \text{ and } x \notin \mathsf{dom}(\sigma) \\ \text{undefined} & \text{otherwise} \end{cases}$$

Hence we return the value of x as given by the topmost frame that contains an entry for x; if no such frame exists the value of x is not defined. In a similar way we can determine the value of an array entry:

$$\vec{\sigma}(A[i]) = \begin{cases} \sigma(A[i]) & \text{if } \vec{\sigma} = \sigma::\vec{\sigma}' \text{ and } A[i] \in \mathsf{dom}(\sigma) \\ \vec{\sigma}'(A[i]) & \text{if } \vec{\sigma} = \sigma::\vec{\sigma}' \text{ and } A[i] \notin \mathsf{dom}(\sigma) \\ \text{undefined} & \text{otherwise} \end{cases}$$

EXERCISE 7.12: Adapt the semantic functions $\mathcal{A}[\![a]\!]$ and $\mathcal{B}[\![b]\!]$ of Chapter 2 to work on memories as defined here.   □

Another key operation on the memory is to update the value of a variable. For a frame we write $\sigma[x \mapsto v]$ for the frame that is as σ except that x has the value v

(provided $x \in \mathrm{dom}(\sigma)$). For memories we shall write the operation as $\vec{\sigma}[x \mapsto v]$ and define it as follows:

$$\vec{\sigma}[x \mapsto v] \;=\; \begin{cases} (\sigma[x \mapsto v])::\vec{\sigma}' & \text{if } \vec{\sigma} = \sigma::\vec{\sigma}' \text{ and } x \in \mathrm{dom}(\sigma) \\ \sigma::(\vec{\sigma}'[x \mapsto v]) & \text{if } \vec{\sigma} = \sigma::\vec{\sigma}' \text{ and } x \notin \mathrm{dom}(\sigma) \\ \text{undefined} & \text{otherwise} \end{cases}$$

Hence we modify the value of x as given by the topmost frame that contains an entry for x; if no such frame exists the resulting memory is undefined. In a similar way we can update the value of an array entry:

$$\vec{\sigma}[A[i] \mapsto v] \;=\; \begin{cases} (\sigma[A[i] \mapsto v])::\vec{\sigma}' & \text{if } \vec{\sigma} = \sigma::\vec{\sigma}' \text{ and } A[i] \in \mathrm{dom}(\sigma) \\ \sigma::(\vec{\sigma}'[A[i] \mapsto v]) & \text{if } \vec{\sigma} = \sigma::\vec{\sigma}' \text{ and } A[i] \notin \mathrm{dom}(\sigma) \\ \text{undefined} & \text{otherwise} \end{cases}$$

DEFINITION 7.13: We are now ready to define the semantics of *Guarded Commands with Blocks*. The semantic domains are

$$\mathbf{Mem_F} \;=\; \mathbf{Frame}^* \text{ where}$$

$$\mathbf{Frame} \;=\; \big(\; \mathbf{Var} \cup \{ A[i] \mid A \in \mathbf{Arr}, \exists n : 0 \le i < n \} \;\big) \hookrightarrow \mathbf{Int}$$

and the semantic function $S_F[\![\cdot]\!] : \mathbf{Act} \to (\mathbf{Mem_F} \hookrightarrow \mathbf{Mem_F})$ is defined as follows for the basic actions:

$$S_F[\![\texttt{skip}]\!]\vec{\sigma} \;=\; \vec{\sigma}$$

$$S_F[\![x := a]\!]\vec{\sigma} \;=\; \begin{cases} \vec{\sigma}[x \mapsto z] & \text{if } z = \mathcal{A}[\![a]\!]\vec{\sigma} \text{ is defined} \\ & \qquad \text{and } x \in \mathrm{dom}(\vec{\sigma}) \\ \text{undefined} & \text{otherwise} \end{cases}$$

$$S_F[\![b]\!]\vec{\sigma} \;=\; \begin{cases} \vec{\sigma} & \text{if } \mathcal{B}[\![b]\!]\vec{\sigma} = \text{true} \\ \text{undefined} & \text{otherwise} \end{cases}$$

$$S_F[\![A[a_1] := a_2]\!]\vec{\sigma} \;=\; \begin{cases} \vec{\sigma}[A[z_1] \mapsto z_2] & \text{if } z_1 = \mathcal{A}[\![a_1]\!]\vec{\sigma} \text{ is defined} \\ & \qquad \text{and } z_2 = \mathcal{A}[\![a_2]\!]\vec{\sigma} \text{ is defined} \\ & \qquad \text{and } A[z_1] \in \mathrm{dom}(\vec{\sigma}) \\ \text{undefined} & \text{otherwise} \end{cases}$$

$$S_F[\![\texttt{var } x]\!]\vec{\sigma} \;=\; \begin{cases} (\sigma[x \mapsto 0])::\vec{\sigma}' & \text{if } \vec{\sigma} = \sigma::\vec{\sigma}' \\ \text{undefined} & \text{if } \vec{\sigma} = \varepsilon \end{cases}$$

$$S_\mathsf{F}[\![\text{array } A[n]]\!]\vec{\sigma} \;=\; \begin{cases} \sigma[A[0] \mapsto 0] \cdots [A[n-1] \mapsto 0] :: \vec{\sigma}' & \text{if } \vec{\sigma} = \sigma :: \vec{\sigma}' \\ \text{undefined} & \text{if } \vec{\sigma} = \varepsilon \end{cases}$$

$$S_\mathsf{F}[\![\text{enter}]\!]\vec{\sigma} \;=\; [\,] :: \vec{\sigma}$$

$$S_\mathsf{F}[\![\text{exit}]\!]\vec{\sigma} \;=\; \begin{cases} \vec{\sigma}' & \text{if } \vec{\sigma} = \sigma :: \vec{\sigma}' \\ \text{undefined} & \text{if } \vec{\sigma} = \varepsilon \end{cases}$$

The first four clauses are straightforward adaptations of the ones in Chapter 2. The next two clauses are adaptations of the ones from Section 7.1; here we would not expect to encounter the cases $\vec{\sigma} = \varepsilon$ when considering program graphs generated by Definition 7.7. The final two clauses provide the formal treatment of the new actions enter and exit; for the latter we would not expect to encounter the case $\vec{\sigma} = \varepsilon$ when considering program graphs generated by Definition 7.7, because of the way the block structure introduces enter and exit as matching pairs of parentheses.

DEFINITION 7.14: As in Definitions 1.10 and 1.11 we define *configurations* to be pairs of nodes and memories, so they have the form $\langle q; \vec{\sigma} \rangle$, and *execution steps* will then have the form

$$\langle q; \vec{\sigma} \rangle \overset{\alpha}{\Longrightarrow} \langle q'; \vec{\sigma}' \rangle$$

whenever α is the action corresponding to an edge from q to q' in the program graph and $S_\mathsf{F}[\![\alpha]\!]\vec{\sigma} = \vec{\sigma}'$. *Execution sequences* are then obtained as the reflexive and transitive closure of the transition relation.

TRY IT OUT 7.15: Assuming that the initial value of x is 4, construct a complete execution sequence for the program of Figure 7.4 using the program graph constructed in Try It Out 7.10. What is the maximal number of frames on the stack in any execution sequence? ☐

EXERCISE 7.16: Assume A is a global array of length 5 and consider the command of Figure 7.6 introducing a local array with the same name but of shorter length. Construct the corresponding program graph and show that a complete execution sequence will update the entry A[3] of the global array to 7. Modify the definition of $\vec{\sigma}[A[i] \mapsto v]$ so that it is undefined when indexing outside the bounds of the most recent declaration of the array A. Make a similar modification of the definition of $\vec{\sigma}(A[i])$ and give an example of a command where this makes a difference. ☐

```
A[3] := 1;
{   array A[2];
    A[3] := 7
}
```

Figure 7.6: Array declarations.

TEASER 7.17: The handling of the break statement becomes more complex in the setting of Guarded Commands with Blocks as we might have to exit a number of blocks as part of jumping to the end of a loop. To handle this, one may keep track of the nesting depth of the block containing the enclosing loop as well as the nesting depth of the construct itself. Specify the construction of program graphs and illustrate the development on an example. Extend the treatment to include the continue construct. ☐

7.3 Procedures with Dynamic Scope

Procedures are named and parameterised commands and the parameters will be local to the procedure. There are many kinds of parameters that can be considered and we shall restrict ourselves to just two parameters. One is an *input parameter* passing values to the procedure, and the other is an *output parameter* passing values out of the procedure.

Syntax   Since parameters are supposed to be local to the procedure it is natural to extend the syntax of Guarded Commands with Blocks.

> DEFINITION 7.18: The syntax of *Guarded Commands with Procedures* is
>
> $$D \quad ::= \quad \texttt{var } x \mid \texttt{array } A[n] \mid \texttt{proc } p(x\,;y)\,C\,\texttt{end} \mid D_1\,;D_2$$
> $$C \quad ::= \quad \{D\,;C\} \mid p(a\,;z) \mid \cdots \text{ as in Definition 2.3 (with arrays)} \cdots$$
> $$GC \quad ::= \quad \cdots \text{ as in Definition 2.3} \cdots$$
>
> The integer n in the array declaration $\texttt{array } A[n]$ is required to be positive.

The *procedure declaration* $\texttt{proc } p(x\,;y)\,C\,\texttt{end}$ introduces a procedure with the name p, *input parameter* x, *output parameter* y and *defining command* C; both x and y are *formal parameters*. The *procedure call* $p(a\,;z)$ calls the procedure p with the *actual parameters* a and z. The call will pass the result of evaluating the arithmetic expression a to the input parameter of p (that is to x) and will pass the resulting value of the output parameter of p (that is y) to the variable z when returning.

```
{ proc fac(x;y)
    if x ≤ 1 → y := 1
    [] x > 1 → { var t;
                    fac(x − 1;t);
                    y := x ∗ t
                }
    fi
  end;
  fac(3;z)
}
```

Figure 7.7: Example program for the factorial function.

> EXAMPLE 7.19: Figure 7.7 defines a factorial program written in Guarded Commands with Procedures. Here x and y are the formal parameters of the procedure and t is a local variable used to hold the result obtained from the recursive call of the procedure. At the top level the procedure is called with the actual parameters 3 and z.

Program graphs   When defining the program graph we need to keep track of the procedures that have been declared and for each procedure we need to record its input parameter, output parameter, entry node and exit node. We shall use an *environment* ρ for this: this is just a partial mapping from procedure names to quadruples consisting of two variables and two nodes, so typically we will have

$$\rho(p) = (x, y, q_n, q_x)$$

for a procedure p with parameters x and y and with q_n being the entry (or initial) node of the procedure body and q_x being the exit (or final) node of the procedure body. It turns out that the way we do this gives rise to something called *dynamic scope*, which will be discussed in more detail in Section 7.4.

The environment ρ will be constructed when we build the program graph for the declarations and, as we shall see shortly, it will be used when we construct the program graph for the commands. We shall therefore let $\mathbf{edges}_{dp2}(q_\circ \rightsquigarrow q_\bullet)[\![D]\!]$ be a function that is supplied with the current environment ρ as parameter and in addition to returning the edges of the program graph for D it will also return an updated version of ρ.

DEFINITION 7.20: For declarations the edges are constructed as follows:

$$\mathbf{edges}_{dp2}(q_\circ \rightsquigarrow q_\bullet)[\![\texttt{var } x]\!]\rho = (\{(q_\circ, \texttt{var } x, q_\bullet)\}, \rho)$$

$$\mathbf{edges}_{dp2}(q_\circ \rightsquigarrow q_\bullet)[\![\texttt{array } A[n]]\!]\rho = (\{(q_\circ, \texttt{array } A[n], q_\bullet)\}, \rho)$$

$$\mathbf{edges}_{dp2}(q_\circ \rightsquigarrow q_\bullet)[\![D_1 ; D_2]\!]\rho =$$
$$\text{let } q \text{ be fresh}$$
$$(E_1, \rho_1) = \mathbf{edges}_{dp2}(q_\circ \rightsquigarrow q)[\![D_1]\!]\rho$$
$$(E_2, \rho_2) = \mathbf{edges}_{dp2}(q \rightsquigarrow q_\bullet)[\![D_2]\!]\rho_1$$
$$\text{in } (E_1 \cup E_2, \rho_2)$$

$$\mathbf{edges}_{dp2}(q_\circ \rightsquigarrow q_\bullet)[\![\texttt{proc } p(x ; y) \, C \, \texttt{end}]\!]\rho =$$
$$\text{let } q_n, q_x \text{ be fresh}$$
$$\rho' = \rho[p \mapsto (x, y, q_n, q_x)]$$
$$E = \mathbf{edges}_{dp}(q_n \rightsquigarrow q_x)[\![C]\!]\rho'$$
$$\text{in } (\{(q_\circ, \texttt{skip}, q_\bullet)\} \cup E, \rho')$$

The first three clauses are much as in Definition 7.2 except that the environment is provided as an additional parameter and is returned as a result.

The last clause takes care of *procedure declarations* and is the clause that updates the environment with information about the procedure defined. It generates a single edge from $q_\circ$ to $q_\bullet$ with a skip action and as a 'side effect' it creates two fresh nodes q_n and q_x to be used as the entry and exit nodes for the program graph for the body of the procedure. This is illustrated in Figure 7.8; at this stage these two parts of the program graph are unconnected but they will become connected when the procedure is called. It turns out that we allow procedures to be recursive ('call themselves') because the environment used for generating the program graph for C is ρ' rather than ρ.

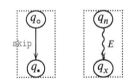

Figure 7.8: Procedure declaration.

Before turning to the procedure calls let us adapt the generation of edges for the other commands and guarded commands to take care of the environment.

ESSENTIAL EXERCISE 7.21: In preparation for dealing with procedure calls you should modify the generation of edges for the remaining commands (that is, Definition 2.7 with arrays) and guarded commands (that is, Definition 2.8) to take care of the environment. For blocks we modify Definition 7.7 to be

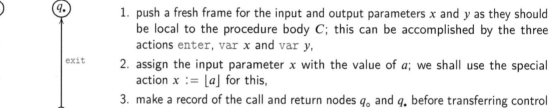

so as to update and make use of the environment. In the clauses you define
there should only be a need to pass the environment around as a parameter (as
was done in the call to $\textbf{edges}_{dp}(q_2 \leadsto q_3)[\![C]\!]\rho_1$ in the above clause).

Consider now a *procedure call* $p(a\,;z)$ of a procedure declared as $\texttt{proc } p(x\,;y)\,C\texttt{ end}$.
Upon execution it should give rise to the following actions, as illustrated in Figure
7.9:

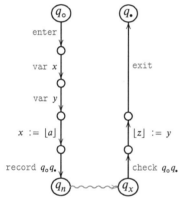

Figure 7.9: Procedure call.

1. push a fresh frame for the input and output parameters x and y as they should
   be local to the procedure body C; this can be accomplished by the three
   actions $\texttt{enter}$, $\texttt{var } x$ and $\texttt{var } y$,

2. assign the input parameter x with the value of a; we shall use the special
   action $x := \lfloor a \rfloor$ for this,

3. make a record of the call and return nodes $q_\circ$ and $q_\bullet$ before transferring control
   to the entry point q_n of the procedure body C; the action $\texttt{record } q_\circ q_\bullet$ will be
   used for this,

4. transfer control from the exit point q_x of the procedure body C if the recorded
   call and return nodes are the appropriate ones; this is ensured by the action
   $\texttt{check } q_\circ q_\bullet$,

5. assign the return variable z the value of the output parameter y using the
   special action $\lfloor z \rfloor := y$, and finally

6. pop the top frame using the action $\texttt{exit}$.

This is achieved by generating program graphs for procedure calls as follows.

DEFINITION 7.22: For commands and guarded commands the edges are constructed as in Essential Exercise 7.21 together with the following clause for
procedure calls:

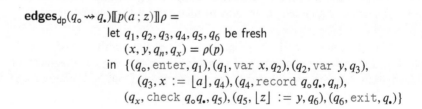

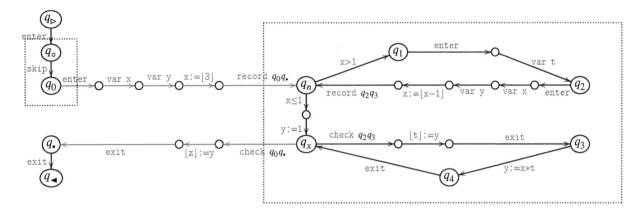

Figure 7.10: Program graph for the factorial function of Figure 7.7; the procedure declaration itself gives rise to the two framed parts of the program graph.

If $\rho(p)$ is undefined (that is, the procedure is not declared) then no program graph can be constructed.

Procedure calls and declarations are best understood together, as in the following example.

EXAMPLE 7.23: Figure 7.10 presents the program graph constructed for the factorial program of Figure 7.7. The procedure declaration gives rise to the framed edge from q_o to q_0 and the framed rightmost part of the graph; it will produce an environment where fac is associated with the information (x, y, q_n, q_x). The procedure call fac(3,z) gives rise to the (red) edges linking q_0 with q_n for the call itself and the (red) edges linking q_x with $q_{\bullet}$ when returning from the call.

The program graph for the procedure body has two parts, corresponding to the two parts of the conditional. When $x \leq 1$ we simply obtain the two edges from q_n to q_x. When $x > 1$ we first have the edges for handling the local declaration of t: the edges from q_1 to q_2 introduce the new frame whereas the edge from q_4 to q_x pops it. The recursive procedure call gives rise to the edges from q_2 to q_n at the call point and the edges from q_x to q_3 at the return point. The edge from q_3 to q_4 takes care of the assignment following the recursive call.

TRY IT OUT 7.24: Construct the program graph for the command of Figure 7.11.□

EXERCISE 7.25: Often we would like to allow procedures to have a number of input parameters $x_1, \cdots, x_n$ (for $n \geq 0$) and a number of output parameters $y_1, \cdots, y_m$ (for $m \geq 0$). Modify the clauses for procedure declaration and procedure call to allow the case $n = 2$ and $m = 1$. □

```
{ proc fib(x; y)
    if x ≤ 1 → y := 1
    [] x > 1 → { var t;
                 var u;
                 fib(x − 1; t);
                 fib(x − 2; u);
                 y := t + u
               }
    fi
  end;
  fib(5; z)
}
```

Figure 7.11: Example program for the Fibonacci function.

TEASER 7.26: Redo Exercise 7.25 in the general case where $n \geq 0$ and $m \geq 0$. □

EXERCISE 7.27: Construct recursive procedures in Guarded Commands with Procedures for computing

(a) the smallest number of steps needed in the game of Towers of Hanoi (see Example 6.2 for a description of the game) to move a stack of n disks from one rod to another,

(b) the Euclidean algorithm for computing the greatest common divisor, and

(c) the binomial coefficients $\binom{n}{k}$; recall that $\binom{n}{k} = \binom{n-1}{k-1} + \binom{n-1}{k}$ when $1 \leq k \leq n-1$ and $\binom{n}{0} = \binom{n}{n} = 1$ for $n \geq 0$.

In each case use the above definitions (and the extensions from Exercise 7.25) to construct the corresponding program graph. □

Semantics The semantics will follow the approach of Section 7.2 and use a memory that is a stack of frames. The semantics of the operations enter and exit are as before so they will push and pop frames from the memory. Similarly the semantics of the declarations var x and array $A[n]$ is as in Section 7.2. We shall now take care of the four new actions used for procedures. So once again consider a procedure call $p(a\,;z)$ of a procedure previously declared as proc $p(x\,;y)\,C$ end.

The key idea behind the $\lfloor\cdot\rfloor$ construct is to bypass the topmost frame on the stack. This is used in the action $x := \lfloor a \rfloor$ when calling a procedure because the actual parameter a needs to be evaluated as if the topmost frame had not yet been pushed, and it is also used in the action $\lfloor z \rfloor := y$ when returning from a procedure because the return parameter z needs to be located as if the topmost frame had already been popped.

The operation record $q_1 q_2$ works much like an assignment $* := (q_1, q_2)$ to a special control variable allocated in the topmost frame, and the operation check $q_1 q_2$ then works much like the test $* = (q_1, q_2)$. Together they ensure that a call returns to the right node; we see an instance of that for the node q_x in Figure 7.10 because the factorial program may be called either globally (in which case we should eventually return to $q_{\blacktriangleleft}$) or recursively (in which case we should eventually return to q_3). This is made precise in the following definition.

DEFINITION 7.28: The semantic function $\mathcal{S}_{\mathsf{F}}\llbracket \cdot \rrbracket : \mathbf{Act} \to (\mathbf{Mem}_{\mathsf{F}} \hookrightarrow \mathbf{Mem}_{\mathsf{F}})$ for Guarded Commands with Procedures is defined by extending Definition 7.13 with the following clauses:

$$\mathcal{S}_{\mathsf{F}}\llbracket x := \lfloor a \rfloor \rrbracket \vec{\sigma} \;=\; \begin{cases} \vec{\sigma}[x \mapsto \mathcal{A}\llbracket a \rrbracket \vec{\sigma}'] & \text{if } \vec{\sigma} = \sigma :: \vec{\sigma}' \\ & \text{and } \mathcal{A}\llbracket a \rrbracket \vec{\sigma}' \text{ is defined} \\ \text{undefined} & \text{otherwise} \end{cases}$$

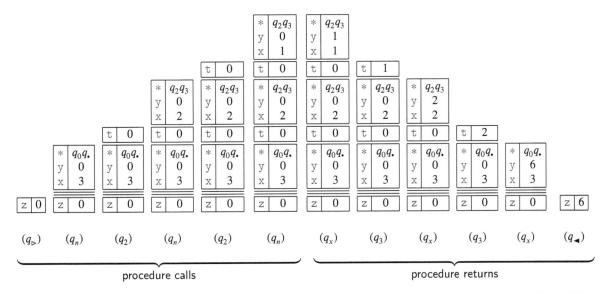

Figure 7.12: Selected memories at different program points for an execution sequence using the program graph of Figure 7.10.

$$\mathcal{S}_{\mathsf{F}}[\![\, \lfloor x \rfloor := a \,]\!]\vec{\sigma} \;=\; \begin{cases} \sigma :: \vec{\sigma}'[x \mapsto \mathcal{A}[\![a]\!]\vec{\sigma}] & \text{if } \vec{\sigma} = \sigma :: \vec{\sigma}' \\ & \text{and } \mathcal{A}[\![a]\!]\vec{\sigma} \text{ is defined} \\ \text{undefined} & \text{otherwise} \end{cases}$$

$$\mathcal{S}_{\mathsf{F}}[\![\, \texttt{record } q_1 q_2 \,]\!]\vec{\sigma} \;=\; \begin{cases} \sigma[* \mapsto (q_1, q_2)] :: \vec{\sigma}' & \text{if } \vec{\sigma} = \sigma :: \vec{\sigma}' \\ \text{undefined} & \text{otherwise} \end{cases}$$

$$\mathcal{S}_{\mathsf{F}}[\![\, \texttt{check } q_1 q_2 \,]\!]\vec{\sigma} \;=\; \begin{cases} \vec{\sigma} & \text{if } \vec{\sigma} = \sigma :: \vec{\sigma}' \text{ and } \sigma(*) = (q_1, q_2) \\ \text{undefined} & \text{otherwise} \end{cases}$$

For this to make sense we need to slightly modify the semantic domains from Definition 7.13 to be

Mem$_\mathsf{F}$ = **Frame*** where

Frame $= \big(\, \mathbf{Var} \cup \{A[i] \mid A \in \mathbf{Arr}, \exists n : 0 \le i < n\} \cup \{*\} \,\big) \hookrightarrow \mathbf{Int} \cup (\mathbf{Q} \times \mathbf{Q})$

where $\sigma \in \mathbf{Frame}$ whenever

$$\sigma \in \big(\, \mathbf{Var} \,\cup\, \{A[i] \mid A \in \mathbf{Arr}, \exists n : 0 \le i < n\} \,\cup\, \{*\} \,\big) \hookrightarrow \mathbf{Int} \cup (\mathbf{Q} \times \mathbf{Q})$$

and $\sigma(\cdot)$ produces a result in $\mathbf{Q} \times \mathbf{Q}$ if and only if its argument is $*$.

EXAMPLE 7.29: Let us consider an execution sequence for the program graph of Figure 7.10 starting with a memory where z has the value 0, as illustrated by the leftmost memory of Figure 7.12. The first time we reach the node q_n we will have the second memory of Figure 7.12: we have added a frame with entries for the formal parameters x and y of the procedure, x has obtained the value 3 and the frame will record that the call and return nodes are $q_0 q_\bullet$. As $x > 1$ holds, the execution will proceed to node q_2 and we will add yet another frame to the memory; it will have an entry for the local variable t, as illustrated in the third memory of Figure 7.12.

The execution will proceed like this, adding a new frame for the formal parameters and the return node each time we pass through q_n and q_2, as illustrated in the left-hand part of Figure 7.12. Eventually the test $x \le 1$ will succeed and we arrive at q_x with a memory where the topmost occurrence of y has the value 1.

The subsequent steps will now pop frames from the memory whenever we reach q_3 or q_x while taking care to update the actual as well as the formal parameter of the procedure call, as illustrated in the right-hand half of Figure 7.12. Eventually we will arrive at the node $q_\blacktriangleleft$ with the memory recording that z has the value 6.

TRY IT OUT 7.30: Construct an execution sequence for the Fibonacci program of Figure 7.11 using the program graph constructed in Try It Out 7.24. ☐

EXERCISE 7.31: Often we would like to allow procedure calls of the form $p(a_1 ; A[a_2])$. Extend the development to allow this. ☐

TEASER 7.32: When constructing the program graphs for procedure calls in Definition 7.22 we have used record $q_\circ q_\bullet$ and check $q_\circ q_\bullet$. An alternative would be to use simply record $q_\bullet$ and check $q_\bullet$. Can you imagine a situation where the alternative choice would be inappropriate? ☐

7.4   Procedures with Static Scope

Dynamic versus static scope   Consider the program in Figure 7.13, where we have a global variable u being set to 1 followed by a block declaring a procedure p with two assignments in its body, together with local variables u and v and concluding with a call to p. What is the final value of the global variable u? This depends on which version of u is updated by p when it is called. The notion of *dynamic scope* says that p should update the occurrence of u that is in scope at the point where p is *called*; this would give rise to the final value of the global variable u being 1. The notion of *static scope* says that p should update the occurrence of u that is in scope at the point where p is *declared*; this would give rise to the final value of the global variable u being 2. We usually expect dynamic scope when using macros and static scope when using procedures.

```
u := 1;
{  proc p(x; y)
      y := x + 1;
      u := 2
   end;
   var u;
   var v;
   p(u; v)
}
```

Figure 7.13: Scope confusion.

ESSENTIAL EXERCISE 7.33: Use the development of Section 7.3 to generate the program graph for the program in Figure 7.13. Next use the semantics to construct a complete execution sequence for the program. Finally conclude that the development of Section 7.3 gives rise to dynamic scope.

Renaming variables   If it is the *same* declaration of a variable that is in scope both when a procedure is *declared* and when it is *called* then there is no distinction between static and dynamic scope. Then we can obtain static scope for a program by first renaming all declarations and formal parameters so that no declaration or formal parameter occurs twice or overlaps with a global variable. This is called *renaming variables apart* and clearly we will have to take care in renaming all other occurrences of variables as well, so that they refer to the appropriate renamed variable.

Renaming variables on the fly   We now show how to rename variables (and arrays) apart while generating the program graph. In the development of Section 7.3 we already used an environment ρ to record crucial information about the procedures declared. We shall now extend the environment ρ to record how variables and arrays have been renamed so as to avoid scope confusion. We begin by renaming on the fly in the case of declarations.

DEFINITION 7.34: For declarations the edges are constructed as follows:

$$\textbf{edges}_{\text{sp2}}(q_\circ \rightsquigarrow q_\bullet)[\![\texttt{var } x]\!]\rho \quad = \quad \begin{aligned}&\text{let } x' \text{ be fresh}\\&\quad \rho' = \rho[x \mapsto x']\\&\text{in } (\{(q_\circ, \texttt{var } x', q_\bullet)\}, \rho')\end{aligned}$$

$$\textbf{edges}_{\text{sp2}}(q_\circ \rightsquigarrow q_\bullet)[\![\texttt{array } A[n]]\!]\rho \quad = \quad \begin{aligned}&\text{let } A' \text{ be fresh}\\&\quad \rho' = \rho[A \mapsto A']\\&\text{in } (\{(q_\circ, \texttt{array } A'[n], q_\bullet)\}, \rho')\end{aligned}$$

$$\textbf{edges}_{\text{sp2}}(q_\circ \rightsquigarrow q_\bullet)[\![D_1 \, ; D_2]\!]\rho \quad = \quad \begin{aligned}&\text{let } q \text{ be fresh}\\&\quad (E_1, \rho_1) = \textbf{edges}_{\text{sp2}}(q_\circ \rightsquigarrow q)[\![D_1]\!]\rho\\&\quad (E_2, \rho_2) = \textbf{edges}_{\text{sp2}}(q \rightsquigarrow q_\bullet)[\![D_2]\!]\rho_1\\&\text{in } (E_1 \cup E_2, \rho_2)\end{aligned}$$

$$\textbf{edges}_{\text{sp2}}(q_\circ \rightsquigarrow q_\bullet)[\![\texttt{proc } p(x \, ; y) \, C \texttt{ end}]\!]\rho \quad = \quad \begin{aligned}&\text{let } q_n, q_x \text{ be fresh}\\&\quad x', y' \text{ be fresh}\\&\quad \rho' = \rho[p \mapsto (x', y', q_n, q_x)]\\&\quad \rho'' = \rho'[x \mapsto x', y \mapsto y']\\&\quad E = \textbf{edges}_{\text{sp}}(q_n \rightsquigarrow q_x)[\![C]\!]\rho''\\&\text{in } (\{(q_\circ, \texttt{skip}, q_\bullet)\} \cup E, \rho')\end{aligned}$$

Thus whenever we encounter a variable or array declaration we provide a fresh name for it and update the environment to keep track of the new names; this also holds for procedure declarations, where we rename the formal parameters. When constructing the edges for the body of the procedure body we make use of the most recent version of the environment in order to enforce static scope.

The clauses for commands show how we make use of the environment on the fly – and update it when needed. In particular we make sure that all the variables (and arrays) are renamed as required by the environment; as explained in more detail below we write $[\![a]\!]\rho$ for the renamed version of the arithmetic expression a and similarly $[\![b]\!]\rho$ for the renamed version of the boolean expression b.

DEFINITION 7.35: For commands the edges are constructed as follows:

$$\textbf{edges}_{sp}(q_\circ \rightsquigarrow q_\bullet)[\![x := a]\!]\rho = \begin{array}{l} \text{let } x' = \rho(x) \\ \quad a' = [\![a]\!]\rho \\ \text{in } \{(q_\circ, x' := a', q_\bullet)\} \end{array}$$

$$\textbf{edges}_{sp}(q_\circ \rightsquigarrow q_\bullet)[\![A[a_1] := a_2]\!]\rho = \begin{array}{l} \text{let } A' = \rho(A) \\ \quad a'_1 = [\![a_1]\!]\rho \\ \quad a'_2 = [\![a_2]\!]\rho \\ \text{in } \{(q_\circ, A'[a'_1] := a'_2, q_\bullet)\} \end{array}$$

$$\textbf{edges}_{sp}(q_\circ \rightsquigarrow q_\bullet)[\![\texttt{skip}]\!]\rho = \{(q_\circ, \texttt{skip}, q_\bullet)\}$$

$$\textbf{edges}_{sp}(q_\circ \rightsquigarrow q_\bullet)[\![C_1 ; C_2]\!]\rho = \begin{array}{l} \text{let } q \text{ be fresh} \\ \quad E_1 = \textbf{edges}_{sp}(q_\circ \rightsquigarrow q)[\![C_1]\!]\rho \\ \quad E_2 = \textbf{edges}_{sp}(q \rightsquigarrow q_\bullet)[\![C_2]\!]\rho \\ \text{in } E_1 \cup E_2 \end{array}$$

$$\textbf{edges}_{sp}(q_\circ \rightsquigarrow q_\bullet)[\![\texttt{if } GC \texttt{ fi}]\!]\rho = \textbf{edges}_{sp}(q_\circ \rightsquigarrow q_\bullet)[\![GC]\!]\rho$$

$$\textbf{edges}_{sp}(q_\circ \rightsquigarrow q_\bullet)[\![\texttt{do } GC \texttt{ od}]\!]\rho = \begin{array}{l} \text{let } b = \texttt{done}[\![GC]\!] \\ \quad b' = [\![b]\!]\rho \\ \quad E = \textbf{edges}_{sp}(q_\circ \rightsquigarrow q_\circ)[\![GC]\!]\rho \\ \text{in } E \cup \{(q_\circ, b', q_\bullet)\} \end{array}$$

$$\textbf{edges}_{sp}(q_\circ \rightsquigarrow q_\bullet)[\![\{D ; C\}]\!]\rho = \begin{array}{l} \text{let } q_1, q_2, q_3 \text{ be fresh} \\ \quad (E_1, \rho_1) = \textbf{edges}_{sp2}(q_1 \rightsquigarrow q_2)[\![D]\!]\rho \\ \quad E_2 = \textbf{edges}_{sp}(q_2 \rightsquigarrow q_3)[\![C]\!]\rho_1 \\ \text{in } \{(q_\circ, \texttt{enter}, q_1)\} \cup E_1 \cup E_2 \\ \quad\quad \cup \{(q_3, \texttt{exit}, q_\bullet)\} \end{array}$$

$$\textbf{edges}_{sp}(q_\circ \rightsquigarrow q_\bullet)[\![p(a\,;z)]\!]\rho \quad = \quad \begin{aligned} &\text{let } q_1,q_2,q_3,q_4,q_5,q_6 \text{ be fresh}\\ &\quad (x,y,q_n,q_x) = \rho(p)\\ &\quad a' = [\![a]\!]\rho\\ &\quad z' = \rho(z)\\ &\text{in } \{(q_\circ,\texttt{enter},q_1),(q_1,\texttt{var } x,q_2),\\ &\qquad (q_2,\texttt{var } y,q_3),(q_3,x := \lfloor a'\rfloor,q_4),\\ &\qquad (q_4,\texttt{record } q_\circ q_\bullet,q_n),\\ &\qquad (q_x,\texttt{check } q_\circ q_\bullet,q_5),(q_5,\lfloor z'\rfloor := y,q_6),\\ &\qquad (q_6,\texttt{exit},q_\bullet)\} \end{aligned}$$

The renaming of the variables and array names has to be enforced everywhere as the memory will provide values only for the renamed variables and array entries. For an arithmetic expression a we write $[\![a]\!]\rho$ for the renamed version of it and some selected cases are:

$$\begin{aligned} [\![x]\!]\rho &= \rho(x)\\ [\![n]\!]\rho &= n\\ [\![a_1 + a_2]\!]\rho &= [\![a_1]\!]\rho + [\![a_2]\!]\rho\\ [\![A[a]]\!]\rho &= \rho(A)[[\![a]\!]\rho] \end{aligned}$$

Similarly, for a boolean expression b we write $[\![b]\!]\rho$ for the renamed version and some selected cases are:

$$\begin{aligned} [\![\texttt{true}]\!]\rho &= \texttt{true}\\ [\![a_1 < a_2]\!]\rho &= [\![a_1]\!]\rho < [\![a_2]\!]\rho\\ [\![b_1 \wedge b_2]\!]\rho &= [\![b_1]\!]\rho \wedge [\![b_2]\!]\rho \end{aligned}$$

TRY IT OUT 7.36: Suppose that $\rho = [x \mapsto x7][y \mapsto y][A \mapsto A']$; which renamed arithmetic expression does $[\![A[x] < (y+2)]\!]\rho$ give rise to? $\qquad\square$

Finally, we show how to rename on the fly in the case of guarded commands.

DEFINITION 7.37: For guarded commands the edges are constructed as follows:

$$\textbf{edges}_{sp}(q_\circ \rightsquigarrow q_\bullet)[\![b \rightarrow C]\!]\rho \quad = \quad \begin{aligned} &\text{let } q \text{ be fresh}\\ &\quad b' = [\![b]\!]\rho\\ &\quad E = \textbf{edges}_{sp}(q \rightsquigarrow q_\bullet)[\![C]\!]\rho\\ &\text{in } \{(q_\circ,b',q)\} \cup E \end{aligned}$$

$$\textbf{edges}_{sp}(q_\circ \rightsquigarrow q_\bullet)[\![GC_1\,[]\,GC_2]\!]\rho \quad = \quad \begin{aligned} &\text{let } E_1 = \textbf{edges}_{sp}(q_\circ \rightsquigarrow q_\bullet)[\![GC_1]\!]\rho\\ &\quad E_2 = \textbf{edges}_{sp}(q_\circ \rightsquigarrow q_\bullet)[\![GC_2]\!]\rho\\ &\text{in } E_1 \cup E_2 \end{aligned}$$

Semantics   The semantic function $\mathcal{S}_F[\![\cdot]\!]$ is as in Definitions 7.13 and 7.28 with the semantic domains as in Definition 7.28. Since the renaming of the variables and array names happens in the construction of the program graphs the semantic functions will not need to know about this.

When implementing programming languages part of the memory is a stack of entries. Entries include values (perhaps 32-bit signed integers instead of our mathematical integers), return addresses (pointers to the code rather than our $q_\circ q_\bullet$) and pointers to the stack.

A so-called *dynamic pointer* is contained in frames corresponding to procedure calls, and points to the frame below the current one so as to facilitate the popping of frames. We did not need this due to our more abstract model of the memory as a stack of frames.

A so-called *static pointer* is contained in frames corresponding to procedure calls, and in general points further down the stack than the dynamic pointer. It is used whenever the values of non-local variables need to be found – assuming that we want to obtain static scope. We did not need this due to our renaming of variables on the fly.

Chapter 8

Concurrency

So far we have been looking at individual programs running on their own. In this chapter we will illustrate how to deal with concurrently running programs that may communicate with one another. Our main focus will be on defining the semantics.

8.1 Shared Variables

We extend the syntax of Guarded Commands from Definition 2.3 to allow commands (called *processes*) that execute concurrently while having a shared memory.

DEFINITION 8.1: The syntax of the programs P, commands C and guarded commands GC of the *Guarded Commands with Concurrency* language are mutually recursively defined using the following *BNF notation*:

$$P \quad ::= \quad \texttt{par } C_1 \, [] \, \cdots \, [] \, C_n \, \texttt{rap}$$
$$C \quad ::= \quad \cdots \text{ as in Definition 2.3 (with arrays)} \cdots$$
$$GC \quad ::= \quad \cdots \text{ as in Definition 2.3} \cdots$$

The number n of concurrent processes is required to be positive.

EXAMPLE 8.2: To illustrate the new constructs we shall consider the *mutual exclusion problem*: two (or more) concurrent processes want to access a shared resource but they cannot be allowed to do so at the same time. The part of each process accessing the shared resource is called the *critical section* of the process. The task of the mutual exclusion algorithm is to ensure that at most one of the processes can be in its critical section at any time. Several such

© Springer Nature Switzerland AG 2019
F. Nielson, H. Riis Nielson, *Formal Methods*, https://doi.org/10.1007/978-3-030-05156-3_8

```
par
   do true →
         x₁ := x₂ + 1;
         if x₂ = 0 ∨ x₁ < x₂ →
               critical section₁
         fi;
         x₁ := 0
   od
[]
   do true →
         x₂ := x₁ + 1;
         if x₁ = 0 ∨ x₂ < x₁ →
               critical section₂
         fi;
         x₂ := 0
   od
rap
```

Figure 8.1: The Bakery Algorithm for two processes.

algorithms exist and one of them is the *Bakery Algorithm* by Leslie Lamport.

Figure 8.1 gives the Bakery Algorithm in the case of just two processes. It makes use of two shared variables x_1 and x_2; each process inspects both variables but only updates one of them.

We shall construct n disjoint program graphs for $\text{par } C_1 [] \cdots [] C_n \text{ rap}$ and each of these is constructed in the manner of Chapter 2.

DEFINITION 8.3: For programs the edges **E** are constructed as follows:

$$\textbf{edges}(q_\rhd^1 \cdots q_\rhd^n \rightsquigarrow q_\blacktriangleleft^1 \cdots q_\blacktriangleleft^n)[\![\text{par } C_1 [] \cdots [] C_n \text{ rap}]\!] =$$
$$\textbf{edges}(q_\rhd^1 \rightsquigarrow q_\blacktriangleleft^1)[\![C_1]\!] \cup \cdots \cup \textbf{edges}(q_\rhd^n \rightsquigarrow q_\blacktriangleleft^n)[\![C_n]\!]$$

where we ensure that all nodes in the vectors $q_\rhd^1 \cdots q_\rhd^n$ and $q_\blacktriangleleft^1 \cdots q_\blacktriangleleft^n$ are distinct.

The remaining parts of the definition of $\textbf{edges}(\rightsquigarrow)[\![ ]\!]$ are as in Definitions 2.7, 2.8 and 2.19. The set of nodes **Q** is defined from **E** as in Section 2.2.

EXAMPLE 8.4: Returning to Example 8.2, we get the program graphs of Figure 8.2 for the program of Figure 8.1; the parts of the graph corresponding to the two critical sections are marked E_1 and E_2, respectively. Note that the two program graphs are disjoint.

When defining the semantics of program graphs we will be looking at configurations consisting of tuples of nodes from the program graphs and memories.

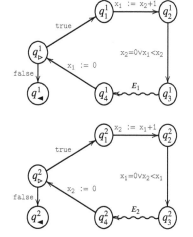

Figure 8.2: Program graphs for the Bakery Algorithm.

DEFINITION 8.5: A *configuration* is a pair $\langle \vec{q}; \sigma \rangle$ with $\vec{q} \in \mathbf{Q}^n$ and $\sigma \in \textbf{Mem}$; an *initial configuration* has $\vec{q} = q_\rhd^1 \cdots q_\rhd^n$ and a *final configuration* has $\vec{q} = q_\blacktriangleleft^1 \cdots q_\blacktriangleleft^n$.

Next we will use the semantics to explain how to move between configurations; this happens whenever one of the concurrent processes may make a move.

DEFINITION 8.6: Whenever $(q_o^i, \alpha, q_\bullet^i) \in \mathbf{E}$ we have an *execution step*

$$\langle q^1 \cdots q_o^i \cdots q^n; \sigma \rangle \overset{\alpha}{\Longrightarrow} \langle q^1 \cdots q_\bullet^i \cdots q^n; \sigma' \rangle \quad \text{if } \mathcal{S}[\![\alpha]\!]\sigma = \sigma'$$

Recall that $\mathcal{S}[\![\alpha]\!]\sigma = \sigma'$ means that σ is in the domain of $\mathcal{S}[\![\alpha]\!]$ as well as that the result of the function is σ'; if σ is not in the domain of $\mathcal{S}[\![\alpha]\!]$ there is no execution step.

EXAMPLE 8.7: Continuing Example 8.4, let us consider an execution of the

Bakery Algorithm and let us write σ_{ij} for the memory where x_1 has the value i and x_2 has the value j. We have the following execution sequence

$$\langle q_{\triangleright}^1 q_{\triangleright}^2; \sigma_{00} \rangle \overset{\text{true}}{\underset{x_1 \, := \, x_2+1}{\Longrightarrow}} \langle q_{\triangleright}^1 q_1^2; \sigma_{00} \rangle \overset{\text{true}}{\underset{x_2 \, := \, x_1+1}{\Longrightarrow}} \langle q_1^1 q_1^2; \sigma_{00} \rangle$$
$$\Longrightarrow \langle q_2^1 q_1^2; \sigma_{10} \rangle \qquad \Longrightarrow \langle q_2^1 q_2^2; \sigma_{12} \rangle$$

where in each step we have non-deterministically selected which process should take the next step. In the configuration $\langle q_2^1 q_2^2; \sigma_{12} \rangle$ the test of the second process evaluates to false, so it will be stuck. However, the first process can proceed and we get

$$\langle q_2^1 q_2^2; \sigma_{12} \rangle \overset{x_2=0 \vee x_1 < x_2}{\underset{x_1 \, := \, 0}{\Longrightarrow}} \langle q_3^1 q_2^2; \sigma_{12} \rangle \overset{\omega_1}{\Longrightarrow}{}^* \langle q_4^1 q_2^2; \sigma_{12} \rangle$$
$$\Longrightarrow \langle q_{\triangleright}^1 q_2^2; \sigma_{02} \rangle$$

where we write ω_1 for the actions of the critical section of the first process. In the configuration $\langle q_{\triangleright}^1 q_2^2; \sigma_{02} \rangle$ the test of the second process evaluates to true so we have a non-deterministic choice as to how to proceed; one possibility is

$$\langle q_{\triangleright}^1 q_2^2; \sigma_{02} \rangle \overset{x_1=0 \vee x_2 < x_1}{\underset{x_2 \, := \, 0}{\Longrightarrow}} \langle q_{\triangleright}^1 q_3^2; \sigma_{02} \rangle \overset{\omega_2}{\Longrightarrow}{}^* \langle q_{\triangleright}^1 q_4^2; \sigma_{02} \rangle$$
$$\Longrightarrow \langle q_{\triangleright}^1 q_{\triangleright}^2; \sigma_{00} \rangle$$

where ω_2 is the sequence of actions of the critical section of the second process.

TRY IT OUT 8.8: Construct another execution sequence for the Bakery Algorithm where you make some other non-deterministic choices. □

EXERCISE 8.9: Construct an execution sequence for the Bakery Algorithm where the values of the two variables x_1 and x_2 become arbitrarily large. □

EXERCISE 8.10: For par $C_1 [] \cdots [] C_n$ rap we constructed (in Definition 8.1) n disjoint program graphs with edges $\mathbf{E} = \mathbf{E}_1 \cup \cdots \cup \mathbf{E}_n$ and nodes $\mathbf{Q} = \mathbf{Q}_1 \cup \cdots \cup \mathbf{Q}_n$ where each $\mathbf{E}_i$ and $\mathbf{Q}_i$ arise from C_i. We then redefined (in Definitions 8.5 and 8.6) the notions of configuration and execution step from Definitions 1.10 and 1.11 so as to provide the semantics of Guarded Commands with Concurrency.

An alternative is to directly construct a single *product program graph* with nodes $\mathbf{Q}_{\text{PPG}} = \mathbf{Q}_1 \times \cdots \times \mathbf{Q}_n$ and edges

$$\mathbf{E}_{\text{PPG}} = \{(q^1 \cdots q_o^i \cdots q^n, \, \alpha, \, q^1 \cdots q_\bullet^i \cdots q^n) \mid (q_o^i, \alpha, q_\bullet^i) \in \mathbf{E}_i, \forall j \neq i : q^j \in \mathbf{Q}_j\}$$

and to retain the notions of configuration and execution step from Definitions 1.10 and 1.11.

Do the two approaches gives rise to the same execution sequences? Are the sizes of $(\mathbf{E}, \mathbf{Q})$ and $(\mathbf{E}_{\text{PPG}}, \mathbf{Q}_{\text{PPG}})$ both linear in the size of the program? □

TEASER 8.11: Another algorithm for mutual exclusion is Peterson's algorithm (see Wikipedia). Formulate it in the language of Guarded Commands with Concurrency and illustrate its semantics by constructing an interesting execution sequence. □

8.2 Asynchronous Communication

We extend the syntax of Guarded Commands with Concurrency from Definition 8.1 to allow channel-based communication between the concurrent processes. For this we introduce two new actions:

- $c!a$: outputs the value of the arithmetic expression a on the channel c, and
- $c?x$: inputs a value on the channel c and assigns it to the variable x.

We shall allow these actions to be used both as commands and as guards – the latter allows us to choose between various communication possibilities in a guarded command, as illustrated in the topmost command of Figure 8.3. Here we also make use of the looping construct loop $\cdots$ pool that differs from the do $\cdots$ od construct in two ways: one is that it allows us to choose between communication possibilities offered in the guards, and the other is that it will never terminate (unless we incorporate constructs like the break of Section 2.5).

```
par
  loop in₁?x →
          ch!(2 * x)
  []    in₂?x →
          ch!(2 * x + 1)
  pool
[]
  loop ch?y →
          if (y rem 2) = 0 →
              out₁!(y div 2)
          [] (y rem 2) = 1 →
              out₂!(y − 1 div 2)
          fi
  pool
rap
```

Figure 8.3: A multiplexer and de-multiplexer.

DEFINITION 8.12: The syntax of the programs P, commands C, guarded commands GC and communicating guarded commands CG of the *Guarded Commands with Communication* language are mutually recursively defined using the following *BNF notation*:

$$
\begin{aligned}
P & ::= \quad \text{par } C_1 \, [] \, \cdots \, [] \, C_n \text{ rap} \\
C & ::= \quad c!a \mid c?x \mid x := a \mid A[a_1] := a_2 \mid \text{skip} \mid \\
  & \qquad C_1 \, ; C_2 \mid \text{if } GC \text{ fi} \mid \text{do } GC \text{ od} \mid \text{loop } CG \text{ pool} \\
GC & ::= \quad b \to C \mid GC_1 \, [] \, GC_2 \\
CG & ::= \quad c!a \to C \mid c?x \to C \mid b \to C \mid CG_1 \, [] \, CG_2
\end{aligned}
$$

where c ranges over an unspecified set of channel names and where the number n of concurrent processes is positive.

Note that a guarded command (GC) is also a communicating guarded command (CG); guards of the form $c!a$ and $c?x$ can be used in if $\cdots$ fi and loop $\cdots$ pool constructs but not in do $\cdots$ od constructs.

EXAMPLE 8.13: The program of Figure 8.3 consists of two processes and makes use of five channels. The first process models a multiplexer that non-deterministically chooses between taking an input from one of the channels

in_1 and in_2 and then encodes the value obtained as an even or odd number and outputs the information on the channel ch. The second process models a demultiplexer; it inputs a value from ch and depending on its parity it will forward the decoded data to one of two channels out_1 and out_2. The encoding is such that input from in_i eventually will be output to out_i (for $i = 1, 2$).

Here we have assumed that our arithmetic expressions have been extended

$$a ::= a_1 \operatorname{rem} a_2 \mid a_1 \operatorname{div} a_2 \mid \cdots \text{ as in Chapter 2} \cdots$$

so as to incorporate remainder and integer division.

Program graphs To generate program graphs we shall admit $c!a$ and $c?x$ as new actions beyond those of the form skip, $x := a$, b and $A[a_1] := a_2$. As an example, for the program of Figure 8.3 we will obtain the program graphs of Figure 8.4. For programs the edges are constructed as in Section 8.1.

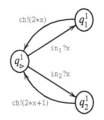

DEFINITION 8.14: For programs the edges are constructed as follows:

$$\mathbf{edges}(q_\rhd^1 \cdots q_\rhd^n \leadsto q_\blacktriangleleft^1 \cdots q_\blacktriangleleft^n)[\![\operatorname{par} C_1 [] \cdots [] C_n \operatorname{rap}]\!] =$$
$$\mathbf{edges}(q_\rhd^1 \leadsto q_\blacktriangleleft^1)[\![C_1]\!] \cup \cdots \cup \mathbf{edges}(q_\rhd^n \leadsto q_\blacktriangleleft^n)[\![C_n]\!]$$

For commands the edges are constructed as in Definitions 2.7 and 2.19 except that we need to handle the new constructs.

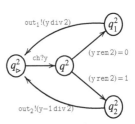

Figure 8.4: Program graphs for Figure 8.3.

DEFINITION 8.15: For commands the edges are constructed as follows:

$$\mathbf{edges}(q_\circ \leadsto q_\bullet)[\![c!a]\!] \quad = \quad \{(q_\circ, c!a, q_\bullet)\}$$

$$\mathbf{edges}(q_\circ \leadsto q_\bullet)[\![c?x]\!] \quad = \quad \{(q_\circ, c?x, q_\bullet)\}$$

$$\mathbf{edges}(q_\circ \leadsto q_\bullet)[\![x := a]\!] \quad = \quad \{(q_\circ, x := a, q_\bullet)\}$$

$$\mathbf{edges}(q_\circ \leadsto q_\bullet)[\![A[a_1] := a_2]\!] \quad = \quad \{(q_\circ, A[a_1] := a_2, q_\bullet)\}$$

$$\mathbf{edges}(q_\circ \leadsto q_\bullet)[\![\operatorname{skip}]\!] \quad = \quad \{(q_\circ, \operatorname{skip}, q_\bullet)\}$$

$$\mathbf{edges}(q_\circ \leadsto q_\bullet)[\![C_1 ; C_2]\!] \quad = \quad \begin{aligned}&\text{let } q \text{ be fresh}\\ &\quad E_1 = \mathbf{edges}(q_\circ \leadsto q)[\![C_1]\!]\\ &\quad E_2 = \mathbf{edges}(q \leadsto q_\bullet)[\![C_2]\!]\\ &\text{in } E_1 \cup E_2\end{aligned}$$

$$\mathbf{edges}(q_\circ \leadsto q_\bullet)[\![\operatorname{if} CG \operatorname{fi}]\!] \quad = \quad \mathbf{edges}(q_\circ \leadsto q_\bullet)[\![CG]\!]$$

$$\mathbf{edges}(q_\circ \rightsquigarrow q_\bullet)[\![\text{do } GC \text{ od}]\!] \;=\; \begin{aligned}[t] &\text{let } b = \text{done}[\![GC]\!] \\ &\qquad E = \mathbf{edges}(q_\circ \rightsquigarrow q_\circ)[\![GC]\!] \\ &\text{in } \; E \cup \{(q_\circ, b, q_\bullet)\} \end{aligned}$$

$$\mathbf{edges}(q_\circ \rightsquigarrow q_\bullet)[\![\text{loop } CG \text{ pool}]\!] \;=\; \mathbf{edges}(q_\circ \rightsquigarrow q_\circ)[\![CG]\!]$$

The clause for the loop $\cdots$ pool construct reflects that it is a looping construct; the clause differs from the usual one for do $\cdots$ od in that there are no edges leading to the node $q_\bullet$.

TRY IT OUT 8.16: In the above definition done$[\![GC]\!]$ is as in Section 2.2. Explain the difficulties in extending the definition to done$[\![CG]\!]$ (which would have allowed us not to distinguish between GC and CG).   □

EXERCISE 8.17: Use the ideas of Section 2.5 to extend the language of Guarded Commands with Communication as follows:

$$C \quad ::= \quad \text{break} \mid \cdots \text{as in Definition 8.12} \cdots$$

Show how this would allow us to dispense with the do GC od command and hence with the guarded commands GC.   □

For communicating guarded commands (and the subcategory of guarded commands) the edges are constructed as in Definition 2.8 except that we need to handle the new constructs.

DEFINITION 8.18: For communicating guarded commands and guarded commands the edges are constructed as follows:

$$\mathbf{edges}(q_\circ \rightsquigarrow q_\bullet)[\![c!a \rightarrow C]\!] \;=\; \begin{aligned}[t] &\text{let } q \text{ be fresh} \\ &\qquad E = \mathbf{edges}(q \rightsquigarrow q_\bullet)[\![C]\!] \\ &\text{in } \; \{(q_\circ, c!a, q)\} \cup E \end{aligned}$$

$$\mathbf{edges}(q_\circ \rightsquigarrow q_\bullet)[\![c?x \rightarrow C]\!] \;=\; \begin{aligned}[t] &\text{let } q \text{ be fresh} \\ &\qquad E = \mathbf{edges}(q \rightsquigarrow q_\bullet)[\![C]\!] \\ &\text{in } \; \{(q_\circ, c?x, q)\} \cup E \end{aligned}$$

$$\mathbf{edges}(q_\circ \rightsquigarrow q_\bullet)[\![b \rightarrow C]\!] \;=\; \begin{aligned}[t] &\text{let } q \text{ be fresh} \\ &\qquad E = \mathbf{edges}(q \rightsquigarrow q_\bullet)[\![C]\!] \\ &\text{in } \; \{(q_\circ, b, q)\} \cup E \end{aligned}$$

$$\mathbf{edges}(q_\circ \rightsquigarrow q_\bullet)[\![CG_1 \,[]\, CG_2]\!] \;=\; \begin{aligned}[t] &\text{let } E_1 = \mathbf{edges}(q_\circ \rightsquigarrow q_\bullet)[\![CG_1]\!] \\ &\qquad E_2 = \mathbf{edges}(q_\circ \rightsquigarrow q_\bullet)[\![CG_2]\!] \\ &\text{in } \; E_1 \cup E_2 \end{aligned}$$

TRY IT OUT 8.19: Imagine that we would like to perform the assignment $\text{y} := \text{A}[27]$ but that the variable y belongs to one process and the array A to another. In the absence of shared variables we will have to use communication to achieve this, and the program in Figure 8.5 is one way to do so. Additionally, it performs a simple check to ensure that we do not index out of bounds (assuming that the array A has length n) and returns an error value otherwise.

Construct the program graphs for Figure 8.5. □

```
par
 loop
  in?x →
   if x < n → ch!A[x]
   [] x ≥ n → ch!−1
   fi
 pool
 []
  ··· in!27 ; ch?y ···
rap
```

Figure 8.5: Protected access to an array.

Semantics We shall equip the language with an *asynchronous* semantics, meaning that whenever an output happens over a channel the value will be stored in a designated buffer and whenever an input happens we will obtain a value from the buffer. The semantics will keep track of all the channel buffers and we shall write $\kappa \in \textbf{Buf}$ for the channel buffers. The idea is that whenever c is a channel name in a finite set **Chan** of channels, then $\kappa(c)$ is the list of values that have been sent and not yet read over that channel; thus we shall take

$$\textbf{Buf} = \textbf{Chan} \rightarrow \textbf{Int}^*$$

or equivalently $\textbf{Buf} = \textbf{Chan} \rightarrow \text{List}(\textbf{Int})$. Whenever we output a value z on the channel c we shall update $\kappa(c)$ to record the new value; this will be written $\kappa[c \mapsto \vec{z} :: z]$ provided that $\kappa(c) = \vec{z}$ before the output – so the value is inserted to the right. We can input from a channel c if $\kappa(c)$ has the form $z' :: \vec{z}$, that is, there is at least one value in the buffer. The input will cause the leftmost value to be removed from the buffer (and assigned to some variable) so as a result of the input action the channel buffers κ will be updated to become $\kappa[c \mapsto \vec{z}]$. In this way we ensure that a value can only be input once.

To make this precise and to define the semantics we need to extend the semantic function $\mathcal{S}[\![\cdot]\!]$ from Definition 2.17 to take care of not only the memories of **Mem** but also the channel buffers of **Buf**.

DEFINITION 8.20: The *asynchronous semantics* for Guarded Commands with Communication has semantic domains

$$\textbf{Mem} = \left(\textbf{Var} \cup \{A[i] \mid A \in \textbf{Arr}, 0 \leq i < \text{size}(A)\} \right) \rightarrow \textbf{Int}$$

$$\textbf{Buf} = \textbf{Chan} \rightarrow \textbf{Int}^*$$

and semantic function $\mathcal{S}_B[\![\cdot]\!] : \textbf{Act} \rightarrow (\textbf{Mem} \times \textbf{Buf} \hookrightarrow \textbf{Mem} \times \textbf{Buf})$ given by

$$\mathcal{S}_B[\![c!a]\!](\sigma, \kappa) = \begin{cases} (\sigma, \kappa[c \mapsto \vec{z} :: z']) & \text{if } z' = \mathcal{A}[\![a]\!]\sigma \\ & \text{and } \kappa(c) = \vec{z} \\ \text{undefined} & \text{otherwise} \end{cases}$$

$$S_B[\![c?x]\!](\sigma, \kappa) = \begin{cases} (\sigma[x \mapsto z'], \kappa[c \mapsto \vec{z}]) & \text{if } \kappa(c) = z' :: \vec{z} \\ & \text{and } x \in \text{dom}(\sigma) \\ \text{undefined} & \text{otherwise} \end{cases}$$

$$S_B[\![\text{skip}]\!](\sigma, \kappa) = (\sigma, \kappa)$$

$$S_B[\![x := a]\!](\sigma, \kappa) = \begin{cases} (\sigma[x \mapsto z], \kappa) & \text{if } z = \mathcal{A}[\![a]\!]\sigma \\ & \text{and } x \in \text{dom}(\sigma) \\ \text{undefined} & \text{otherwise} \end{cases}$$

$$S_B[\![b]\!](\sigma, \kappa) = \begin{cases} (\sigma, \kappa) & \text{if } \mathcal{B}[\![b]\!]\sigma = \text{true} \\ \text{undefined} & \text{otherwise} \end{cases}$$

$$S_B[\![A[a_1] := a_2]\!](\sigma, \kappa) = \begin{cases} (\sigma[A[z_1] \mapsto z_2], \kappa) & \text{if } z_1 = \mathcal{A}[\![a_1]\!]\sigma \\ & \text{and } z_2 = \mathcal{A}[\![a_2]\!]\sigma \\ & \text{and } A[z_1] \in \text{dom}(\sigma) \\ \text{undefined} & \text{otherwise} \end{cases}$$

Configurations need to be changed from Definition 8.5 to take buffers into account and so does the definition of execution step in Definition 8.6.

DEFINITION 8.21: A *configuration* is a triple $\langle \vec{q}; \sigma, \kappa \rangle$ with $\vec{q} \in \mathbf{Q}^n$, $\sigma \in \mathbf{Mem}$ and $\kappa \in \mathbf{Buf}$. We have an *execution step*

$$\langle q^1 \cdots q_\circ^i \cdots q^n; \sigma, \kappa \rangle \overset{\alpha}{\Longrightarrow} \langle q^1 \cdots q_\bullet^i \cdots q^n; \sigma', \kappa' \rangle \quad \text{if } S_B[\![\alpha]\!](\sigma, \kappa) = (\sigma', \kappa')$$

whenever $(q_\circ^i, \alpha, q_\bullet^i) \in \mathbf{E}$.

EXAMPLE 8.22: To illustrate the semantics, let us consider the program graphs of Figure 8.4 and let us assume that initially the buffers are as follows:

$$\kappa_0 = [\text{in}_1 \mapsto 1\,2\,3; \text{in}_2 \mapsto 2\,4\,6; \text{ch} \mapsto \epsilon; \text{out}_1 \mapsto \epsilon; \text{out}_2 \mapsto \epsilon]$$

so that the buffer for in_1 contains three values, the buffer for in_2 contains three values and the remaining three buffers are empty. We then have an execution sequence where the first process takes a number of rounds without the second process taking any actions. So we have the following execution sequence

$$\langle q_\triangleright^1 q_\triangleright^2; \sigma, \kappa_0 \rangle \overset{\omega}{\Longrightarrow}{}^* \langle q_\triangleright^1 q_\triangleright^2; \sigma[x \mapsto 2], \kappa_0[\text{in}_1 \mapsto 3][\text{in}_2 \mapsto 4\,6][\text{ch} \mapsto 2\,5\,4] \rangle$$

where we have read two values from in_1 and one value from in_2. At this stage the second process may take a round and we may arrive at the configuration

$$\langle q_\triangleright^1 q_\triangleright^2; \sigma[x \mapsto 2][y \mapsto 2], \kappa_0[\text{in}_1 \mapsto 3][\text{in}_2 \mapsto 4\,6][\text{ch} \mapsto 5\,4][\text{out}_1 \mapsto 1] \rangle$$

TRY IT OUT 8.23: Construct an execution sequence for the program graphs constructed for the program in Figure 8.5 in Try It Out 8.19 (where you make suitable assumptions about the initial values of the buffers). ☐

EXERCISE 8.24: The above semantics assumes that the buffers can have arbitrary size. Assume now that there is a positive bound k on the size of the buffers. Modify the semantics to reflect that. What happens when one of the buffers is full? ☐

8.3 Synchronous Communication

Let us reconsider the Guarded Commands with Communication language and replace the asynchronous semantics of the previous section with a synchronous semantics. Here the outputs and inputs happen at the same time: if one process is ready to execute an output $c!a$ then it can only proceed if there is another process that is ready do do an input $c?x$ over the same channel c – they will then exchange the value in *one joint action*, written $c!a?x$, before they proceed. Thus we will no longer have the need for the buffers of the semantics of Section 8.2.

For this development the syntax is exactly as in Definition 8.12 and the generation of the edges of the program graphs is still as in Definitions 8.14, 8.15 and 8.18 – so in particular, the joint actions will never appear in the program graphs but only in execution sequences.

> EXAMPLE 8.25: In Figure 8.6 we have repeated the processes for the multiplexer and demultiplexer of Figure 8.3 and just added two processes producing data on the channels in_1 and in_2 and two processes consuming data on the channels out_1 and out_2. The program graphs for the producers and consumers are shown in Figure 8.7. Having all six processes available allows us to express the joint actions of the system. As an example, the joint actions $in_1!u_1?x$, $ch!(2*x)?y$ and $out_1!(y\,div\,2)?z_1$ correspond to the three synchronous communications required to send a value from a producer to a consumer via the multiplexer and demultiplexer.

As for the semantics, we need to define the meaning of the actions, the form of the configurations and the execution steps, as they will be different from those of Section 8.2. For the actions we return to the semantic function $\mathcal{S}[\![\cdot]\!]$ from Definition 2.17 and Essential Exercise 2.20.

DEFINITION 8.26: The *synchronous semantics* for Guarded Commands with Communication has semantic domain

$$\mathbf{Mem} = \big(\ \mathbf{Var} \cup \{A[i] \mid A \in \mathbf{Arr}, 0 \le i < \text{size}(A)\}\ \big) \to \mathbf{Int}$$

```
par
  loop in₁!u₁ → u₁ := u₁ + 1
  pool
[]
  loop in₂!u₂ → u₂ := u₂ + 2
  pool
[]
  loop in₁?x →
          ch!(2 * x)
    []   in₂?x →
          ch!(2 * x + 1)
  pool
[]
  loop ch?y →
          if (y rem 2) = 0 →
            out₁!(y div 2)
          [] (y rem 2) = 1 →
            out₂!(y − 1 div 2)
          fi
  pool
[]
  loop out₁?z₁ → skip
  pool
[]
  loop out₂?z₂ → skip
  pool
rap
```

Figure 8.6: A multiplexer and demultiplexer with two producers and two consumers.

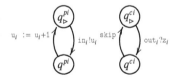

Figure 8.7: Program graphs for the i'th producer and i'th consumer of Figure 8.6.

and semantic functions $S[\![\alpha]\!] : \mathbf{Mem} \hookrightarrow \mathbf{Mem}$ (for α of the form skip, $x := a$, b or $A[a_1] := a_2$) and $A[\![a]\!] : \mathbf{Mem} \hookrightarrow \mathbf{Int}$ as defined in Section 2.3.

As for the configurations, we return to those of Section 8.1; we then have a more complex treatment of the execution steps as there will be two different types: one type is due to actions of the form skip, $x := a$, b or $A[a_1] := a_2$, where only one process participates in the step, and the other type of execution step is for the joint actions of the form $c!a?x$, where two processes participate.

DEFINITION 8.27: A *configuration* is a pair $\langle \vec{q}; \sigma \rangle$ with $\vec{q} \in \mathbf{Q}^n$ and $\sigma \in \mathbf{Mem}$.

We have an *individual execution step*

$$\langle q^1 \cdots q^i_o \cdots q^n; \sigma \rangle \overset{\alpha}{\Longrightarrow} \langle q^1 \cdots q^i_\bullet \cdots q^n; \sigma' \rangle$$

whenever we have

$\sigma' = S[\![\alpha]\!]\sigma$, and

$(q^i_o, \alpha, q^i_\bullet) \in \mathbf{E}_i$ and α is of the form skip, $x := a$, b or $A[a_1] := a_2$.

We have a *synchronous execution step*

$$\langle q^1 \cdots q^i_o \cdots q^j_o \cdots q^n; \sigma \rangle \overset{c!a?x}{\Longrightarrow} \langle q^1 \cdots q^i_\bullet \cdots q^j_\bullet \cdots q^n; \sigma' \rangle$$

whenever we have

$\sigma' = \sigma[x \mapsto z]$ and $z = A[\![a]\!]\sigma$,

$(q^i_o, c!a, q^i_\bullet) \in \mathbf{E}_i$,

$(q^j_o, c?x, q^j_\bullet) \in \mathbf{E}_j$, and

either $i < j$ or $i > j$.

It is not intended that the occurrence of i before j in the configuration should suggest that i is smaller than j.

EXAMPLE 8.28: Returning to the system of Figure 8.6, with programs graphs in Figures 8.4 and 8.7, the initial configuration will have the form

$$\langle q^{p1}_\triangleright q^{p2}_\triangleright q^1_\triangleright q^2_\triangleright q^{c1}_\triangleright q^{c2}_\triangleright; \sigma \rangle$$

where we first list the nodes of the two producers, then those of the multiplexer and demultiplexer and finally the nodes of the two consumers.

The first step of the execution sequence will be a joint action between one of the producers and the multiplexer. So assuming that σ maps u_1 to 7 we have the following execution steps:

$$\langle q_{\triangleright}^{p1} q_{\triangleright}^{p2} q_{\triangleright}^1 q_{\triangleright}^2 q_{\triangleright}^{c1} q_{\triangleright}^{c2}; \sigma \rangle$$

$$\xrightarrow{\text{in}_1!u_1?x} \langle q^{p1} q_{\triangleright}^{p2} q_1^1 q_{\triangleright}^2 q_{\triangleright}^{c1} q_{\triangleright}^{c2}; \sigma[x \mapsto 7] \rangle$$

$$\xrightarrow{\text{ch}!(2*x)?y} \langle q^{p1} q_{\triangleright}^{p2} q_{\triangleright}^1 q^2 q_{\triangleright}^{c1} q_{\triangleright}^{c2}; \sigma[x \mapsto 7][y \mapsto 14] \rangle$$

$$\xrightarrow{u_1 := u_1 + 1} \langle q_{\triangleright}^{p1} q_{\triangleright}^{p2} q_{\triangleright}^1 q^2 q_{\triangleright}^{c1} q_{\triangleright}^{c2}; \sigma[x \mapsto 7][y \mapsto 14][u_1 \mapsto 8] \rangle$$

$$\xrightarrow{(y\,\text{rem}\,2)=0} \langle q_{\triangleright}^{p1} q_{\triangleright}^{p2} q_{\triangleright}^1 q_1^2 q_{\triangleright}^{c1} q_{\triangleright}^{c2}; \sigma[x \mapsto 7][y \mapsto 14][u_1 \mapsto 8] \rangle$$

$$\xrightarrow{\text{out}_1!(y\,\text{div}\,2)?z_1} \langle q_{\triangleright}^{p1} q_{\triangleright}^{p2} q_{\triangleright}^1 q_{\triangleright}^2 q^{c1} q_{\triangleright}^{c2}; \sigma[x \mapsto 7][y \mapsto 14][u_1 \mapsto 8][z_1 \mapsto 7] \rangle$$

Here we start with a synchronisation between the first producer and the multiplexer and then a synchronisation between the multiplexer and the demultiplexer. Next, the first producer continues on its own and so does the demultiplexer. The last step in the above execution sequence is a synchronisation between the demultiplexer and the first consumer.

TRY IT OUT 8.29: Construct an execution sequence for the program graphs constructed for the program in Figure 8.5 in Try It Out 8.19. □

EXERCISE 8.30: Extend the channel-based communication to allow channels where tuples of values can be communicated, as in $c!a_1, \cdots, a_m$ and $c?x_1, \cdots, x_m$. □

EXERCISE 8.31: Discuss the difference between the synchronous semantics of the present section and the asynchronous semantics of Section 8.2 where all buffers have length 1 (as discussed in Exercise 8.24). Explain how to construct an asynchronous execution sequence corresponding to every synchronous execution sequence. □

8.4 Broadcast and Gather (Bonus Material)

We shall now extend the syntax of Guarded Commands with Communication from Definition 8.12 to allow communication actions involving more than one receiver or more than one sender (but not both simultaneously). The construct $c \mathbin{!!}_k a$ is a *broadcast* version of $c!a$ that in a synchronous manner outputs to *all* processes able to do an input on the channel c (using $c?$); the index k is a non-negative integer that requires that at least k processes are able to do an input on c, otherwise the action is stuck.

Dually $c \mathbin{??}_k A\,x$ is a *gathering* version of $c?x$ that in a synchronous manner inputs from *all* processes able to do an output on the channel c (using $c!$); the index k is a non-negative integer that requires that at least k processes are able to do an output on c, otherwise the action is stuck. The received values are placed in the array A and the variable x is set to the number of values received; if the array is too short the remaining values are discarded and x is set to the length of the array.

Sensor$_i$:
```
loop
    req?t_i → rep!Reg_i[t_i]
[]
    true → ··· update Reg_i ···
pool
```

Control :
```
req !!_10 temp;
rep ??_10 A x;
i := 0;
s := 0;
do i < x →
    s := s + A[i];
    i := i + 1
od;
avg := s/x
```

Figure 8.8: Specification of sensors and controller.

Sensor$_i$:

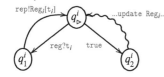

Control:

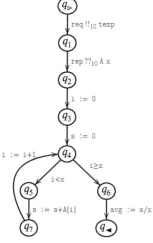

Figure 8.9: Program graphs for sensors and controller.

DEFINITION 8.32: The syntax of the programs P, commands C, guarded commands GC and communicating guarded commands CG of the *Guarded Commands with Broadcast* language are mutually recursively defined using the following *BNF notation*:

$$P \quad ::= \quad \text{par } C_1 \,[] \, \cdots \, [] \, C_n \text{ rap}$$

$$C \quad ::= \quad c\,!!_k\,a \mid c\,??_k\,A\,x \mid \cdots \text{ as in Definition 8.12} \cdots$$

$$GC \quad ::= \quad \cdots \text{ as in Definition 8.12} \cdots$$

$$CG \quad ::= \quad \cdots \text{ as in Definition 8.12} \cdots$$

where c ranges over an unspecified set of channel names, the number n of concurrent processes is positive and the number k of required participants is non-negative.

EXAMPLE 8.33: The following program describes a system consisting of 16 sensors and one controller running concurrently:

$$\text{par } Sensor_0 \,[] \, \cdots \, [] \, Sensor_{15} \,[] \, Control \text{ rap}$$

The processes *Sensor$_i$* and *Control* are defined in Figure 8.8. Each sensor is able to measure temperature, pressure and humidity and 'continuously' updates the measurements in the array Reg$_i$. Additionally it can be asked about a measurement, which it will then report.

The controller merely wants to compute the average temperature among at least 10 of the 16 sensors. It broadcasts a request (for example the number 0) for the temperature measurement and, having obtained at least 10 measurements, computes the average.

Turning to the generation of the edges of the program graphs, we extend Definitions 8.14, 8.15 and 8.18 to deal with the two new constructs $c\,!!_k\,a$ and $c\,??_k\,A\,x$.

DEFINITION 8.34: For commands we additionally generate edges as follows:

$$\textbf{edges}(q_\circ \rightsquigarrow q_\bullet)[\![c\,!!_k\,a]\!] \quad = \quad \{(q_\circ, c\,!!_k\,a, q_\bullet)\}$$

$$\textbf{edges}(q_\circ \rightsquigarrow q_\bullet)[\![c\,??_k\,A\,x]\!] \quad = \quad \{(q_\circ, c\,??_k\,A\,x, q_\bullet)\}$$

EXAMPLE 8.35: The program graphs for the sensors and controller of Example 8.33 are displayed in Figure 8.9. The update of the measurements performed by the sensors is modelled by the curly edge.

The semantics, configurations and execution steps extend Definitions 8.26 and 8.27 to deal with the constructs $c\,!!_k\,a$ and $c\,??_k\,A\,x$. For the semantics we reuse the semantic functions $\mathcal{S}[\![\cdot]\!]$ and $\mathcal{A}[\![\cdot]\!]$ from Definition 8.26. Also configurations, individual execution steps and synchronous execution steps are as in Definition 8.27.

Let us first consider the extension of the semantics to handle the broadcast. As in Section 8.3, we shall introduce a joint action $c \,!!_k\, a\,?\,x_1 \cdots x_h$, which only occurs as part of execution steps but not in any of the program graphs; it represents the merge of a single output action $c \,!!_k\, a$ with a number of input actions $c?x_1, \cdots, c?x_h$. The broadcast is successful if one of the processes of the system is ready to perform the action $c \,!!_k\, a$ and at the same time at least k processes are ready to perform an action of the form $c?x_j$. If so, the value of a will be assigned to the variables x_j of the h participating processes. This is formalised in the following definition.

DEFINITION 8.36: We have a *broadcast execution step*

$$\langle q_o^1 \cdots q_o^n; \sigma \rangle \overset{c \,!!_k\, a\,?\,x_1 \cdots x_h}{\Longrightarrow} \langle q_\bullet^1 \cdots q_\bullet^n; \sigma' \rangle$$

whenever we have

$(q_o^i, c \,!!_k\, a, q_\bullet^i) \in \mathbf{E}_i$

$z = \mathcal{A}[\![a]\!]\sigma$

$\{j_1, \cdots, j_h\} = \{j \neq i \mid \exists x, q : (q_o^j, c?x, q) \in \mathbf{E}_j\}$

$h \geq k$ and all j_l are pairwise distinct

$(q_o^j, c?x_j, q_\bullet^j) \in \mathbf{E}_j$ whenever $j \in \{j_1, \cdots, j_h\}$

$\sigma' = \sigma[x_{j_1} \mapsto z] \cdots [x_{j_h} \mapsto z]$

$q_\bullet^l = q_o^l$ whenever $l \notin \{j_1, \cdots, j_h, i\}$

EXAMPLE 8.37: Returning to Examples 8.33 and 8.35, let us consider the configuration

$$\langle q_2^0 q_\triangleright^1 q_\triangleright^2 q_2^3 q_\triangleright^4 q_\triangleright^5 q_2^6 q_\triangleright^7 q_\triangleright^8 q_2^9 q_\triangleright^{10} q_\triangleright^{11} q_2^{12} q_\triangleright^{13} q_\triangleright^{14} q_2^{15} q_\triangleright; \sigma \rangle$$

where the controller is at its initial node ($q_\triangleright$) and so are exactly 10 of the 16 sensors ($q_\triangleright^i$), while the remaining 6 sensors are updating their information (that is, at node q_2^i). Then the action $\mathtt{req}\,!!_{10}\,\mathtt{temp}$ can be executed and the new configuration will be

$$\langle q_2^0 q_1^1 q_1^2 q_2^3 q_1^4 q_1^5 q_2^6 q_1^7 q_1^8 q_2^9 q_1^{10} q_1^{11} q_2^{12} q_1^{13} q_1^{14} q_2^{15} q_1; \sigma' \rangle$$

where σ' is as σ except that each of the variables $t_1, t_2, t_4, t_5, t_7, t_8, t_{10}, t_{11}, t_{13}$ and t_{14} will have obtained the value $\sigma(\mathtt{temp})$.

TRY IT OUT 8.38: Redo the above example in the case where the configuration is such that 12 of the 16 sensors are at their initial node and so is the controller. What happens if only 8 of the 16 sensors are at their initial nodes? □

TEASER 8.39: Modify the semantics of the broadcast operation $c\,!!_k\,a$ such that exactly k processes able to perform an input $c?$ will participate. (Hint: It does not suffice to change $h \geq k$ to $h = k$.)   ☐

Turning to the gathering action, we shall introduce a joint action as above; it has the form $c\,!\,a_1 \cdots a_h\,??_k\,A\,x$ and only occurs as part of execution steps and not in any of the program graphs. It represents the merge of a number of output actions $c!a_1, \cdots, c!a_h$ with a single input action $c\,??_k\,A\,x$. The gathering is successful if one of the processes of the system is ready to perform the action $c\,??_k\,A\,x$ and at the same time at least k processes are ready to perform an action of the form $c!a_j$. When it is successful, the entries of the array A will be assigned the values of the expressions a_j from the h participating processes in some arbitrary order (while dropping some values if $h > \mathsf{length}(A)$) and the variable x will be assigned the number of entries placed in the array. This is formalised in the following definition.

DEFINITION 8.40: We have a *gathering execution step*

$$\langle q_o^1 \cdots q_o^n; \sigma \rangle \overset{c\,!\,a_1\cdots a_h\,??_k\,A\,x}{\Longrightarrow} \langle q_\bullet^1 \cdots q_\bullet^n; \sigma' \rangle$$

whenever we have

$(q_o^i, c\,??_k\,A\,x, q_\bullet^i) \in \mathbf{E}_i$

$\{j_1, \cdots, j_h\} = \{j \neq i \mid \exists a, q : (q_o^j, c!a, q) \in \mathbf{E}_j\}$

$h \geq k$ and all j_l are pairwise distinct

$(q_o^j, c!a_j, q_\bullet^j) \in \mathbf{E}_j$ and $z_j = \mathcal{A}[\![a_j]\!]\sigma$ whenever $j \in \{j_1, \cdots, j_h\}$

$h' = \min(h, \mathsf{length}(A))$

$\sigma' = \sigma[A[0] \mapsto z_{j_1}] \cdots [A[h'-1] \mapsto z_{j_{h'}}][x \mapsto h']$

$q_\bullet^l = q_o^l$ whenever $l \notin \{j_1, \cdots, j_h, i\}$

EXAMPLE 8.41: Continuing Example 8.37, we can now perform the action $\mathtt{rep}\,??_{10}\,A\,x$ from the configuration

$$\langle q_2^0 q_1^1 q_1^2 q_2^3 q_1^4 q_1^5 q_2^6 q_1^7 q_1^8 q_2^9 q_1^{10} q_1^{11} q_2^{12} q_1^{13} q_1^{14} q_2^{15} q_1; \sigma' \rangle$$

as the control is at node q_1 and exactly 10 sensors are at node q_1^i. The new configuration is

$$\langle q_2^0 q_\rhd^1 q_\rhd^2 q_2^3 q_\rhd^4 q_\rhd^5 q_2^6 q_\rhd^7 q_\rhd^8 q_2^9 q_\rhd^{10} q_2^{11} q_\rhd^{12} q_\rhd^{13} q_2^{14} q_\rhd^{15} q_2; \sigma'' \rangle$$

where σ'' is as σ' except that the array A and the variable x have been updated. The first 10 entries of the array have been updated so that the i'th entry has the value of $\sigma'(\text{Reg}_i[\sigma'(\mathbf{t}_i)])$ (for $0 \leq i < 10$) and the value of $\mathbf{x}$ has been updated to be 10.

TRY IT OUT 8.42: Redo the above example in the case where the configuration is such that 12 of the 16 sensors are in the node q_1^i. What happens if only 8 of the 16 sensors are in this configuration? □

TEASER 8.43: Modify the semantics of the gathering operation $c \,??_k\, A\,x$ such that exactly $\min(k, \text{length}(A))$ processes able to perform an output $c!$ will participate. (Hint: It does not suffice to change $h \geq k$ to $h = k$.) □

EXERCISE 8.44: Extend the broadcast action to allow channels where tuples of values can be communicated as in $c \,!!_k\, a_1, \cdots, a_m$ and $c?x_1, \cdots, x_m$. Similarly, extend the gathering action to allow channels where tuples of values can be communicated as in $c!a_1, \cdots, a_m$ and $c \,??_k\, A_1, \cdots, A_m\, x$. In both cases you may decide to choose $m = 2$ for simplicity. □

Epilogue

We will provide a few pointers for where to find more advanced material on some of the topics covered in this book.

Program Verification   Program verification is being explored in many directions with tool support for the discovery of proofs as well as for checking proofs.

For an in-depth study of semi-automated program verification using the *Isabelle* proof assistant you may consult the advanced book

> Tobias Nipkow, Gerwin Klein: *Concrete Semantics*. Springer, 2014.

For an in-depth study of semi-automated program verification using the *Coq* proof assistant you may consult the advanced book

> Adam Chlipala: *Certified Programming with Dependent Types*. MIT Press, 2013.

For an overview of some of the many tools developed you may consult the web-page

> https://en.wikipedia.org/wiki/Proof_assistant

which categorises the tools with respect to some of the features supported.

Program Analysis   Program analysis (sometimes called static analysis) is widely used in software development.

For an in-depth study of program analysis you may consult the advanced book

> Flemming Nielson, Hanne Riis Nielson, Chris Hankin: *Principles of Program Analysis*. Springer, 2005.

© Springer Nature Switzerland AG 2019
F. Nielson, H. Riis Nielson, *Formal Methods*, https://doi.org/10.1007/978-3-030-05156-3

which provides a thorough overview of some of the key approaches to program analysis as well as some of the algorithms needed for computing the solutions. It covers Data Flow Analysis, Constraint-Based Analysis, Abstract Interpretation and Type and Effect Systems with a view to exploring their similarities and differences.

For an overview of the many tools developed you may consult the web-page

https://en.wikipedia.org/wiki/List_of_tools_for_static_code_analysis

which categorises the tools with respect to the programming languages supported.

Model Checking   Model checking is a fast-growing area with a lot of tool support.

For an in-depth study of model checking you may consult the advanced book

> Christel Baier, Joost-Pieter Katoen: *Principles of Model Checking.* MIT Press, 2008.

which provides a thorough overview of transition systems and logics such as Computation Tree Logic (CTL) and Linear Time Logic (LTL). It covers the algorithms needed for dealing with the 'state explosion problem' through the use of symbolic data structures and ways of reducing the size of the transition system by exploiting various similarities and symmetries. It also covers timed systems and probabilistic systems.

For an overview of the many tools developed you may consult the web-page

https://en.wikipedia.org/wiki/List_of_model_checking_tools

which categorises the tools with respect to whether or not they support features such as probabilities, real-time behaviour and continuous stochastic behaviour.

Semantics of Procedures and Concurrency   Semantics aims at describing the behaviour of programming languages, taking care of all subtle issues that may arise.

The approach taken in this book is based on program graphs but there are other approaches that are more structural in nature. For an introductory textbook taking another approach you may consult

> Hanne Riis Nielson, Flemming Nielson: *Semantics with Applications: An Appetizer.* Springer Undergraduate Topics in Computer Science, 2007.

which presents operational semantics, denotational semantics and axiomatic verification. For an intermediate book covering concurrency and reactive systems you may consult

Luca Aceto, Anna Ingólfsdóttir, Kim Guldstrand Larsen, Jiří Srba: *Reactive Systems: Modelling, Specification and Verification.* Cambridge University Press, 2007.

which covers process algebras and timed automata.

Appendix A

The MicroC Language

In this appendix we shall introduce MicroC, a C-like language, and we shall present a series of tasks performing some of the developments that were done for the Guarded Commands language.

Simple statements   A program in MicroC is simply a *statement* and as in Section 2.1 we shall specify the form of the abstract syntax trees. We shall feel free to use traditional *round brackets* for expressions and *curly brackets* for statements in order to disambiguate the syntax, as shown in Figure A.1.

```
y := 1;
while (x > 0)
  { y := x * y;
    x := x − 1;
  }
```

Figure A.1: Example program for the factorial function.

The syntax of the statements S, arithmetic expressions a and boolean expressions b of MicroC are defined using the following BNF notation (where we have included some of the brackets usually found in C) :

$$
\begin{aligned}
S \quad ::= \quad & x := a\,; \mid A[a_1] := a_2\,; \mid S_1\ S_2 \\
& \mid \quad \texttt{if}\ (b)\ S_0 \mid \texttt{if}\ (b)\ S_1\ \texttt{else}\ S_2 \mid \texttt{while}\ (b)\ S_0 \\
a \quad ::= \quad & n \mid x \mid A[a_0] \mid a_1 + a_2 \mid a_1 - a_2 \mid a_1 * a_2 \mid a_1 / a_2 \\
b \quad ::= \quad & \texttt{true} \mid a_1 = a_2 \mid a_1 > a_2 \mid a_1 \geq a_2 \mid b_1 \wedge b_2 \mid \neg b_0
\end{aligned}
$$

The syntax for variables x and numbers n is left unspecified.

In addition to the two kinds of assignments that are familiar from the Guarded Commands language, MicroC has sequencing, conditional and iteration constructs that are inspired by similar constructs in C. As in the Guarded Commands language, we shall distinguish between arithmetic and boolean expressions (rather than following C, where they are merged into one syntactic category). The arithmetic and boolean expressions are as in Chapter 2 and so are the associated semantic functions.

We shall be interested in extensions of MicroC with additional iteration constructs

129

© Springer Nature Switzerland AG 2019
F. Nielson, H. Riis Nielson, *Formal Methods*, https://doi.org/10.1007/978-3-030-05156-3

and loop control constructs from C and with exceptions from C++. The extensions are summarised by

$$S \quad ::= \quad \ldots \quad | \quad \text{do } S_0 \text{ while } (b) \,|\, \text{for } (S_1\, b;\, S_2)\, S_0$$
$$| \quad \text{break}; \,|\, \text{continue}; \,|\, \text{skip};$$
$$| \quad \text{try}\{S_0\}\, H \,|\, \text{throw } s;$$

$$H \quad ::= \quad \text{catch}(s)\{S\} \,|\, \text{catch}(s)\{S\}\, H$$

The first line contains the iteration constructs. The construct

$$\text{do } S_0 \text{ while } (b)$$

```
z := 1;
y := 0;
t := 0;
for (i := 0; i < x; i := i + 1;)
   { t := z;
     z := y;
     y := t + z;
   }
```

Figure A.2: Example program for the Fibonacci function.

will execute the statement S_0 and will continue doing so as long as the test b holds. The construct

$$\text{for } (S_1\, b;\, S_2)\, S_0$$

is a looping construct with S_1 being the initialisation step, b being the iteration condition for the loop, S_2 being the increment/decrement step of the loop and finally S_0 being the body of the loop. Figure A.2 shows a program using the for-construct; it computes in y the x'th Fibonacci number.

The second line lists the two loop control statements of C. Here break terminates the immediately enclosing loop whereas continue skips the remainder of the loop body and evaluates the loop condition once more. It is also convenient to introduce a skip action to represent the direct transfer of control from one program point to another (as in the Guarded Commands language).

The third line introduces the exception constructs of C++. Here s is the exception name (whose syntax we leave unspecified) and it is defined by a construct of the form

$$\text{try}\{S_0\}\text{catch}(s_1)\{S_1\} \cdots \text{catch}(s_n)\{S_n\}$$

for $n > 0$. If the exception s_i is thrown (using the construct throw s_i) within S_0 then the execution of S_0 is terminated and S_i is executed instead. In the case where several constructs are embedded within one another it is always the syntactically innermost exception that is caught.

TASK A.1: Construct program graphs for MicroC in the manner of Chapter 2. Gradually extend the construction to deal with the extensions listed above. □

TASK A.2: Generate proof obligations for MicroC in the manner of Chapter 3. □

TASK A.3: Develop the detection of signs analysis of Chapter 4 for MicroC. □

TASK A.4: Adapt the security analysis of Chapter 5 to work for MicroC. □

Declarations and functions   Another extension of MicroC introduces declarations and functions as in C; the suggested syntax is as follows:

$$D \quad ::= \quad \text{int } x; \mid \text{int } A[n]; \mid \epsilon \mid D_1 \; D_2$$
$$\mid \quad \text{int } f \; (\text{int } y) \; \{ D \; S \};$$
$$S \quad ::= \quad ... \mid \{ \; D \; S \; \} \mid \text{return } a; \mid x := f(a);$$

The first line gives the format for declarations of variables and arrays; for the sake of simplicity we shall assume that they always have type int. These declarations may appear at the top level as well as within nested blocks of statements, that is, within blocks of the form { *D S* }.

At the top level we may additionally have function declarations of the form

$$\text{int } f \; (\text{int } y) \; \{ D \; S \}$$

as illustrated in Figure A.3. Here f is the name of the function and y is its formal parameter (of type int) and the function returns a value of type int. The body of the function is a block of the form { *D S* } and hence it may introduce new (local) variables and arrays. Occurrences of statements of the form

$$\text{return } a$$

determine the value returned by the function. The function is called using an assignment of the form

$$x := f(a)$$

Here a is the actual parameter whose value will be bound to the formal parameter of the function before its body is executed; the value returned by the function will eventually be assigned to the variable x.

Following C, functions can only be declared at the top level and they are mutually recursive. One of the declared functions must be called main and this is the one that is called (with actual parameter 0) when the program is executed.

```
int fac (int x)
   { int t;
      if (x < 1) return 1;
      else t := fac(x − 1);
               return (x * t);
   }
```

Figure A.3: Declaration of the factorial function.

TASK A.5: Specify the semantics for this extension of MicroC in the manner of Chapter 7; you may do so in a gradual manner, starting with simple variable and array declarations and ending with function declarations. As part of this you have to design an appropriate memory model, to introduce appropriate actions together with their semantics and to construct program graphs making use of these actions. □

Appendix B

Programming Projects

In this appendix we present a sequence of programming projects aimed at implementing central parts of the development of Chapters 1 to 5. The projects may focus on the Guarded Commands language studied in the main part of the book, or on the MicroC language of Appendix A. In the formulation we envisage the use of a functional language like F# but the programming projects can be adapted to use other implementation languages. Our own realisation in Appendix C makes use of F# and forms the core of the electronic learning tool *Formal Methods – A Learning Environment* that goes with the book.

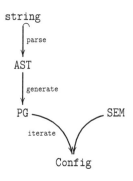

The core development The starting point of the development is illustrated in Figure B.1. It assumes that the program of interest is available as a string of characters (of type `string`) and it is the job of the parser to turn it into its representation as an abstract syntax tree. Thus a main task will be to define an abstract data type AST representing the abstract syntax of programs. Appropriate techniques for constructing the parser are covered in other books; here we just note that the type of the parsing function can be written

```
parse: string -> AST option
```

where we use the `option` data type constructor to take care of ill-formed strings.

Figure B.1: The core of the implementation.

The next step is to introduce a data type for program graphs PG and to define a function constructing a program graph from an abstract syntax tree. The type of this function will be

```
generate: AST -> PG
```

This function will need a mechanism for generating the fresh nodes needed in the

133

© Springer Nature Switzerland AG 2019
F. Nielson, H. Riis Nielson, *Formal Methods*, https://doi.org/10.1007/978-3-030-05156-3

construction of program graphs.

The third step is to specify the semantic domain and the semantic functions giving the meaning of the actions of the program graphs – the latter involves among others things the specification of how expressions are evaluated. Writing SEM for the type of semantic functions and Config for the type of configurations, we can construct a function

$$\texttt{iterate: PG -> SEM -> Config -> int -> Config}$$

which, given a program graph, an initial configuration and an integer bound, will execute the program for at most that number of steps and return the resulting configuration. If the semantics is non-deterministic the function will also need a way of resolving this in a random way.

Program verification　　The aim of our implementation of the verification technique of Chapter 3 will be to extract the relevant proof obligations, as illustrated in Figure B.2. The key function has functionality

$$\texttt{extract: PG -> PredAssign -> ProofObl}$$

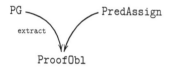

Figure B.2: The verification implementation.

Given a program graph and a partial predicate assignment (represented by values of type PredAssign) it constructs (a sequence of) proof obligations of type ProofObl. There are several points to consider in doing so.

One is concerned with how to obtain the partial predicate assignments. One possibility is to annotate the programs with the required predicates and hence obtain a program graph as well as a partial predicate assignment from the program. An alternative would be to supply the partial predicate assignment directly and simply check that its domain covers the program graph and only produce a proof obligation in that case.

Another choice concerns the format of the proof obligations. In the simplest version they may simply be shortest path fragments. More refined implementations may introduce a small language (a version of first-order logic) for the predicates and use it in the proof obligations; even more ambitious implementations may incorporate ideas from Teaser 3.12.

The program analysis　　The implementation of the program analysis of Chapter 4 is in two parts. The first is independent of the actual analysis being performed and is illustrated in Figure B.3. The key function has functionality

$$\texttt{analyse: AnaSpec -> PG -> AbsMem Set -> AnaAssign}$$

Its first argument is the analysis specification (of type AnaSpec) and when applying the function later we shall supply the actual analysis – this may be the detection of signs analysis, the parity analysis or yet another analysis. The second parameter of the function is the program graph of interest and the third is the set of initial abstract memories (of type AbsMem). The function will compute the corresponding analysis assignment (of type AnaAssign). The types AbsMem and AnaAssign can be parametric and hence knowledge about the actual analysis being performed is not needed when implementing the function analyse.

The second part of the implementation is then concerned with the actual analysis being performed. For the detection of signs analysis we shall construct an element

signSpec: AnaSpec

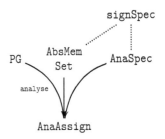

Figure B.3: The program analysis implementation.

that specifies how to compute with signs and in particular how the abstract memories (now recording the signs of variables and arrays) are modified by the actions of the program graph; supplying this element as an argument to analyse will give us a detection of signs analysis. In a similar way we can specify an element parSpec of type AnaSpec and obtain a parity analysis when supplying it as an argument to analyse.

The security analysis   The starting point for the implementation of the security analysis of Chapter 5 is abstract syntax trees, as illustrated in Figure B.4. The admitted flows are specified in the data type Flow and the function secure will check whether the program adheres to it:

secure: AST -> Flow -> Secure

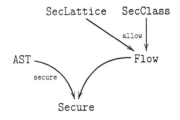

Figure B.4: The security analysis implementation.

The result may be a simple yes/no answer or more detailed information may be given – we use the type Secure for this.

The permitted flows can be generated from a security lattice and a security classification; writing SecLattice and SecClass for the data type with this information, the function allow can construct the permitted flows:

allow: SecLattice * SecClass -> Flow

Combining these functions allows us to check a number of confidentiality and integrity properties.

Appendix C

Realisation in F#

In this appendix we document our implementation in F# of the programming projects proposed in Appendix B. The development focuses on the Guarded Commands language studied in the main part of the book. The appendix provides the functionalities and types of the key functions used in our implementation. The implementation also forms the core of the electronic learning tool *Formal Methods – A Learning Environment* that goes with the book.

C.1   The Core Development

Our first step is to construct a generic *interpreter* for program graphs, thereby providing an implementation of Chapter 1, as illustrated in Figure C.1. We shall choose data types that are parametric in the type of the nodes as well as the actions of the program graphs and we shall also ensure that the semantics is parametric in the type of the memory.

Our second step will then be to instantiate this setting to use the actions of the Guarded Commands language and the associated semantics. On top of this we then introduce the Guarded Commands language itself and the functions for generating program graphs and for running their semantics – together these provide us with an implementation corresponding to the development of Chapter 2.

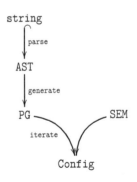

Figure C.1: The core of the implementation.

A generic interpreter   The first step is to choose a data structure for program graphs, as specified in Definition 1.2. Edges are represented as triples and in F# we take

```
type ('q,'a) PG = 'q list * ('q * 'a * 'q) list * 'q * 'q
```

137

© Springer Nature Switzerland AG 2019

F. Nielson, H. Riis Nielson, *Formal Methods*, https://doi.org/10.1007/978-3-030-05156-3

where 'q is the type of the nodes and 'a is the type of the actions.

The next step is to choose a data structure for the semantics, as specified in Definition 1.6. The data structure is a function type and in order to model that the meaning of an action may be a partial function we use the option type of F# and take

```
type ('a,'m) SEM = ('a -> 'm -> 'm Option)
```

where now 'm is the type of the memory.

We can now implement the transitions of the semantics, as specified in Definition 1.11. For this we introduce a function

```
transition: ('q,'a) PG -> ('a,'m) SEM -> ('q * 'm)
            -> ('q * 'm) list
```

where 'q * 'm is the type of the configurations. As input it takes a program graph, a semantics and a configuration and the result is a list of the potential next configurations.

The next step is to implement the execution sequences of Definition 1.13. The function iterate of type

```
iterate: ('q,'a) PG -> ('a,'m) SEM -> ('q * 'm) -> int
         -> ('q * 'm)
```

will construct an execution sequence starting in the supplied configuration; the integer argument will bound its length and the function returns the resulting configuration, which may be a final configuration, a stuck configuration or just the configuration that was reached after the given number of steps. The function makes use of the function transition introduced above and will randomly choose one of the possible next configurations in case there is more than one.

Actions: syntax and semantics   We shall now introduce the abstract syntax of the actions, as introduced in Chapter 2. We shall assume that variables and array names have type Ident (which may be defined as strings) and take

```
type AExp = Num  of int
          | Var  of Ident
          | Arr  of Ident * AExp
          | Add  of AExp * AExp
          | Sub  of AExp * AExp
          | Mul  of AExp * AExp
          | Div  of AExp * AExp
```

```
type BExp = True
          | Eq   of AExp * AExp
          | Gt   of AExp * AExp
          | Gte  of AExp * AExp
          | And  of BExp * BExp
          | Neg  of BExp

type Action = VAsgn of Ident * AExp
            | AAsgn of Ident * AExp * AExp
            | Skip
            | Test  of BExp
```

Turning to the semantics, we shall represent the memory as a pair of lists of pairs as suggested in Section 2.3; the first component holds the values of the variables and the second component holds the values of the arrays represented as a list of integers:

```
type Mem = (Ident * int) list * (Ident * int list) list
```

We can now define an auxiliary function for looking up the values of variables and array entries as well as for updating the value of variables and array entries. With these functions in place we can implement functions for evaluating arithmetic and boolean expressions; they will have types

```
AEval: AExp -> Mem -> int Option
BEval: BExp -> Mem -> bool Option
```

These functions are partly defined in the text of Section 2.3 and in Exercise 2.20. The semantics of actions in Definition 2.17 gives rise to the function sem of type

```
sem: SEM<Action,Mem>
```

The function `iterate` can now be specialised to use these functions, as for example in `iterate pg sem (q,m) k`.

We have chosen to use the normal F# integers `int` when defining the memory Mem and should be aware that they behave much like a 32-bit version of our signed bytes from Section 1.5. To get as close as possible to the behaviour of mathematical integers we might use the F# full-precision integers `bigint` when defining the memory.

Guarded Commands and program graphs   Turning to the Guarded Commands language, the first step is to introduce types for the abstract syntax. We shall follow Definition 2.3 closely and take

```
type AST  = Assign   of Ident * AExp
          | AAssign  of Ident * AExp * AExp
          | SkipGC
          | Seq      of AST * AST
          | If       of GAST
          | Do       of GAST
and  GAST = Cond     of BExp * AST
          | Choice   of GAST * GAST
```

A parser for the language will then have to construct abstract syntax trees that can be represented in this data structure:

```
parse: string -> AST Option
```

We shall not go into further details and only mention that various libraries in F# support this development.

In the construction of program graphs we shall write Node for the type of the nodes of the programming graphs; a simple choice is to take this to be integers. Definition 2.7 will then give rise to a function for commands of type

```
edges: AST -> Node -> Node -> (Node * Action * Node) list
```

and it will make use of a corresponding function for guarded commands. The definition of these functions is fairly straightforward except for the generation of fresh nodes; this can be solved by using an imperative variable to keep track of the next unused node. Using the edges function we can then define the overall function

```
generate: AST -> PG<Node,Action>
```

Making use of the previously defined functions, the interpreter can be implemented by combining the parse, generate, sem and iterate functions.

The above implementation are easily extended to handle the extensions of the language considered in Section 2.5. It is also possible to implement a deterministic version of the language following the approach of Section 2.4.

C.2   Program Verification

The starting point for this programming project is a version of the Guarded Commands language annotated with predicates as suggested in Section 3.4. We can then obtain a program graph and a partial predicate assignment, the aim of the programming project is then to obtain a set of proof obligations, as described in Section 3.3. The overall development is summarised in Figure C.2.

Guarded Commands with Predicates We shall first introduce types for the expressions and predicates to be used for formulating the properties of interest; here we shall follow Section 3.1. We shall distinguish between (program) array names and logical array names as they both may appear in expressions and predicates, so we take

```
type Array = AName of Ident
           | LName of Ident
```

Both kinds of array names can be used when indexing into array names, just as they can occur as arguments to predefined mathematical functions and predefined predicates – the names of the latter have type Name, which may be just strings. Thus we take

```
type Exp  = PNum of int
          | PVar of Ident
          | LVar of Ident
          | PArr of Array * Exp
          | ...
          | PFun of Name * Array list * Exp list

type Pred = PTrue
          | ...
          | PPred of Name * Array list * Exp list
```

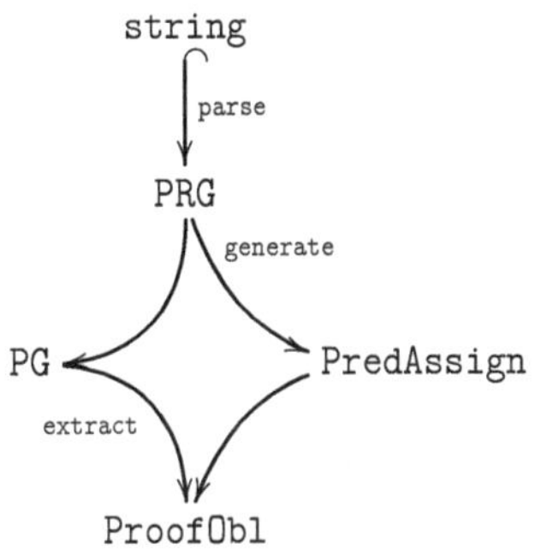

Figure C.2: Generating proof obligations.

The actual choice of expressions and predicates is fairly open but must include the arithmetic and boolean expressions of the Guarded Commands language. In particular, we shall need functions mapping the data structures for the arithmetic and boolean expressions into the above data structures.

With this in place we can now modify the abstract syntax introduced in Section C.1 for the Guarded Commands language to include predicates for the iteration construct and the overall program. So the types will now be:

```
type AST = Assign of Ident * AExp
         | ...
         | Do      of Pred * GAST
and  GAST = ...

type PRG = Pred * AST * Pred
```

The function generate is now modified to construct a program graph together with a partial predicate assignment of type

```
type PredAssign = (Node * Pred) list
```

So the overall functions will be

```
parse:    string -> AST Option
generate: PRG -> PG<Node,Action> * PredAssign
```

where generate amounts to an implementation of Definitions 3.32 and 3.33.

Proof obligations   In order to generate proof obligations we shall first compute the short path fragments as presented by the algorithm of Figure 3.3; the corresponding function is

```
paths: PG<Node,Action> * PredAssign
       -> (Node * Action list * Node) list
```

It returns a list of triples where the first and the third components are nodes in the program graph and the second component is a list of actions. It is now easy to extract the proof obligations using the partial predicate assignment so we can obtain the function

```
extract: PG<Node,Action> * PredAssign
         -> (Pred * Action list * Pred) list
```

We can now combine the parse, generate and extract functions to generate a list of proof obligations for the guarded commands. The actual checking of the obligations is beyond the scope of this implementation.

The above implementation is easily extended to handle the extensions of the language considered in Section 2.5. It is also possible to extend the implementation to work directly on program graphs as suggested in Section 3.5; then the input to the system could be a program graph and a partial predicate assignment; one could then check whether the corresponding set of nodes covers it and construct the proof obligations if that is the case.

C.3   Program Analysis

This programming project consists of two parts. In the first we develop a generic analysis function for program graphs; it is parameterised on a specification of the analysis of interest and builds on the algorithms of Section 4.5. In the second part of the project we specify the detection of signs analysis (and parity analysis) for the actions of the Guarded Commands language; similar specifications can be written for other analyses, for example the parity analysis of the exercises of Chapter 4. The overall development is summarised in Figure C.3.

Analysing program graphs We shall assume that program graphs have the type given in Section C.1 and we shall now replace the semantics and the associated iteration function with an analysis specification and a technique for computing the analysis result. The first step is to specify data structures corresponding to the analysis specifications of Definition 4.21. The analysis functions will have type

```
type ('a,'m) AnaSpec = ('a -> 'm Set -> 'm Set)
```

where as before 'a is the type of the actions and now 'm is the type of the abstract memories. Following Definition 4.5 we can now introduce the following type for analysis assignments:

```
type ('q,'m) AnaAssign = ('q * 'm Set) list
```

Here 'q is the type of the nodes of the program graph.

We can then define a function implementing the algorithm of Figure 4.16; it will have type

```
solve: AnaSpec<'a,'m> -> PG<'q,'a> -> Set<'m> ->
                    -> AnaAssign<'q,'m>
```

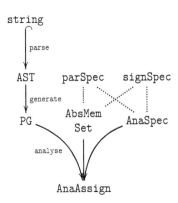

Figure C.3: The program analysis implementation.

and thus require three parameters, namely the analysis functions for the actions ($\widehat{S}[\![\cdot]\!]$ in Figure 4.15), the program graph of interest and the initial analysis information for the initial node ($\widehat{\mathbf{Mem}}_{\triangleright}$ in Figure 4.15). It is now straightforward to define the function

```
analyse: AnaSpec<'a,'m> -> PG<'q,'a> -> Set<'m> ->
                    -> AnaAssign<'q,'m>
```

as it simply amounts to a call of solve with the same parameters.

Detection of signs analysis In order to specify the detection of signs analysis we shall first introduce the necessary types and functions for calculating with signs. The signs are represented by an enumeration type:

```
type Sign = Nsign | Zsign | Psign
```

It is straightforward to specify a function sign corresponding to **sign : Int → Sign** (of Section 4.1).

We can now specify the abstract operations $\tilde{op}$ of Section 4.3 corresponding to the arithmetic, relational and binary operators of the expressions. Corresponding to Figures 4.10 and 4.11 we can define functions of type

```
signAdd: Sign * Sign -> Sign Set
signGte: Sign * Sign -> bool Set
```

and we shall need similar functions for the other operators. Note that when specifying the analysis of arithmetic and boolean expressions we shall need extensions of these functions that take pairs of sets of signs, respectively, pairs of sets of booleans, as parameters; for this it is convenient to introduce a generic function (taking special care of the short-circuit operators).

Following Section 4.1 we shall introduce the type

```
type SignMem = (Ident * Sign) list *
               (Ident * Sign Set) list
```

for abstract memories (AbsMem in Figure C.3). As was the case when we implemented the semantics in Section C.1, it is helpful to introduce auxiliary functions for looking up the sign of variables and the set of signs of arrays. It will also be useful to define a function

```
signOf: Mem -> SignMem
```

corresponding to the function η of Definition 4.2.

We are now ready to define functions for analysing arithmetic and boolean expressions as well as actions, and here we shall follow Section 4.3. We shall define functions with types

```
ASign:    AExp -> SignMem -> Sign Set
BSign:    BExp -> SignMem -> bool Set
signSpec: AnaSpec<Action, SignMem>
```

In the case of arithmetic expressions the function directly reflects the definition in Section 4.3; in the case of boolean expressions it relies on Exercise 4.16. When specifying the analysis of actions it may be useful first to define an auxiliary function taking an action and a single abstract memory as arguments and returning a set of abstract memories as result; then signSpec can be obtained by lifting this function to take a set of abstract memories as argument.

By supplying the function analyse with the argument signSpec we have a detection of signs analysis for program graphs obtained from the Guarded Commands language; combining it with the functions parse and generate we obtain a detection of signs analysis for Guarded Commands.

A similar development can be performed for the parity analysis developed in Exercises 4.4, 4.17 and 4.20. This amounts to specifying a type ParMem for the abstract memories of the parity analysis and developing the various functions for calculating with parities including specifying the function

```
    parSpec: AnaSpec<Action, ParMem>
```

By supplying the function `analyse` with the argument `parSpec` we obtain an implementation of the parity analysis.

C.4 Language-Based Security

In this programming project we shall implement the security analysis of Chapter 5. We shall take a syntax-directed approach and develop the analysis for the Guarded Commands language as described in Section 5.3. The project has two parts. The first is concerned with extracting the actual flows of a Guarded Commands program and checking them against a given permissible flow. The second part constructs the permissible flows from a security specification consisting of a security lattice and a security classification. The overall development is illustrated in Figure C.4.

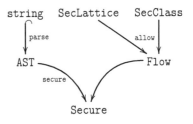

Figure C.4: The security analysis implementation.

Constructing the flows As a preparation our first step will be to define functions extracting the free variables of arithmetic and boolean expressions

```
    fvA: AExp -> Ident Set
    fvB: BExp -> Ident Set
```

where AExp and BExp are the types for expressions introduced in Section C.1.

We can now define the type of flows to be

```
    type Flow = (Ident * Ident) Set
```

We can then define a function corresponding to the operation $X \rightrightarrows Y$ of Section 5.1; it will have type

```
    make_flow: Ident Set -> Ident Set -> Flow
```

The next step will be to define functions corresponding to Definitions 5.12 and 5.13. Here we have two choices. One is to supply the permitted flows as an argument to the functions and another possibility is to collect the actual flows of the commands and then check them subsequently – we shall take the latter approach. The types of the functions thus are

```
    sec:  AST  -> Ident Set -> Flow
    secG: GAST -> BExp * Ident Set -> Flow * BExp
```

The function `secure` will then compute the actual flow and check whether it is a subset of the allowed flows, so it has type

```
secure: AST -> Flow -> Secure
```

A simple solution takes Secure to be the type bool but more elaborate choices are also possible; as an example one might return the offending flows.

Security specification   The first component of a security specification is a security lattice. It is defined by its ordering so we shall take

```
type SecLattice = (SecLevel * SecLevel) list
```

where SecLevel is the type of the security levels. Some examples are

```
confidentiality = [(public,private)]
integrity       = [(trusted, dubious)]
classical       = [(low,high)]
```

Not every element of type SecLattice is a partially ordered set and there are several ways to deal with this. One possibility is to introduce a function checking whether or not the element is a partially ordered set, and only proceed if this is the case. Another possibility is to construct a partially ordered set from the given element if this is indeed possible; then we would get a function

```
make_pO: SecLattice -> SecLattice Option
```

that performs the required checks on its argument and constructs a partially ordered set from it. The steps could be as follows: first remove all reflexive components from the argument, then construct the transitive closure and check its intersection with the identity relation. If this test succeeds the function returns the reflexive transitive closure of its argument, and otherwise it fails.

Following the development of Section 5.4 we shall specify a security classification as an element of type

```
type SecClass = (Ident * SecLevel) list
```

that to each variable and array name associates a security class (from the security lattice); it is useful to provide a function checking that only security classes from the given security lattice are indeed used.

The permissible flows can then be obtained as all pairs of variables (and array names) that, according to the security classification, have security classes that are ordered in a way permitted by the partial ordering obtained from the security lattice:

```
allow: SecLattice * SecClass -> Flow
```

The security validation now amounts to supplying the permitted flows as an argument to the function secure defined earlier.

Appendix D

A Learning Environment

We now introduce the learning environment available at FormalMethods.dk, where one can play with the development of many of the chapters of the book. This is useful for checking one's understanding of the examples and exercises and is useful for exploring further examples to those found in the book. Our main focus is on the system at FormalMethods.dk/fm4fun, which supports the first five chapters of the book. The welcome screen is shown in Figure D.1.

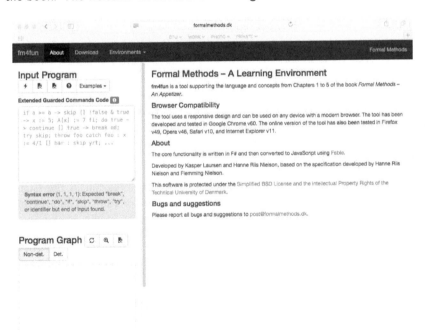

Figure D.1: The welcome screen – when first starting the system.

149

© Springer Nature Switzerland AG 2019
F. Nielson, H. Riis Nielson, *Formal Methods*, https://doi.org/10.1007/978-3-030-05156-3

D.1   The Welcome Screen

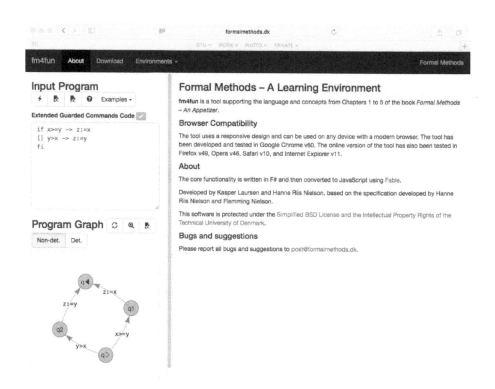

Figure D.2: The welcome screen – with an example program and program graph.

When you have written a program you get the view in Figure D.2. You can always navigate back to this view by pressing the About button in the top line, and when you press the Download button in the top line you will be offered the opportunity to download a version of the system that will run locally in the browser even when not connected to the Internet.

The top part of the left pane is the place to write the program in the Guarded Commands language. You can write directly in the box or you can choose one of the available example programs by clicking on Examples.

The bottom part of the left pane displays the program graph. You can choose the semantics to be used for this: the usual non-deterministic semantics of Guarded Commands or the deterministic version covered in Section 2.4.

The buttons in the left pane offer you a number of ways to interact with the system:

⚡   To pretty print the program that you wrote.

🖼   To download the program or program graph to a file.

🖼   To upload a program from a file.

❓ To get an overview of the syntax supported.

🔄 To redraw the program graph.

🔍 To open a separate window where you can rearrange the program graph.

D.2 Step-Wise Execution

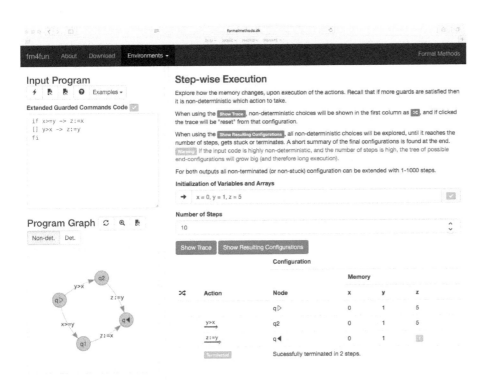

Figure D.3: The Step-wise Execution screen – with an execution sequence.

When you click on `Environments` in the first line you get the possibility to choose `Step-wise Execution`, as covered in Chapters 1 and 2. Here you should specify initial values for all the variables and array entries in your program.

You can then choose to see an example execution and you can control the number of steps to be carried out. This is shown in Figure D.3. If the execution sequence resolves a non-deterministic choice the symbol ⤬ indicates the point where it happens and if you click it the system will redo the choice.

You can also choose to see all the resulting configurations from all non-deterministic executions and you can control the depth of the computation tree.

D.3   Verification Conditions

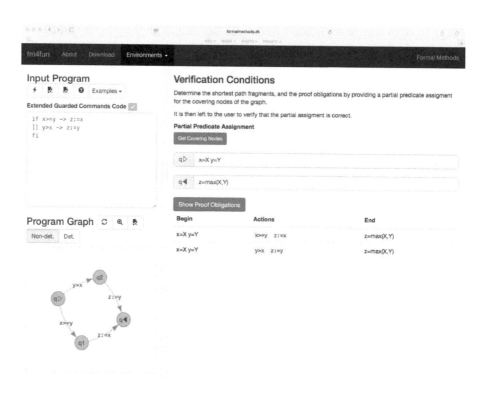

Figure D.4: The Verification Conditions screen – with a partial predicate assignment.

When you click on Environments in the first line you get the possibility to choose Verification Conditions, as covered in Chapter 3.

By pressing Get Covering Nodes you will get a list of the covering nodes: you have the option of replacing their names with a textual presentation of the predicate that should hold there and this corresponds to providing a partial predicate assignment.

By pressing Show Obligations you will then get a list of all the short path fragments, presented in the form of a list of proof obligations (if you chose to write the partial predicate assignment). This is shown in Figure D.4.

D.4 Detection of Signs Analysis

Figure D.5: The Detection of Signs Analysis screen – with an analysis assignment.

When you click on Environments in the first line you get the possibility to choose Detection of Signs Analysis, as covered in Chapter 4.

First you need to specify the collection $\overset{\frown}{\mathbf{Mem}}_{\triangleright}$ of abstract memories holding initially. Each abstract memory should be written on a separate line and you can use ⊞ to add additional lines.

When you click Show Sign Analysis you then get the least solution to the analysis problem. This is shown in Figure D.5.

D.5 Security Analysis

Figure D.6: The Security Analysis screen – with an example confidentiality analysis.

When you click on Environments in the first line you get the possibility to choose Security Analysis, as covered in Chapter 5. You will be forced to choose the deterministic semantics in order for the security analysis to work.

First you should specify the security lattice and then the security classification for variables and arrays. By clicking on Show Security Analysis you then get the result of the security analysis. This is shown in Figure D.6.

Symbols

Some of the symbols used in this book may be unfamiliar, and it may not be so obvious how to 'read them aloud', so here is a bit of help.

$\mathcal{A}$ curly A
$\mathcal{B}$ curly B
$\mathcal{S}$ curly S
$\widehat{\mathcal{A}}$ curly A hat
$\widehat{\mathcal{B}}$ curly B hat
$\widehat{\mathcal{S}}$ curly S hat

$q_{\triangleright}$ initial node
$q_{\blacktriangleleft}$ final node
$\triangleright$ initial
$\blacktriangleleft$ final
$q_{\circ}$ q circle / source node
$q_{\bullet}$ q bullet / target node

Φ (Greek capital) Phi
Ψ (Greek capital) Psi
α (Greek) alpha
η (Greek) eta
γ (Greek) gamma
ϕ (Greek) phi
π (Greek) pi
σ (Greek) sigma
ς (Greek) varsigma / written sigma
ω (Greek) omega

$[\![\ ]\!]$ semantic brackets
$(\ )$ parentheses

$\longrightarrow$ long arrow / goes to
$\longrightarrow^{*}$ goes to in many steps

© Springer Nature Switzerland AG 2019
F. Nielson, H. Riis Nielson, *Formal Methods*, https://doi.org/10.1007/978-3-030-05156-3

$\Longrightarrow$	double long arrow / goes to
$\Longrightarrow^*$	goes to in many steps
$\Rightarrow$	implies
$[\mapsto]$	update
$\mapsto$	maps to
$\rightarrow$	arrow / maps to / flows to
$\rightsquigarrow$	leads to
$\hookrightarrow$	partially maps to
$\rightrightarrows$	double arrow / flows to
$\wedge$	and
$\vee$	or
$\neg$	not
&&	short-circuit and
||	short-circuit or
^	exponentiation
[]	or
:=	becomes
?	question mark / input
!	exclamation mark / output
$\subseteq$	subset of
$\not\subseteq$	not subset of
$\sqsubseteq$	less than or equal to
$\sqsubset$	strictly less than
$\cup$	union
$\sqcup$	join / least upper bound
$\cap$	intersection
$\sqcap$	meet / greatest lower bound
$\oplus$	oplus
$\setminus$	set minus
{ }	empty set
$\exists$	exists
$\forall$	for all
$\models$	models
$\times$	times
@	at
#	hash
$\lfloor\;\rfloor$	floor of

Index

157

© Springer Nature Switzerland AG 2019
F. Nielson, H. Riis Nielson, *Formal Methods*, https://doi.org/10.1007/978-3-030-05156-3